3D Photorealism Toolkit

3D Photorealism Toolkit

Bill Fleming

WILEY COMPUTER PUBLISHING

JOHN WILEY & SONS, INC.

New York • Chichester • Weinheim • Brisbane • Singapore • Toronto

Publisher: Robert Ipsen
Editor: Cary Sullivan
Assistant Editor: Kathryn A. Malm
Managing Editor: Brian Snapp
Electronic Products, Associate Editor: Michael Sosa
Text Design & Composition: North Market Street Graphics, Lancaster, PA

This publication is designed to provide accurate and authoritative information in regard to the subject matter covered. It is sold with the understanding that the publisher is not engaged in professional services. If professional advice or other expert assistance is required, the services of a competent professional person should be sought.

Library of Congress Cataloging-in-Publication Data:
Fleming, Bill, 1969–
    3D photorealism toolkit / Bill Fleming.
      p.   cm.
    Includes index.
    ISBN 0-471-25346-4 (pbk. : alk. paper)
    1. Computer graphics. 2. Photo-realism. 3. Three-dimensional display systems. I. Title.
1385F59   1998
006.6'93—dc21   97-52083
                                         CIP

Printed in the United States of America.

10 9 8 7 6 5 4 3 2 1

Contents

CHAPTER 3

Material—What's It Made Of?   **51**

CHAPTER 4

Construction—How's It Assembled?   **73**

CHAPTER 5

Movement—What Are the Mechanics of Objects?   **87**

CHAPTER 6

Beveling—The Key to Specular Reality   **99**

CHAPTER 7

Dents and Dings—Aging Your Models   **117**

Introduction

Have you ever sat and stared at the wall of 3D books on store shelves, wondering which one to purchase? I can't even count the number of hours I've wasted trying to find specific information on 3D rendering. All the books seem to repeat the same things but never explore any one topic with enough detail to satisfy the readers.

Everyday, it seems, there is yet another 3D book added to bookstore shelves. The majority of them are merely rewrites of the program manual. Sure, they point out a few things that aren't covered in the manual but you are still faced with a small amount of information for a large number of topics. How many times have you read a 3D book only to be left wanting more? If you're like me, this happens all too often. That's why I decided to write the *3D Photorealism Toolkit.*

So, who am I? Some would say I'm the most neurotic artist they've ever met. Others call me a perfectionist. They are both correct, but I like to refer to myself as a 3D Chaotician. A *3D Chaotician* is someone who focuses his or her efforts on developing photorealistic 3D images by applying the chaos of reality. Call it an obsession—my wife does. I probably spend 14 hours a day glued to my computer screen. There is something about the challenge of creating digital realities that intrigues me. I've always been impressed by the 3D artists who have taken the time and energy to ensure their images were truly photorealistic. It takes a serious commitment to be a photorealistic 3D artist. You don't have to commit 14 hours of your day but you do need to take the time to add the subtle detail and nuances that make images realistic. I refer to photorealistic 3D rendering as a "visual smorgasbord." A properly constructed photorealistic image has tremendous depth. It provides viewers with a seemingly never ending source of enjoyment—they just sit there and marvel at the attention to detail. It gives me great satisfaction to see the reaction of the people who view a truly photorealistic 3D image. They are literally lost in the image.

Being a photorealistic 3D artist actually entails more attention to detail than artistic talent. To be honest, I haven't done traditional art in more than 20 years.

I probably couldn't even sketch a simple chair without wearing holes in the paper where I've erased the mistakes. The skill I bring to my 3D work is neurotic attention to detail. I'm a firm believer that the term "neurotic" is not always a bad thing. It's important that you are committed to the details or your 3D efforts will fall short of being photorealistic. You have to spend an equal amount of time researching the work as you do creating it. The goal of a photorealistic 3D artist is to capture reality—to harness its chaos and reflect it in your work. That's what the *3D Photorealism Toolkit* is all about. This book focuses on discovering the subtle, and sometimes not so subtle, nuances of reality and incorporating them into every 3D image you create.

I use photorealistic techniques every day in my professional career as a 3D artist. I remember the difficulty I encountered when trying to create photorealistic images for the first time. I also remember the questions I asked in an attempt to ease the pain of making the transition to a photorealistic 3D artist. I've tried to answer all of those questions, and more, in this book. I've made every effort to provide you with all the information you'll need to create photorealistic 3D images.

The *3D Photorealism Toolkit* was written for 3D artists, by a 3D artist. It will provide you with a wealth of insight into the creation of photorealistic 3D images.

Overview of the Book and Technology

New technology is steadily being developed that expands the capabilities of 3D products. Even the most basic 3D programs possess many of the essential tools for creating photorealistic 3D images. While the capabilities of 3D programs will continue to grow, the principles of 3D photorealism will always remain constant. This book covers countless universal techniques for creating photorealistic 3D images. These techniques are not fixed to any one specific program; they can be used with any 3D program on the market. The surfacing and lighting capabilities will vary from the low-cost amateur programs to the high-cost professional programs, but the techniques for photorealistic 3D modeling and staging remain the same.

This book covers the when and where of 3D photorealism. Rather than focusing on how the technique is done in your specific program, it focuses on the objective—when and where to use the technique. For example, a Boolean operation is the same regardless of the program you own. Therefore, this book covers where and when to use Booleans instead of illustrating how to perform the operation. It would consume far too much space to demonstrate the Boolean operations for every 3D program.

If you use any of the following programs you should read this book: SoftImage, Alias, LightWave, 3D Studio MAX, 3D Studio, Strata, ElectricImage, Ray Dream, trueSpace, Extreme 3D, Animation Master, Houdini, Imagine, and even POV-RAY.

How This Book Is Organized

This book is divided into five parts that will take you logically through the process of developing photorealistic images. Each part is a complete concept, allowing you to reach closure at the end. You don't have to read one part to understand another. If you are interested only in the principles of photorealistic modeling, you can read Part II and skip the other parts of the book. I do recommend that you read the entire book if you are interested in the complete process of developing photorealistic 3D images.

Part I: Reality Is Chaos

Part I contains a single chapter, yet it is probably the most important chapter in this book. Before you can begin to develop photorealistic scenes you need to have a complete understanding of the elements that make an image realistic. This part focuses on showing you how to identify the critical elements of a photorealistic scene.

Chapter 1: Chaos—A Reality Primer

Here is where you lay the foundation for a photorealistic 3D image. Chapter 1 identifies the ten principles of photorealistic 3D images. You will examine several photorealistic 3D images and learn to identify the elements that make them appear realistic. It's all about taking the time to experience the chaos of reality. By the end of this chapter you will be looking at real-world objects in an entirely different way than you ever have before.

Part II: Photorealistic Modeling Techniques

Modeling is where the photorealistic 3D process begins—it's the foundation of a photorealistic 3D scene. A solid model is paramount in creating a photorealistic object. Part II includes six chapters that cover the modeling techniques that are a fundamental part of developing photorealistic models. Whether you are using polygons, splines, or nurbs, the information in this chapter will help you add photorealistic detail to your 3D models.

Chapter 2: Detail—The Main Component of Reality

One of the major flaws in most 3D models is the lack of detail. Real objects are typically covered with detail. Just examine any multimedia component in your house and you'll quickly see that detail is a necessary part of photorealistic 3D modeling. Chapter 2 covers the basic details of photorealistic 3D models and shows you how to apply them to your models.

Chapter 3: Material—What's It Made Of?

Where are the seams? That's the first question that comes to mind when I see 3D objects. How often do you actually see a seam in an object? Rarely does a 3D object have seams, yet all objects in reality are assembled from parts and therefore contain seams. Chapter 3 covers the importance of adding seams to your models so they appear manufactured. You'll learn simple techniques for adding seams to your existing models.

Chapter 4: Construction—How's It Assembled?

What happens when you pull all the screws out of your TV? It falls apart! Keeping this in mind, most 3D scenes should appear as piles of parts since the models rarely have anything holding them together. Real-world objects are assembled, which means they need something to hold them together. This is just another of those details that makes a model realistic. Chapter 4 covers the technique of adding nuts, bolts, screws, and even glue to your models to make them realistic.

Chapter 5: Movement—What Are the Mechanics of Objects?

Have you ever seen a car move without an axle? You will in most 3D animations. One of the major elements modelers forget to add to 3D models is the mechanics of movement. For an object to be photorealistic it must possess the mechanics for the motion it's making. All too often you'll see a robot that is just a collection of tubes and spheres with no presence of any mechanical hardware for movement. Chapter 5 focuses on developing motion mechanics for your 3D models. You'll learn how to add mechanical detail to your models so they appear realistic.

Chapter 6: Beveling—The Key to Specular Reality

Beveling is one element that is rarely seen in most 3D models. In the real world, bevels are simply a treatment to the edge of an object to remove the harsh right angle that is quite often a hazard. Nearly every object that is manufactured has beveled edges. This makes it mandatory that you incorporate beveled edges in your 3D models to make them realistic. Chapter 6 covers where and when to use beveled edges on your models.

Chapter 7: Dents and Dings—Aging Your Models

How many new things do you own? I mean objects that have no scratches, dents, or dings. How polished and clean is the world around you? Well, if your world is anything like mine it could use a visit from "Mr. Clean." The most common problem with 3D images is that everything is too perfect. All the objects are clean and free of any blemishes. Chapter 7 focuses on the techniques for aging your 3D models. You'll learn how to beat some reality into them, but more important, you'll learn where and when to create dents and dings.

Part III: Photorealistic Surfacing Techniques

Photorealistic surfacing is by far the most complicated aspect of the photorealistic process. There are many factors to take into consideration when creating photorealistic surfacing. The six chapters in Part III focus on planning your surfaces and determining the appropriate surfacing technique to use with your model.

Chapter 8: Photorealistic Surfacing Fundamentals

The first step in surfacing your models is to completely understand the elements that make a surface photorealistic. Once you have a handle on these elements, you can determine how to select the surfaces on your object and which surface mapping method to use. Chapter 8 will help you understand the photorealistic surfacing fundamentals so you can determine which surfaces to create and how they will be mapped.

Chapter 9: Image Map Surfaces

Image map surfaces are the most commonly used photorealistic surfacing technique. They offer you an unlimited level of detail while providing you with the means to create photorealistic surfaces. There are eight types of image map surface that are discussed in Chapter 9: color, luminosity, diffusion, secularity, glossiness, reflection, transparency, and bump. You will also learn how to create multiple surface types on a single surface, such as plastic and metal, using image maps.

Chapter 10: Procedural Textures

Procedural textures are an essential tool for creating photorealistic surfaces. They can save you hours of time that would be spent trying to create the same effects with image maps. Because procedural textures are truly 3D they offer unlimited potential for adding photorealistic detail to surfaces. They can be used to create brushed metal or add dirt to a polished surface to make it appear tarnished. They are by far the most flexible surfacing method. Chapter 10 explores the most common procedural textures and how they can be used to create realistic surface detail.

Part IV: Photorealistic Staging Techniques

How many images have you seen where everything was in complete order? Nearly every 3D image is too organized. Reality is chaotic. Don't let the term fool you. Reality isn't complete havoc; it's just a bit disorganized. There is order in chaos. For example: The whole chessboard is neatly arranged except for one piece that is off center. Now that's realistic staging. Part IV has two chapters that focus on developing realistic scenes by creating chaos and disorder. You'll learn how to create imperfections in your staging that look natural and help create a photorealistic scene.

Chapter 11: Planning Your Scene

Planning your scene is a very important step in the 3D photorealism process. A poorly planned scene can look artificial in spite of the model and surface quality. The foundation of proper scene planning is an in-depth exploration of the characters responsible for creating the scene. Not you, but the fictional characters— whether they are present in the image or not. Once you understand their personality, you can properly stage the scene so it makes sense. Chapter 11 explores the five major personality types and how they can be used to plan your scenes so they appear photorealistic and believable.

Chapter 12: Adding Chaos—Creating Clutter

Chaos is a fundamental ingredient of photorealistic 3D images. Nothing makes a scene look more artificial than uniformity. In order for a scene to look photoreal it needs to have an element of chaos. Knock over one of the chess pieces, hang the picture on the wall crooked, move a chair away from the table, you get the idea. There is order in chaos but not uniformity. Chapter 12 shows you how to stage a scene so it doesn't look planned or artificial.

Part V: Photorealistic Camera and Lighting Techniques

Camera and lighting techniques are the cornerstones of a quality photorealistic 3D image. They influence the mood of the image. If you shot a clown from a low angle with dim lighting he'll end up looking dark and sinister. The same clown from a higher camera angle in bright light looks happy. The two chapters in Part V focus on illustrating techniques for properly lighting a scene and demonstrating the proper camera angles for nearly every occasion.

Chapter 13: Camera Positioning

One of the major flaws in most 3D images is a poor camera angle. The camera angle helps depict the mood of the scene. All too often 3D scenes are shot from sterile camera angles that flatten the depth of the scene. Chapter 13 will explain where and when to use specific camera angles. You will also learn how to use camera zoom and focal lengths to change the mood of the image.

Chapter 14: Lighting for Every Occasion

Lighting can make or break a photorealistic scene. There are many different lighting possibilities depending on where the scene is located; that is, indoors or outdoors. Your scene may require direct sunlight or it may need a soft and subtle diffused light. Using the wrong lighting can make your scene appear artificial even though you may have incredibly photorealistic models and textures. Chapter 14 focuses on determining the proper lighting technique for every scene. You'll learn where and when to use different types of lighting.

Appendixes

The six appendixes cover resources for modeling source material, surface attributes for metal, plastic, and a variety of other surfaces, index of refraction values for transparent surfaces, and a complete visual reference of the bonus items on the companion Web site.

Appendix A: Modeling and Surfacing Source Material

Photorealistic modeling requires good source material. It can be very difficult to find high-quality color images of objects you wish to model and surface. Appendix A contains a comprehensive listing of resources for visual modeling reference. These books contain outstanding visual references for thousands of common items ranging from insects to military weapons.

Appendix B: Procedural Metal Attributes

Creating the right surface attributes for metals can be very time consuming. I spent months perfecting the values for more than 30 common metals. In Appendix B, you'll find a complete listing of the surface attributes for those metals. The information includes surface color, diffusion, secularity, glossiness, reflectivity, and bump values.

Appendix C: Procedural Plastic and Rubber Attributes

Creating the right surface attributes for plastics and rubber is no less time consuming than metals. In Appendix C, you'll find a complete listing of the surface attributes for 15 forms of plastic and rubber. The information includes surface color, diffusion, secularity, glossiness, reflectivity, and bump values.

Appendix D: Index of Refraction Values for Transparent Materials

One of the most common problems with 3D photorealism is simulating the natural index of refraction that occurs with transparent materials. Appendix D gives you a complete listing of Index of Refraction values for 25 transparent materials ranging from glass to lead crystal.

Appendix E: Light Colors Rated in Kelvins

Determining the proper light colors can be very difficult, particularly when there are so many variations. Fortunately there is an answer. You'll find a very comprehensive listing of the light sources and their Kelvin rating in this chart.

Appendix F: The Companion Web Site

Refer to Appendix F for a listing of everything you'll find on the companion Web site, including bonus models and map textures.

Who Should Read This Book

This book is for all 3D artists who desire to take their images to the next level. If you are truly dedicated to making photorealistic 3D images you should read this book. Most of the 3D books I've read seem to throw the word *photorealistic* around like the multimedia industry once did with the word *interactive*. It's easy to call an image photorealistic; it's another thing to take the time to really make the image realistic. I have a simple definition for photorealism: if it looks like a photograph, it's photorealistic—no more, no less. A 3D television isn't photorealistic unless it has seams and screws holding it together. A couch isn't photorealistic unless the seat cushions have a depression in the middle. And, of course, nothing is photorealistic if it's perfect. If you want to create 3D images with unprecedented levels of photorealistic detail then this book is for you.

If you fall into any of the categories below you should read this book:

Seeking a Career in 3D: If you are seeking a career in 3D graphics this book is a must. Although there are literally thousands of 3D artists seeking work, only a handful are capable of generating photorealistic 3D images. A proficiency in creating photorealistic images puts you at the top of the stack of resumes in the major studios. You should read the book cover to cover because it will give you a distinct advantage in the job market.

Multimedia/Games: If you are in the multimedia or game industry you are well acquainted with 3D graphics. 3D effects have permeated every aspect of your industry. Where it was once acceptable to use 2D or low-quality 3D graphics it is now required that you create photorealistic effects. Competition is fierce, forcing you to keep improving the quality of your 3D graphics. In this book, you'll discover hundreds of techniques for wowing your customers and clients with photorealistic 3D effects.

Film/Broadcast: No industry is more particular about the quality of 3D work than yours. Every form of visual media is being saturated with 3D graphics, whether it's needed or not. From virtual sets to animated stunt characters, 3D effects have become a part of nearly every film and broadcast production. Traditional special effects are being replaced with digital effects. This book will provide you with the knowledge to create photorealistic sets and props for your next project or production.

Print Media: Computer graphics have taken your industry by storm. More 3D graphics are popping up in print media every day. Your industry is probably the most challenging when it comes to photorealistic 3D. Unlike the film industry where most things move by you too fast to really get a good look, your work lies there motionless so even the smallest flaw can stand out like a beacon. This book will show you countless techniques for creating eye-popping photorealistic images that will keep your viewers glued to the page.

3D Modelers: You are the foundation of every 3D image. It all starts with modeling. If you want to know the secrets of making photorealistic models, you should dive right into Part II. You'll discover dozens of proven techniques for adding photorealistic detail to your models.

3D Texture Artists: There is no more important element of photorealistic 3D than the textures. You are saddled with the responsibility of creating the eye candy. It's up to you to create realistic textures that make the model photorealistic. You've mastered the painting technique but now you want to learn the elements that make a texture realistic. You should skip ahead to Part III where you'll learn how to add subtle nuances to your texture to make them undeniably realistic.

3D Staging and Lighting Technicians: You're sitting there with a pile of 3D models that have beautiful textures and now it's up to you to package them in a photorealistic environment. Part IV will show you how to mimic the chaos of reality in your scenes. You'll learn techniques for making your scene look natural, not staged. You'll also learn techniques for lighting every situation you'll encounter.

Hobbyists: You've been experimenting with 3D and you really want to do something spectacular. Let's face it, you want to show the world what you're capable of doing. You want to leave them dumbfounded when they look at your 3D images. Well, you're only 300+ pages away from doing just that! Remember this, photorealistic 3D entails more attention to detail than artistic talent. Let everyone else be artistic; you'll be photorealistic.

Whether you are an amateur or a professional you will benefit from reading this book. In short, if you are a 3D artist who's interested in creating photorealistic images, read this book!

Tools You Will Need

You will, of course, need a 3D program to take advantage of the information this book has to offer. Any 3D program is fine—the principles and techniques are not limited to any one program. I do recommend that you purchase SoftImage, Alias, LightWave, or 3D Studio MAX if you are interested in exploring all the resources described in this book. The lower-priced programs typically lack a few of the surfacing and lighting features that make photorealistic 3D images possible. You can still create great looking photorealistic images with the lower-priced programs; the quality just won't be as high as the professional programs.

You will require a working knowledge of the modeling, surfacing, staging, and lighting aspects of your 3D program to grasp the concepts in this book. The main focus of this book is to illustrate the principles and techniques of 3D photorealism. It doesn't cover product-specific examples. If you are just beginning to explore 3D you should become more acquainted with your program before beginning to read this book.

You will also need a painting program such as Photoshop. This is an important tool when creating the different types of image maps. Some Photoshop techniques are described in Part III, but the same techniques can be applied with Fractal Painter and Corel's Photopaint.

The last item you need is dedication. You have to be dedicated to creating photorealistic 3D images. It doesn't happen overnight. It takes practice and experimentation. In time, it will become second nature. You won't even have to think about doing it.

What's on the Web Site

The companion Web site contains a variety of support materials for creating photorealistic 3D images. The support materials of the examples discussed in this book are provided in a common format that can be used by any program on any platform. The bonus models on the Web site are available in several common formats. The bonus Image Maps are in a TGA format.

Here's what you'll find on the Web site:

- Support materials for exercises discussed in the book
- A 3D photorealism gallery
- Free photorealistic models
- Free photorealistic image map textures
- Update to the book
- And links to dozens of photorealism resources

The *3D Photorealism Toolkit* companion Web site is located at www.wiley.com/compbooks/fleming.

Color Plates

Inside you'll find several photorealistic images on the Color Plates. These images are provided to give you an idea of what is possible if you closely follow the principles of 3D photorealism. Sure, they're a bit complicated and highly detailed, but these elements will become second nature to you in very little time. You'll soon find yourself applying painstaking detail to your images so they become ultra-realistic.

Getting Started

Photorealistic 3D can be the hardest thing you'll ever accomplish if you don't understand the techniques and principles. Fortunately, you currently have these techniques and principles at your fingertips. After reading this book you'll find 3D photorealism to be one of the easiest endeavors you've undertaken. You are only 300+ pages away from knowing everything you'll need to create stunning photorealistic 3D images. What are you waiting for—dive in!

PART I
Reality Is Chaos

I remember a conversation I had with one of my modelers several months ago. We were critiquing an image I had just completed for an animated short film. While he was very impressed with the photorealistic quality of the image, he was also concerned that it was too cluttered . . . too cluttered? Let's examine that statement. Saying that a photorealistic image is too cluttered is sort of an oxymoron. That's like saying a ball is too round. 3D artists have become accustomed to seeing purity in computer-generated images. We've seen so much of it that it has altered our perception of reality. We've come to accept neat and spotless images as photorealistic. The term *photorealistic* implies that the image resembles a photograph. In other words, it mimics reality. Somewhere along the line the term *photorealistic* has been downgraded to meaning something that's close to realistic but not quite there. The same thing happened with the term *interactive* in the multimedia industry. Suddenly every program was interactive! The reality was that only a handful of the programs were actually interactive. As 3D artists we need to strive for more. We can't stop at close to photorealistic and make the jump to realistic by simply calling it photorealistic. The difference between a near photorealistic image and one that's truly realistic is marginal. It's all a matter of taking the time to add the subtle detail that transforms the image into something photorealistic. If you are willing to dedicate yourself to taking that extra step toward realism then turn the page and get ready for a little chaos!

VISIT THE COMPANION WEB SITE FOR COLOR IMAGES.

Before you begin Part I, go to Appendix F and learn about the companion Web site, located at www.wiley.com/compbooks/fleming. All of the figures shown in this book are included, in color, on the companion Web site. I recommend you visit the site and view the images while you read the book, or download the images for faster reference. There will be details in the figures that you can't see in the printed image.

1 *Chaos—A Reality Primer*

What makes an image photorealistic? Actually there are literally thousands of things that make an image photorealistic but they all fall into 10 categories that I call "The Principles of 3D Photorealism." These principles are the guidelines to ensure that an image is photorealistic.

The 10 Principles of 3D Photorealism

1. Clutter and Chaos
2. Personality and Expectations
3. Believability
4. Surface Texture
5. Specularity
6. Dirt, Dust, and Rust
7. Flaws, Scratches, and Dings
8. Beveled Edges
9. Object Material Depth
10. Radiosity

All you need to do is take a look at your image and compare it with the 10 principles of 3D photorealism. Your image must conform to at least eight of the principles for your image to be considered truly photorealistic. For example, an out-of-the-box-, factory-new object, would not require principles 6 and 7 because it is new, but it would still need the other eight principles to be photorealistic.

There you have it. Ten simple principles to use as guidelines in your 3D photorealism endeavors. What are they all about? I was hoping you would ask. This chapter briefly outlines each of the principles so you have a basic understanding of their application. We will be doing an in-depth exploration of each principle in the coming chapters.

Let's take a moment to examine each of these principles by seeing how they were applied to this book's cover image. Before we get started with the principles, it's important to understand the background behind the image. This helps you to understand how and why the principles of 3D photorealism were applied to the image.

Dwellers is a 3D animated short film currently in production at Komodo Studio, a 3D studio in Southern California. It's about a race of cognitive thinking robotic creatures that were created by an old toy maker named Papagaio. Papagaio created the first Dweller, Gizmo, in his basement workshop. To make a short story even shorter, Papagaio built Gizmo out of discarded junk and parts he scavenged from both new and old items. The Dwellers are built from actual real-world parts. This helps to establish their photorealistic credibility. This also helps determine the modeling and surfacing attributes . . . not to mention the mechanics of motion.

Figure 1.1 shows Gizmo on Papagaio's workbench where he was created. The scene takes place at around 1 AM in the basement of Papagaio's house. He doesn't want anyone to find out about the Dwellers, so he uses only a shop light to illu-

Figure 1.1 *Gizmo in Papagaio's workshop.*

minate the workbench. He's just finished adding the circuit board that is Gizmo's brain. The scene has captured the moment at which Gizmo comes to life.

Now that you have a basic understanding of the story behind the scene, let's take a look at those Principles of 3D photorealism and see how they were applied to the Dwellers image.

Principle 1: Clutter and Chaos

There is much more to photorealism than applying real image textures to your objects. The way that you stage a scene can impact the realism. For example, a table with all the chairs rotated at 90-degree angles and moved to the exact same distance from the table looks too planned. Even if the textures are amazingly real the scene will end up looking like a shot of Barbie's dream house. It just won't look natural. It is important to add chaos and clutter to your 3D scenes to paint a little reality in the picture.

Clutter is one of the most obvious traits of reality. The common problem in most 3D rendered scenes is the lack of clutter—they are too sterile. Everything is neatly arranged. I don't know about your world but the world I live in is in complete chaos. Look around your home or office. What do you see? Well, if it's anything like my studio you see stacks of reference books, piles of papers, floppies, zips, and an assortment of knick-knacks. Basically, pure CHAOS.

Reality is pure chaos. Chaos doesn't mean that everything is completely disorganized. There is actually order in chaos. Chaos means that everything in the scene cannot be aligned perfectly. You can create order by putting all the chess pieces on the board but chaos dictates that they will be rotated at slightly different angles and none of them will be in the middle of their space. There is no uniformity in reality yet, for some reason, 3D rendered scenes defy reality by neatly arranging everything. Actually, the reason is simple. 3D programs present us with countless tools for engineering our creations. Because we are submersed in this engineering environment we feel compelled to be linear in our thinking. It's far too easy to get caught up in the rigidity of 3D engineering. You need to break loose of the engineering binds of 3D and experience the creative side.

Try to make it a habit to place things out of alignment in your scenes. Not dramatically out of alignment, because that would be too much chaos, but a little out of alignment. You'll see it makes a big difference in the photorealism of the scene.

TELL ME MORE

In Chapter 12, you'll learn a number of techniques for applying clutter and chaos to your scenes.

COMBINE BOTH CHAOS AND ORDER TO CREATE WINNING PHOTOREALISTIC SCENES.

While it's important to add clutter it is also equally important to add balance. If a scene is too out of balance it will be uncomfortable to view. A solid photorealistic 3D scene combines the chaos of reality with the balance we desire. For example: Placing chairs around a table is order, rotating them all to slightly different angles is chaos. Reality formula: Order + Chaos = Reality.

Now let's see how the clutter and chaos principle was applied to the workbench scene. Take another look at Figure 1.1. You'll notice an abundance of clutter. This is a workbench, and I haven't seen a workbench that is neatly arranged . . . particularly when it's in use. There are nuts, bolts, and screws scattered everywhere. And yet, there is still an element of order in the tools that are neatly stored on the wall rack. You can't go wrong by combining chaos and order. Notice the subtle chaos in the scene. One of the two batteries has fallen over. The camera box is turned away from the wall slightly. The needle-nose pliers are open and the red wire isn't coiled perfectly. Probably the best use of chaos is the hot soldering iron that is burning the workbench. I don't recommend doing this in your workshop, but I don't recall the last time I saw anyone use a heat synch with a soldering iron . . . that would be too much of a hassle for the busy craftsman.

Speaking of the craftsman, it's very important to understand the personality of the characters involved in your scene. This takes us to the next principle of 3D photorealism: personality and expectations.

Principle 2: Personality and Expectations

What does personality have to do with 3D photorealism? Everything! It's important to realize that people create their environments. In this world, few sanctuaries exist that people have not altered. Because of this, nearly every 3D scene has some element of human intervention. Of course, it's not just people we're talking about here. It could be animals, aliens, or even insects. Every creature has a distinct personality that it reflects in its environment. They have a particular way of doing things. It may be sloppy, neat, or completely chaotic, but they definitely have a way they like to structure their environment. You need to dedicate some time to exploring the theoretical creators of your scene. Even though a character may not be featured in the scene, it was most definitely created by someone or something. You need to understand their personality to properly construct a photorealistic scene.

Expectation Is a Large Part of Photorealism

When exploring the personality of your scene's creators, it's important to consider the viewer's expectation. We have come to stereotype nearly everyone and everything. While stereotypes may not always be flattering, they do provide you with perfect guidelines for developing your photorealistic scenes. Stereotypes don't limit your creativity; instead they provide you with simple guidelines for ensuring your work will be recognized as photorealistic.

For example, we assume that intelligent people are neat. And, of course, that less intelligent people are sloppy. While this may be true in some cases it certainly doesn't apply to everyone. Still, when developing a scene created by an intelligent character you should aim for neatness to make the scene believable to the viewers. Another example would be how the intelligent character looks. What would happen if you made a scientist a buff, handsome hunk? The answer is simple—nobody would believe he was smart. Hollywood has conditioned us to believe scientists are skinny, nerdy-looking guys with glasses and pocket protectors. We've also been programmed to believe that muscle-bound macho men are dumb as dirt. You can't escape the stereotypes and expect the scene to be credibly photorealistic. Even though it may be completely realistic looking there will still be some doubt in the viewers' mind due to their expectations. It would be like fighting millions of years of evolution. Everyone has been stereotyped . . . even 3D artists.

Let's see if we can extract Papagaio's personality from the workbench scene. Take a look at Figure 1.1. Immediately you can see that he has a neat side to his personality since there are tools carefully hung on the wall rack. This tells you that he respects his tools and workspace. You'll see some aging on the tools but they are still in great condition. The workbench surface is dirty but it doesn't have a lot of damage like paint stains and gouges. Even the wire is coiled up neatly as opposed to being knotted. These are all subtle expressions of his personality. We have to assume that Papagaio is rather intelligent since he has created an artificial life form capable of cognitive thought. Therefore, by stereotype definition, he is neat. But because he is an inventor, a messy stereotype, his workspace is cluttered while he is working. He probably cleans it up after he's done. We can also assume, since he is an inventor, that he will have reference books piled on his workbench. This justifies the book in the scene.

You can see how the scene is starting to make a great deal of sense based on the personality of Papagaio. It's very important to get inside the head of the characters responsible for the development and maintenance of the scene you are creating. It's also a lot of fun.

Working with the Viewer's Expectations

It is also important to get inside the heads of your viewers to understand their expectation of the scene. We have come to expect certain attributes of particular scenes and environments. For instance: We expect an industrial factory to be dark and dirty; a movie theater to be littered with popcorn and empty cups; spaceships to be covered in grease stains; monsters to be very ugly with huge fangs; and dinosaurs to be earthtone colors—you get the idea. We have been conditioned by our experiences to make assumptions about the nature of things. The media have played a major role in defining our expectations. When was the last time you saw a spotless factory in the media? Probably never, but there are actually many factories that are extremely clean. Yet, if I were to show you a spotless factory scene you would say it didn't look realistic because there wasn't any dirt. How can a factory operate without making a mess? We can't accept a spotless factory, because the media has taught us that it isn't possible for a factory to be clean.

►► UNDERSTAND THE VIEWER'S EXPECTATIONS BEFORE YOU BEGIN YOUR PROJECT.

People have predefined expectations of things. Over time they are conditioned by their environment to expect certain attributes in real objects. For instance: Grass is green and the sky is blue. It's what they are used to seeing. If you include objects in your scene that have unexpected attributes you will lose photorealistic credibility . . . even if it looks great. An aurora borealis would be unrealistic to people who haven't seen one.

Here's a great example of the expectations we create ourselves: If I showed you a render of a dinosaur with bright colors you would say it was artificial, in spite of the fact that dinosaurs were most likely very colorful. Because of their size and skin texture, we tend to compare dinosaurs to current day behemoths like elephants. But these are also pachyderms—pachyderms don't have colorful skin. These skin colors wouldn't make sense for a dinosaur since they were reptilian and reptiles are very colorful, particularly the males. They were depicted with subtle tones by the media because we wouldn't expect them to be colorful. This brings up an important point. You need to conform to people's expectations in spite of the fact that they may be occasionally misguided. It's all part of making the scene believable, which just happens to be the next principle of 3D photorealism.

►► TELL ME MORE

You'll learn more about designing scenes based on personality and expectation in Chapter 11, "Planning Your Scene."

Principle 3: Believability

What makes a 3D scene believable? Probably the most important aspect of believability is recognition. The objects and/or surfaces in the scene must be recognizable to be believable. They must be familiar to the viewer. Otherwise they have no basis for determining the photorealism of the scene.

There are two types of believability: models and surfaces. You don't need to have both to make an object believable. For example, a futuristic spaceship isn't a real object, but if the surfaces are something we expect, the object becomes believable. The opposite also applies. If you had a photoreal model of a computer screen that was painted with psychedelic colors it would still seem believable, in spite of the strange colors, because a computer monitor is a familiar object. It would be a bizarre choice of coloration but the computer just might belong to a Grateful Dead fanatic.

Another good example of believable surfaces would be the dinosaur we discussed earlier. A colorful dinosaur wouldn't be believable even if the model was physiologically perfect. We just don't accept the colors. On the other hand, an earthtone dinosaur with flaws in the physical design would be believable. There are only a few cases where we have preconceived notions for the physical structure of a dinosaur. The T rex is a perfect example of a dinosaur's physical structure that we have come to expect. The media has told us that the T rex has tiny arms. Any deviation from that structure and the creature becomes less believable. We wouldn't buy into a T rex with large upper arms, even if the surfacing is something we expect.

Let's take another look at Figure 1.1. What makes this scene believable? Actually there are many things. First and foremost, the scene is comprised of all real-world objects. Most of the objects in the scene are recognizable to everyone, particularly the tools. They lay a solid foundation for believability. The book is another element of believability. It adds credibility because it is easily recognized as a real-world object. All of these items add a great deal of believability to the scene but the batteries really bring it home. Take a look at the batteries in Figure 1.2. They are the most recognizable objects in the scene. This helps build photorealistic credibility for the entire scene. Key photorealistic objects, like the batteries, are referred to as object anchors.

Using Photorealistic Object Anchors to Make Your Scenes Believable

One of the best ways to ensure viewers perceive your scene as photorealistic is to use object anchors. An *object anchor* is a recognizable object that has undeniable photorealistic attributes. More often than not, it's a simple object, usually one that is surfaced with real-world texture maps. These are the easiest objects to

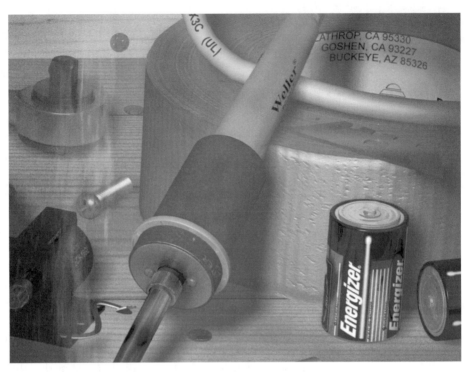

Figure 1.2 *Believable objects are a necessary element of photorealistic scenes.*

make photorealistic. It can be as simple as a product box with scanned textures or may be a book with a commonly seen cover.

It's important to make the distinction between objects that are recognizably photorealistic and those that appear realistic. For example, a chair is not an object anchor because it isn't immediately recognizable. We know that it's a chair, but we probably haven't seen the specific chair that's in the scene. While it may be realistic, it isn't recognizably photorealistic. Objects like furniture are not good object anchors because their styles are too varied. An effective object anchor needs to have detailed familiarity. It needs to be a very specific object that we frequently see in our daily lives. A box of cereal is an excellent object anchor, particularly if the textures were scanned from an actual box. Who hasn't seen a Wheaties box? The cereal box is a great object anchor because all cereal boxes are constructed the same way. It's the object's construction that makes it a solid object anchor.

It's important to note that the texture you apply to the object anchor must fall into the guidelines of what the viewer expects. This means you can't change the basic layout of a cereal box without losing its photorealistic credibility. We are accustomed to seeing a specific layout for cereal boxes; for example, the manufacturer's name at the top of the box; a product name underneath the manufacturer's name; a picture of the cereal under the product name; a nutritional label on one side panel; and something gimmicky on the other side panel; and, of course, some kind of bonus offer on the back. If you dramatically alter this design with your textures you'll negate the object's credibility.

Another excellent object anchor is a battery. All batteries are basically shaped the same. They are commonly seen items and the viewer is actually fairly flexible on the texture design. Figure 1.1 makes good use of a battery to establish believability.

ALWAYS ANCHOR YOUR SCENE WITH RECOGNIZABLE OBJECTS.

Recognizable objects lend credibility to a photorealistic scene. They add that undeniably realistic anchoring element. If viewers are convinced that one object is real they are likely to assume all the other objects are real, thereby becoming less critical of the scene's photorealism.

To see a closer view of the batteries, take another look Figure 1.2. While the model is nice, it's the textures that makes it believable. The object's surfacing matches the real-world object so well that you can't tell the difference. Adding a believable object like this gives the whole image great leverage in convincing the viewer that it's real. If viewers believe that one object in the scene is real, they are likely to assume the whole thing is real. This can be a great benefit when creating photorealistic scenes. Object anchors are a critical part of every photorealistic scene.

While the object anchor is crucial to the scene's believability, it doesn't need to be the main focus of the scene. The batteries in Figure 1.1 are a very small element in the scene. Gizmo, the robot, is the main focus of the scene. The batteries were added to anchor the photorealism of the scene, and build more credibility for the fantasy robot object. Actually, there are several anchors in this scene. The book and camera box are also powerful object anchors that solidify the scene's photorealism. Books and product packages are very familiar objects that make them perfect object anchors. This brings us to another aspect of believability: object familiarity.

Using Familiar Objects to Make Fantasy Objects Photorealistic

Familiar objects play a major role in a scene's photorealistic credibility. Familiar objects are a little different from object anchors. Object anchors are used as a foundation of the scene's photorealism. *Familiar objects* are used to make fantasy objects appear realistic. For instance, to make a futuristic car that flies appear realistic, we add familiar components to the body such as: headlights, running lights, turn signals, bumpers, windshield wipers, rear view mirrors, and so forth. These are all familiar objects that make the fantasy object appear realistic. Gizmo, the robot, is a great example of a fantasy object that incorporates familiar objects.

Take a look at Figure 1.3. Even though Gizmo isn't a real-world object, he is comprised of very familiar real-world parts. You can immediately identify his right arm as a Swiss Army knife, and the speaker on his back is quite familiar as well. If you take a closer look you'll recognize his feet as headphone speakers. And, of course, his body is an oilcan—it even says it on the label. All of these real-world objects help to make Gizmo believable in spite of the fact that he is completely imaginary.

You should make an effort to include familiar objects in the construction of all your fantasy objects. There will be cases where the fantasy object is too sophisticated or too old to incorporate familiar objects. In these situations, you need to focus your efforts on creating believable surfaces. 3D photorealism principles 4 to 7 explore the surfacing guidelines.

Principle 4: Surface Texture

All real-world objects have surface texture. Now don't confuse the term *texture* with the reference commonly used in the 3D industry. Texture does not mean the coloration of the object. In fact, the proper term for texture is the roughness or smoothness of the object surface. It's the surface attribute that you can feel. All objects have some form of surface texture. Yes, including the smooth ones.

A common problem with the 3D objects surfacing is that they are almost always too smooth. Frequently you will see polished wood that's as smooth as glass. This just isn't realistic. The varnish will conform to the natural texture of the wood's grain, leaving very subtle variations in the varnish texture. The only way to get smooth varnish is to coat the wood with several layers and then sand the final layer smooth. This just isn't done unless you want to mortgage your house to buy a wooden desk. You could hypothesize that the wood is an artificial veneer but then nobody would want to admit to using artificial wood in their scene. You could try sanding the wood until it is completely smooth, but this wouldn't work well either. Wood has a natural grain. To completely remove any surface texture, you would have to sand all the wood away . . . this just isn't a very practical solution. Keep in mind that just because you can't feel a texture doesn't mean it's not there. The texture may be too subtle to feel, but it will definitely show up in the object's specularity—particularly if the object is animated.

>> **ADD SURFACE TEXTURE TO EVERY PHOTOREALISTIC OBJECT.**

Every object in your photorealistic scenes should have some level of surface bump mapping. It can be procedural or image based but it must be included to make the objects realistic. Without surface bumps, the objects' specularity will appear unrealistic.

Figure 1.3 *Object recognition is an important part of 3D photorealism.*

13

Another factor of varnished wood is the very subtle bump that the varnish itself creates. When the varnish dries there are very tiny air bubbles trapped under the surface; you can't see these from any distance but if you plan to shoot a close-up of an object on a varnished table, you'll need to add the varnish bump. Once again, you won't really see the bump but you will see the visual impact on the specularity and reflectivity of the wood.

Take a look at Figure 1.4. This is a close-up shot of the tools on Papagaio's workbench. You can see a subtle bump texture on the wrenches against the wall. Shop tools are primarily made of chrome alloy. Chrome alloy usually has a slightly rough surface that is quite often brushed. There are also many chrome alloys that have an irregular bumpiness to their surface. This texture is essential for the tools to appear photorealistic. There is also a very subtle brushed bump map on the neck of the light. This texture is not really obvious in a still shot, but it's very apparent when the neck is animated. It affects both the specularity and the reflection. Of course, there is a subtle texture on the wood. You have to look close, but you will see small lines between the larger grain lines. This is that tiny texture that can't be felt but can be seen upon close inspection. While this texture isn't necessary for distance shots it becomes an important part of close-up shots.

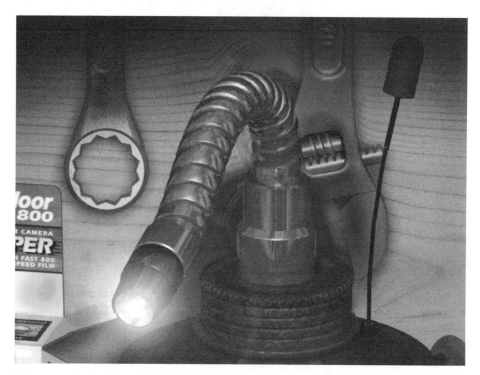

Figure 1.4 *Real-world objects have surface texture.*

I know I've been picking on wood, but it's not the only surface that requires a bump map. You'll need to add surface texture to all the photorealistic objects in your scene—particularly surfaces such as plastic, rubber, metals, fabric, and even paper. Take a look at any multimedia component in your house. You'll notice the plastic has a minor roughness to its surface. If you don't incorporate that texture into the 3D-rendered version of that object, it won't be photorealistic. Even smooth plastic objects have minor surface distortion that impacts their specularity. Specularity is a critical element of surface realism. It's also the fifth principle of 3D photorealism.

 TELL ME MORE

You'll see many examples on applying surface textures in Chapter 9; "Image Map Surfaces," and Chapter 10, "Procedural Textures."

Principle 5: Specularity

Simply put, *specularity* is the reflection of the light source on the object's surface. It's a bright spot that the human eye uses to determine the surface's shininess and hardness. Specularity is a very important aspect of 3D photorealism. It's necessary to add specularity to mimic the real-world attributes of the surface. Without specularity, the object would appear dull, soft, and flat. While this may be good for cloth it doesn't do much for metal or plastic. Specularity and surface texture work together to simulate real-world surfaces. For example: Plastic has a rough surface texture. When specularity is applied, it adds specular highlights to the tops of the surface bumps. This does two things: It gives the surface bump a 3D feel and provides you with a visual reference for hardness.

Let's take a look at how specularity impacts the model photorealism in the workbench scene. Take another look at Figure 1.4. Notice how there is a soft white spot on the leading edge of each segment in the light's neck. This subtle specular highlight is essential for the photorealism of the object. The light's neck is made of chromed aluminum, which, like all metals, has a low specular level because it reflects light. The subtle specular highlight helps the human eye identify the surface as metal.

Just behind the light neck you'll see the head of a crescent wrench. You'll notice a very subtle specular highlight on peaks of the rounded parts. The wrench has a lower specular level than the light neck because it's a different metal surface. The wrench is made of chromed alloy, which has a lower specular level and a rough surface texture. The low specular level spreads the highlight over the surface of the object, which is then softened by the rough surface texture.

Take a look at the open-end wrench to the left of the light neck. It too is made of chrome alloy, so the specularity is spread out over the surface. The entire head of the wrench is covered in a soft specular highlight because it's a flat surface that is parallel to the light source. This is a case where the surface texture is necessary to maintain the photorealism of the metal surface. Without a texture, the surface would be completely washed out by the specular highlight, covering all the surface attributes. The specular highlight is broken up by the surface texture, which helps maintain the integrity of the surface.

SPECULARITY ISN'T AN OPTION, IT'S A REQUIREMENT.

The human eye uses specularity to determine the hardness of an object. This is a crucial element in creating photorealistic surfaces like metal, plastic, wood, paper, and cloth. You need to add specularity to every object in your scene or they will not appear photorealistic.

While specularity is important to simulate many real-world textures, there are cases where you don't want parts of an object to be specular. For instance: You would want metal to be specular but what if it was covered in corrosion? Corrosion isn't normally specular. Therefore you would need to make the metal specular but not the corroded areas. This is accomplished with specular image maps, which we discuss in Part III, "Photorealistic Surfacing Techniques." There are occasions where the corrosion would be specular due to humidity or water; in these cases you would need to add specularity to the corrosion. As you can see, it's important to identify the environmental conditions of the scene to properly apply specularity.

While we're on the subject of corrosion, let's take a look at the sixth principle of 3D photorealism: dirt, dust, and rust.

Principle 6: Dirt, Dust, and Rust

Dirt, dust, and rust are very important aspects of an object's surface, which are commonly referred to as *aging.* There are very few clean surfaces in reality. Just look around your home or office and you'll find almost everything is covered in dust. If you have small children, it's likely that you have stains on the carpet and handprints on the walls. I'm willing to bet that your glass tabletops have smudges and there might even be cobwebs in the ceiling corners. If you have brass, copper, or silver items they are likely to be tarnished. I haven't seen a TV yet that doesn't have a layer of dust on the screen. Picture tubes are dust magnets! You can't see it while the TV is on but when you turn it off, well, it's not a pretty sight.

APPLY AGING TO ALL YOUR OBJECTS WHEN RENDERING CLOSE-UPS.

All objects, regardless of how new they are, will show signs of aging. These signs may not be visible from a distance shot but they are obvious when viewed up close. You should make an effort to add subtle layers of dust to your objects when shooting close-ups.

It's not that we are lazy and don't clean our houses. It's just a fact of life: Dirt is everywhere and we can't escape it—unless we live in a plastic bubble. Yet it seems nearly every 3D scene created has somehow captured the precise moment after which it was visited by Mr. Clean. That's a whole lot of great timing. Spotless scenes just aren't natural. It may look great but it doesn't look realistic. It's important to add aging to your scenes. The level of aging depends on the scene's background. If you are creating a factory scene you should bury everything in a layer of dirt and grime. If you are rendering a hospital operating room you can probably get away with making the scene spotless—well, one would hope it would be spotless. You need to consider the environment of the scene when planning your surfaces.

Let's take another look at the workbench scene in Figure 1.1 and see where the aging was added. Remember when we discussed Papagaio's personality? He's an intelligent inventor, and that makes him neat with a tendency to get a little disorganized. His personality needs to be reflected in the scene's surfaces. Notice how the workbench is covered in burn marks and dirt stains. Even though Papagaio is neat, it would be nearly impossible to avoid making stains on the workbench. You'll notice they aren't huge stains, just a little dirty. This is a reflection of Papagaio's personality. We need to zoom in to the picture more to see some of the aging detail.

Take a look at the image in Figure 1.5. This is a close-up of Gizmo's oilcan body. You'll notice the top of the can is covered in rust and corrosion. This is a very important element of the scene. It justifies a great deal of the dirt in the rest of the scene. We have to assume that Papagaio has been handling Gizmo. If so, the rust and corrosion have likely rubbed off on his hands. This dirt will be transferred to the objects Papagaio handles. You can see evidence of this by looking back at Figure 1.2. Here you can see that the rust and corrosion from Papagaio's hands have rubbed off on the soldering iron grip. You can see that he handled the duct tape because there is grime on the left side and dirt on the center roll.

Let's explore the workbench scene a little more to see if we can find additional evidence of Papagaio's grimy grasp. Take a look at Figure 1.6. Here we have a close-up of the reference book. Notice how there are dirt stains on the cover. This is another subtle sign of aging, but it's important to ensure the scene makes sense. A spotless book on a cluttered and dirty workbench would stand out like

Figure 1.5 *You begin by determining the source of the aging.*

a sore thumb. You need to sit back and examine a scene after you have staged it, to determine where and how to apply the aging.

Keeping with the idea that Papagaio is spreading the dirt with his hands, there is another object in the scene that needs some specific aging. Take a look at Figure 1.7. Here we have a close-up of the camera box. Since the camera box is open, we have to assume Papagaio handled it. Therefore it needs to have dirty fingerprints. If you look close you'll see a couple fingerprints around the opening on the right side of the box, and a couple on the opposite side where he held the box while opening it. These may be subtle details but they add an extraordinary amount of photorealism to the scene. It's this attention to detail that makes the scene photorealistic. If you take a closer look at Figure 1.1, you'll notice that there are grime and dirt marks on all of the tools that Papagaio has handled.

As you can see, aging is a critical aspect of a photorealistic 3D scene. Before you add the aging, take some time to explore your scene to find out what kind of aging to add, where it is coming from, and how it's being spread. It may seem like a lot of work but it's actually a lot of fun. How often do you get the opportunity to make a mess without having to clean it up? If you're like me, it's not often enough.

Figure 1.6 *Only certain objects will be affected by the aging source.*

There is still another element of aging that we haven't covered: flaws, scratches, and dings. As you have probably guessed, that's the topic of the next principle of 3D photorealism.

 TELL ME MORE

Part III, "Photorealistic Surfacing Techniques," will show you many techniques for applying aging to your models.

Principle 7: Flaws, Scratches, and Dings

Nothing makes an object look more artificial that a flawless surface. Even brand-new objects have occasional subtle flaws. Computer graphics have made it far too easy to create perfect objects. The problem is that reality isn't perfect. It's important that you add a little wear and tear to your objects to make them realistic. I can't count the number of 3D wooden tables I've seen, yet, not a single one has a dent or ding on its surface. All wooden objects, unless they are new, have some

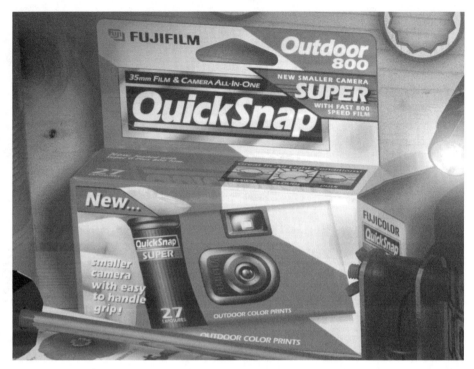

Figure 1.7 *You need to follow the aging source through the scene.*

form of flaw. In fact, even the new ones can be flawed since the delivery people are more than willing to help you apply them.

Applying flaws to your objects requires that you first explore the nature of the scene. You must consider the following questions in the order presented here, to determine if and when to apply flaws:

1. *What is the object material?* This is the most important question. The material makes a major impact on the type of flaws you'll need to apply. Wood is the most likely surface to be flawed. Plastic and papers, such as cardboard, frequently have dents and dings. Metal, on the other hand, usually has minimal flaws. Hard metals, like steel, are typically scratched; softer metals like lead, aluminum, copper, and brass are usually dented and dinged. Objects that are dented and dinged are commonly referred to as *peened*. You will see a lot of peened metals in industrial images. The last of the major material types is fabric. Fabric frequently has rips and tears, though you will see knotted threads on occasion. Take a moment to consider the object's material when you are applying its surfacing.

2. *How often is the object handled?* Most objects are handled at some point. It's necessary to determine how often the object is handled to accurately

apply the flaws. Objects such as household appliances, tools, sports equipment, recreational items, and clothing are frequently handled. These items are likely to have flaws. I've seen many 3D characters wearing jeans, but I've yet to see a worn spot on the knees. If the item is frequently handled, it really needs to have flaws, even if they are minor. I've also seen an abundance of flawless tools, which is very unlikely. Be sure to invest a little time in determining how often the object is handled before you surface it.

3. *Who is handling the object?*   This is a question 3D artists rarely consider when applying surfacing to their objects. It's important to take into consideration the personality of the individual who handles the objects. If the person is an auto body shop worker, it's likely the tools are very flawed. They've been dropped, banged, and pounded against everything in the garage. If the objects are surgeon's instruments, there are likely to be very few flaws. If the object is a child's toy, you can count on some serious dents and dings . . . not to mention the damage to the rest of the scene. Think about the personality of the characters handling the object before you apply aging.

4. *Where is the object located?*   The placement of objects will determine the magnitude of flaws. The location of the object can have a large impact on the surface aging. For example: If you place objects high on a shelf they are likely to remain flawless. If they are located within reach they will probably have some minor flaws. If they are within reach of children, well, plan for the worst. This, of course, is an obvious example, so let's look at one that's not so obvious. Let's say you have a car parked under a carport. The carport has posts that hold it in place. What are the odds you'll ding one of these posts when backing out the car? Okay, so you're an excellent driver. Now, what about the guy in the parking lot that dings your car door for you? Tell me this hasn't happened to you at least once. Get the idea? You need to be creative with your aging. The more creative you are the more likely it will appear realistic.

Now it's time for a little fun. Let's ask these questions of an object in the workbench scene. Take a look at Figure 1.8. Here we have a close-up of Gizmo's body. Let's explore the aging of the Swiss Army knife.

Gizmo is made from many discarded parts. We will assume the knife was an object Papagaio found in a city street gutter. It probably fell out of someone's pocket. This gives us the location. This also tells us the object was handled frequently, though in this case, most of the damage would come from falling in the gutter. We also know the case is plastic so it tends to dent easily. This covers the object material. The last remaining question is who was handling the knife. Well, in this case it's a question of what, not who. It was the gutter that handled the knife. Yes, it's unusual but we must assume that it spent a while in the gutter before it

Figure 1.8 *Flaws, dents, and dings are necessary tools of aging.*

caught Papagaio's eye. The water running through the gutter pushed the knife for some time before it was discovered. This would add quite a few flaws to the plastic case. Take another look at the knife in Figure 1.8. You'll notice it is littered with dents and dings. This adds a great deal of natural photorealism to the model.

There is another great example of surface flaws in Figure 1.8. Take a look at the hip joint on the left side of the image. This object is showing quite a few flaws in the form of dings. I wonder how they got there? Actually, this object is a new item. So why does it have dings? Well, it was stored with several other metal items, such as screws and bolts, in the tin can on the left side of the workbench scene. Since it's a softer metal, it was dinged by the other harder metal items when they were dropped on it. It also received damage when Papagaio would shake the can to find the object he was seeking.

As you can see, it requires some planning to determine the proper use of aging. It's a bit of work, but the time is well spent when you consider the final result is a truly striking photorealistic image. Just remember not to get carried away with aging items. If you apply too much aging, the items will tend to look unrealistic. Just apply enough to break up the surface. Nobody will buy into an object that is completely mutilated . . . unless it's a post–nuclear war environment.

We've covered all the staging and surfacing principles, now it's time to take a look at the modeling principles.

   TELL ME MORE

You'll learn how to age your models with dents and dings in Chapter 7, "Dents and Dings—Aging Your Models."

Principle 8: Beveled Edges

What is the one feature that is missing in nearly every 3D object? Beveled edges. Very rarely will you see beveled edges on a 3D model. This, of course, is a problem since nearly every real-world object that's manufactured has beveled edges. In the real world, beveling is done to shave off the harsh right angle that can cause injury. In the 3D world beveling becomes necessary for two reasons: The first is that the objects need to mirror the features of their real-world counterparts; the second becomes an issue of specularity. As we discussed earlier, specularity is the reflection of the light source on the object's surface. What this means is there will be very subtle specular highlights on the beveled edges. These highlights become particularly noticeable when the object is animated. We are accustomed to seeing these highlights on real-world objects. Without them, the 3D object will seem artificial.

Let's take a look at how beveled edges were used in the workbench scene. Look at Figure 1.9. You'll see a close-up of several hex nuts. This is a simple yet effective use of beveled edges. You can see a small bevel on the outer edge of the nut. Notice how the beveled edges closest to the light source have a specular highlight. These are fairly obvious bevels. Now let's look at a less obvious, but no less important bevel. Take a close look at the edge surrounding the blade lever on the X-acto knife. You can see a very fine line of specularity on this small beveled edge. You can even see the specular reflection in the brass lever grip. This gives the X-acto knife a refined and manufactured look.

Okay, those are the more obvious bevels. Not it's time for a really subliminal bevel. Take a look at the edge of the sheath around the copper wire that's facing you. You'll notice a smooth look to the edge. This is an extremely small bevel, but it helps make the object realistic. When you cut a sheath with trimmers, you'll compress the edge where it was cut. The beveling on the 3D object creates that compressed look. If it didn't have the bevel, it would be flat. This would cause the end of the sheath to be washed out by a specular highlight, making it look unnatural. Even though it's a minor element in the scene, your eye would be drawn to it because of the irregular specular highlight. You can see how even the smallest of details can have a large impact on the photorealism of the scene.

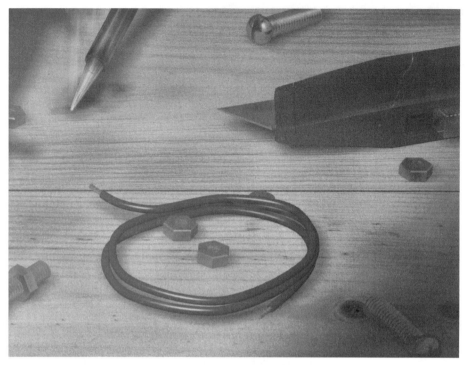

Figure 1.9 *Using beveled edges to create specular reality.*

ADD BEVELED EDGES TO ALL YOUR MANUFACTURED OBJECTS.

Real-world, manufactured, items have beveled edges. You need to add beveled edges to all your models that resemble manufactured items.

While beveled edges are important, they are not necessary for all models. Only objects that appear manufactured require beveled edges. Beveling is done to only three material types: metal, wood, and plastic. If your model is made of another material, it's likely you won't need to add beveled edges. Now it's time to explore the other modeling principle: object material depth.

TELL ME MORE

You'll learn how to add beveled edges to your models in Chapter 6, "Beveling—The Key to Specular Reality."

Principle 9: Object Material Depth

One of my major complaints about 3D objects is their lack of material depth. I'm not talking about their depth on the z axis. I'm speaking of the physical depth of the material. I've seen far too many objects where their material was thin as paper. This problem is mainly seen in character clothing, where the clothing resembles paper hanging off the model's body. While this is great for keeping the model cool during the summer, it's not a very photorealistic look. All real-world object materials have depth. There are only a few objects that have a depth that would resemble the thickness of a single polygon. This, of course, would be paper.

Take a look at Figure 1.10. Here you'll see a close-up of the camera box from the workbench scene. This is a great example of object material depth. Notice how the cardboard tabs have thickness. If you take a closer look you'll notice that the surface texture of the box label doesn't go all the way through the material, making it possible for you to see the cardboard surface. This is a critical aspect of object depth in regard to box labels. For a 3D box to appear photorealistic, you need to show both the label and cardboard surface. Real-world labels are printed on the surface of the cardboard, not as a part of the cardboard. If you ran the label surface all the way through the depth of the material, it would look artificial.

Now take a look at the other end of the box. You'll see that there are actually folded tabs that give the box the look of being assembled. We have all seen way too many 3D product boxes that were merely scanned images mapped to a simple cube. This obviously doesn't look realistic because there is no depth to the material. In fact, there is no visible way to open the box. This makes the box lose all photorealistic credibility, in spite of the scanned texture maps. For 3D product boxes to be realistic, they need to have material depth and signs of being manufactured. They also need to have slightly rounded edges that display specularity. The hard edge of a simple cube is completely unrealistic.

YOU NEED TO PLAN FOR OBJECT MATERIAL DEPTH.

For 3D objects to appear realistic they need to have material depth. This attribute of your model must be planned before you begin the modeling process. It's unlikely you'll be able to add it after the model is completed.

As you can see, material depth has a profound impact on the realism of a model. Adding material depth is relatively simple but you must plan ahead. It's far easier to add the material depth when you are just beginning the model than

Figure 1.10 *Object material needs to have depth.*

waiting until you've completed it. Take a moment to consider the material of the object before you begin modeling it.

Well, that does it for the modeling principles. Now let's take a look at the final principle of 3D photorealism: radiosity.

 TELL ME MORE

You'll learn many ways for adding depth to your models in Chapter 2, "Detail—The Main Component of Reality," including how to fold a 3D product package.

Principle 10: Radiosity

Radiosity is the most critical of the 10 principles of 3D photorealism. It was saved until last because few 3D programs have the capability to render radiosity lighting. *Radiosity* is defined as the radiation leaving a surface per unit time per unit area. Did that clear it up for you? Well, it didn't work for me either. Simply put, radiosity is the indirect light that is distributed between objects. Most real-world objects reflect light.

You'll be surprised to know that the majority of illumination in any room comes from the light reflected off objects, not directly from the source. For example: Let's say we built a room with four walls, painted with semigloss paint, and a floor tiled with linoleum. We'll call it a dining room. We then place a table in the middle of the room and light it with a single light source directly above. Can we see the legs? In fact, we can. You see—the light was reflected off the table, then the walls, and finally the floor, thereby illuminating the table legs. This is radiosity. Now try the same test with a standard point light in a 3D scene. Can you see the legs? Unfortunately, you can't. The objects in the scene did not reflect the light. This is why radiosity is necessary for creating truly photorealistic scenes.

Now that you understand the concept of radiosity, you can see why it's so critical for photorealism. Unfortunately, nearly ever 3D scene suffers from a lack of reflected light. This has nothing to do with the artist. It's a limitation of nearly every 3D program. Why, you ask. It's simple really. Radiosity is the most complex lighting formula to create, not to mention that it also adds considerably to your render times. The good news is that many of the more popular 3D programs are working on radiosity solutions. So what do you do until radiosity is a feature in your 3D program? You fake it.

 TELL ME MORE

In Chapter 14, "Lighting for Every Occasion," you will learn how to fake radiosity lighting in your scenes to give them that ultrarealistic look. You'll also learn how to light nearly every conceivable situation.

Getting Your Hands Dirty

Well, there you have it, the 10 principles of 3D photorealism. See, it wasn't that bad. Well, not too bad, anyway. Now the fun begins. You've seen how these principles were applied to the workbench scene to make it photorealistic; now it's time to take a look at how you can apply these same principle to your own images. The following chapters will take you even deeper into each of the principles, and show you, by example, several ways you can incorporate them into every 3D image you create. So sit back, relax, and take a deep breath. You're about to go where no 3D artist has gone before. Okay, so it's a bit melodramatic, but you should be excited because you are about to learn very simple and practical techniques for turning your 3D creations into ultraphotorealistic images.

PART II

Photorealistic Modeling Techniques

Modeling is the foundation of every photorealistic 3D image. Unfortunately, it's where most 3D artists skimp on detail. Sure, it can be complicated to model real-world objects, but without a high level of model detail you can't have photorealistic images. Objects in reality have a great deal of subtle detail. Even the simplest object is complex in design. Take a book for instance. It's a relatively simple object but there are details you must add to the model or it won't be photorealistic.

Take a look at any hardbound book in your studio and you'll see that it actually has a great deal of detail. Sure, it's basically a bunch of pages glued together, but take a closer look and you'll see that the top and bottom of the spine have been dented from use. My books look like they've been through a battle, probably because they're fighting for space on my desk. Now take a closer look at that book and you'll notice that cover material is actually thicker than the spine. It's a subtle detail but it's there nonetheless. Don't forget the cloth liner that's inside the spine—nobody ever considers this item. While we're here, take a look at how the pages actually curve a bit where they are glued to the spine. In fact, take a look at the other side of the book and you'll notice a slight curvature to the end of the pages.

As you can see, even the most simplistic object has an abundance of detail, which is required to make the object photorealistic. Yes, you can skimp on the detail, but realize that every thing you skip lessens the photorealistic credibility of the model. If your goal is to inspire the viewer with a wealth of photorealistic detail, you have a bit of work to do. It's not that difficult to add photorealistic details to your models. It's just a matter of discipline. It's far too easy to quit before you reach the level of photorealistic detail. In fact, it's usually just a few steps away.

The following chapters cover a wealth of issues regarding photorealistic modeling. We'll even do a couple exercises that are designed to illustrate techniques for adding detail to your models. While the modeling techniques may change from one program to another, the concepts remain the same—regardless if you are using polygons, splines, or nurbs. The exercises in these chapters will be done with polygons since they are the most common modeling method. Tutorial models will be provided in DXF or 3DS file format since these are accepted by nearly every program. You might have to use an import filter to use them.

Enough talk and more action! Let's get started.

VISIT THE COMPANION WEB SITE FOR TUTORIAL FILES.

Before you begin Part II, go to Appendix F and learn about the companion Web site. All of the TUTORIAL FILES referenced are located on the companion Web site. You should also download the color figures from the companion Web site since they will be easier to review than the grayscale images printed in this book. The site is located at www.wiley.com/ compbooks/fleming.

2 *Detail—The Main Component of Reality*

What is the one key element of reality that is missing from nearly every 3D model? If you said detail, you are correct. (Did you cheat by looking at the title of this chapter?)

Have you noticed that very few 3D models contain enough detail to be photorealistic? This problem runs amuck in the 3D industry. While it's true that a lot of detail can be added when surfacing the model, you still need to lay a solid foundation of model detail, or the object won't be photorealistic. The one consistent thing about every object in reality is that they are very detailed, whether they are manmade or natural.

So why is detail so important? Well, because the viewer expects it.

Working with the Viewer's Expectations

Since we've all been around reality for some time now, though a few of us have drifted into Bizarro World, we have become accustomed to seeing a certain level of detail in the objects around us. Naturally we don't spend a lot of time studying the objects in our environment, but we have seen them enough times to expect certain details. For instance: I'm sure you haven't taken the time to analyze your TV's remote control, but I'll guarantee you that you would expect a 3D model of one to have several buttons, a battery door, and an infrared port on the end. These are the basic details of a remote control. Without these, a 3D model won't be photorealistic. Look at the difference between a typical 3D TV remote and one that is photorealistic. (See Figure 2.1).

As you can see, the difference in detail is subtle but difference in photorealistic credibility is significant. Take a look at the remote on the left. Notice how it lacks detail. In fact, the infrared port has been created by simply creating a stencil on the surface of the remote's body, rather than actually creating a hole and placing an object within. Now look at the buttons. While they are placed in actual holes, they seem out of place on the barren surface of the remote. In general, this is a very simple model, but a typical representation of what you'll find in most 3D images. Now let's take a look at the remote on the right.

Notice how this one appears photorealistic because it has more detail—particularly the detail we expect in a TV remote. I'm sure you saw the distinctive battery door with a nice thumb grip for removing it. This is a very cool detail that adds credibility to the object. Now look at the distinctive button panel that makes the buttons appear more natural. It's a simple recess but it does a great job of braking up the surface. Electronics manufacturers spend millions on designers who are charged with creating designs that are comfortable for the end user. Did you notice the seam around the body? This adds awesome credibility to the object since you'll rarely see a 3D model that shows signs of being assembled. We'll take a look at techniques for making objects appear like they are manufactured in Chapter 3, "Material—What's It Made Of?"

Now take a look at the edge around the infrared port. This is a subtle detail, but necessary to make the object photorealistic. In reality, the infrared port is manufactured separately and installed in the remote upon assembly. Therefore we need to cut a hole in the remote and install the infrared port much the same way it's done in reality. Now for the last of the details, take a look at the "Made in" text window at the base of the remote. Every electronic item has this feature—typically they say "Made in Japan" or "Made in Taiwan." This remote happened to be made in Malaysia. Yes, this could have been created with a bump map but it wouldn't have been very believable, at least not nearly as much as actual geometry.

ALWAYS CONFORM TO THE VIEWER'S EXPECTATIONS.

The viewers of your models will have expectations of detail, particularly if the model is a recognizable real-world object. You need to meet the viewer's expectations for the model to be photorealistic. Don't worry, you aren't limited in creativity by these expectations; you just need to include the familiar details to anchor the object's photorealistic credibility.

All of these are common elements you'll find on every remote. Sure, the styles may change but they are present nonetheless. If you fail to include these elements, the remote will appear artificial. You have to comply with the viewer's expectations if you intend for the object to be photorealistic. Once again, we have expectations about nearly every object in existence. You do have a certain level of freedom when creating objects but you'll need to incorporate the expected items if you want the object to be photorealistic. Let's take a look at a common object, about which viewers have expectations. Take a look at Figure 2.2.

Here we have a very detailed model of an office phone; of course, we have misplaced the receiver but we won't be making any calls in this chapter anyway. Let's take a look at some of the items the viewer will expect in an office phone. Realize that viewers don't consciously expect things from the models; it's done on a subconscious level, which means they'll find fault with the object, but won't likely know why. In their mind they have a visual representation of an office phone, which the subconscious compares to the image. Of course, the subconscious usually doesn't bother to inform them of the exact problem. The viewer simply feels uncomfortable with the image.

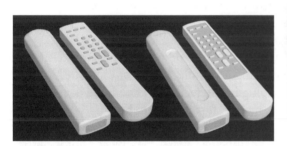

Figure 2.1 *A typical 3D TV remote compared to a photorealistic version.*

Figure 2.2 *Working with a viewer's expectations.*

Figure 2.3 *A phone with expected detail.*

Figure 2.4 *The surfaced, photorealistic phone model.*

The most obvious element of an office phone is the colorful "Hold" button, which is the orange button on this model. Another thing viewers expect is a collection of speed-dial buttons, which you'll find in the upper right of the phone. Of course, they'll expect a couple "Line" buttons, since it's an office phone. You'll find three of these just under the speed-dial buttons. These are the obvious things; there are a couple not so obvious elements that they expect but might not consciously realize. These items include the little microphone in the lower right corner and the receiver lock at the bottom of the upper receiver cup. Of course, there actually is a flaw in this model, which undermines its photorealistic credibility. What is it?

Well, what are three features that are common to nearly every phone? They are a pulse/tone select, ringer volume option, and someplace to plug in the receiver cord. You'll be hard-pressed to find a phone that doesn't have a receiver jack. Where are these features usually located? Typically they are located on the side of the phone where the receiver sits. This brings us to the flaws in the phone in Figure 2.2. It doesn't have these options. In fact, it's a three-line phone so it should have three ringer volume switches. An updated version of the phone, which features these items, is shown in Figure 2.3.

In FIgure 2.3 we see several switches on the side panel. That's more like it. You'll find a pulse/tone switch and a ringer volume switch for each line. And, of course, we now have someplace to plug in the receiver. The phone is now truly photorealistic. Well, the model is at any rate. It still needs to be surfaced but that's a topic for Part III, "Photorealistic Surfacing Techniques." Let's take a look at a final render to see how the model detail helped make the object photorealistic. Take a look at Figure 2.4.

As you can see, the model detail has made a large impact on the photorealistic credibility of the object. While the surfaces are important, they are also relatively simple, which means they rely heavily on the model to create photorealistic credibility.

We've seen that the viewer's expectations dictate a large degree of the object's detail. What about objects that aren't found in reality? Something like spaceships? Well, then we need to incorporate a little familiar detail work.

Using Familiar Detail to Make Fantasy Objects Photorealistic

What are familiar details? They are simply familiar parts on objects. They can be complex objects like radar antennas or simple objects like doors and access panels. Familiar details become a necessary element when creating fantasy objects like spaceships because we have expectations about these objects, too. I don't think there is a viewer out there who hasn't seen a major science fiction film. Of course, these films are filled with highly detailed spaceships. While the spaceships may not exist in reality, we have been conditioned by the media to expect a certain amount of detail. Besides, it's difficult for us to picture a high-tech object that doesn't have tons of detail.

Of course, you can't just start randomly throwing miscellaneous parts on a spaceship model to make it photorealistic. While you do have a certain amount of freedom since it's a fantasy object, you still need to have parts that are recognizable. For instance: You would need to have some point of access to the ship, which is something the viewer expects. You'll need to have some external representation of a communications device like an antenna or satellite dish. Of course, you'll need an abundance of access panels and ventilation ducts, which are commonplace items on current space vehicles and traditional aircraft like planes and jets. These are all very familiar details to the viewer. No, they don't have to meet any predefined expectation as far as appearance goes, they just need to be easily identifiable as doors, antennas, and access panels.

➤➤ ALWAYS INCLUDE FAMILIAR DETAILS IN YOUR FANTASY MODELS.

In spite of the fantasy nature of the object, the viewer will have expectations for detail. Nearly all fantasy objects have some sort of real-world element that is used to make them believable. It doesn't have to be the main focus of the object, just something to enhance its credibility.

Once you have laid a foundation of familiar details, you can start to have a little fun with the random, chaotic objects, which are referred to as *nurnies*. Yep, that's right—nurnies. It's a term that was pioneered by the special effects industry for the pointless details they added to spaceships to make them appear high-tech. Don't ask me why they call them nurnies, though I feel it has something to do with pulling all-nighters. You'll find things get a little weird after 36 hours with no sleep.

So what do nurnies look like? Well, they are usually no more than a bunch of cylinders, boxes, tubes, and spheres that are piled together in a somewhat organized and logical fashion. They are basically a collection of simple objects, that when combined, create a single complex object. In fact, the Star Trek Borg ship is one giant mass of nurnies. To get a better idea of what nurnies are, let's take a look at them in action.

Figure 2.5 shows a collection of nurnies on a spaceship. All of the darker objects in the image are nurnies. They are just a collection of simple objects, yet when surfaced properly they become photorealistic components. You should

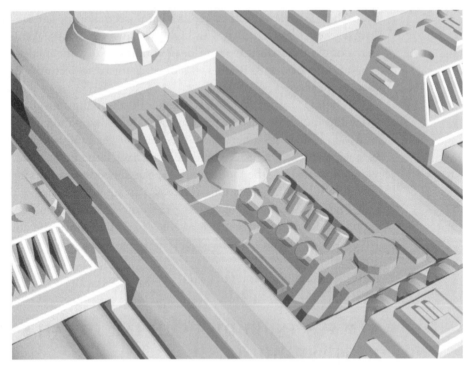

Figure 2.5 *A collection of nurnies put to good use.*

make an effort to include nurnies on all your high-tech objects. This doesn't apply only to spaceships; it can also mean machines, factories, and robots. Let's take a look at an object that utilizes both nurnies and familiar details to make it appear high-tech and photorealistic (see Figure 2.6).

Wow, now that's what I call detail. This, of course, is a very complicated spaceship, but this is actually necessary for the object to be believable. I doubt anyone would expect a spaceship to be simple, particularly one that is suited for combat. Maybe this one is a bit complex; but you have to admit, it does look high-tech. What we have here is a Roid Runner patrol gunship, which is used to protect the mining colonies on Saturn's satellites. Let's take a moment to explore the familiar details and expected objects on this model. We'll start with the wings.

Take a look at the wing on the large model in the lower right corner. You can see that there are several guns on the front of the wing. From their appearance, we can assume they shoot a standard projectile round. If this is the case, there needs to be a place where the ammunition can be loaded. If you look directly behind the guns you'll notice three access panels. The one in the center, with the hinges, is the most readily accessible so it must be the door to the armory. Now take a look under the guns and you'll see a large vent, which is used to cool the

Figure 2.6 *Creating photorealistic fantasy objects with familiar detail.*

guns that get hot during use. You can see that these are very logical items on the spaceship. They are also expected items for those with any knowledge of machinery or weapons.

Follow the wing back to the engine of the spaceship. Notice the hinge where the wing connects to the engine. This allows the wing to move up and down for maneuvering. This helps to add high-tech detail to the spaceship, which is expected by viewers. They probably don't expect the wings to be movable but they sure do expect a lot of detail. The people viewing your images will expect high-tech objects to have a lot of detail and I can't think of anything more high-tech than a spaceship. Now follow the engine back and you'll see a recess where there is a lot of detail. This is a nurnie zone. Here we have completely pointless detail that makes the spaceship appear high-tech. In fact, there are nurnies all over this object.

Take a look at the main body of the ship, behind the cockpit, and you'll see an abundance of nurnies in a recess. Speaking of the cockpit. Did you take a look inside it? Talk about detail. The interior of the cockpit is littered with details, which include a pilot, flight controls, display panel, and, of course, a bunch of nurnies. We could spend all day talking about the details on this model but we have much to cover.

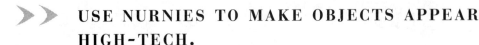

USE NURNIES TO MAKE OBJECTS APPEAR HIGH-TECH.

Nurnies are nothing more than a bunch of cylinders, boxes, tubes, and spheres that are piled together in a somewhat organized and logical fashion to create a single complex object. Use nurnies to make your industrial and high-tech objects photorealistic. Nothing quite says industrial like pointless pipes and power boxes.

Boy, that was some object. As you can see, both familiar details and nurnies are necessary to make high-tech objects appear photorealistic. How exactly do we create detail in our objects? Most of the detail you'll create will be done with Boolean operations. Let's take a look at how they work.

Creating Detail with Booleans

Boolean operations are the primary tool for creating object details. Boolean operations will merge, split, carve, and join objects. To create Booleans you must have two overlapping objects. One is the effector and the other is the recipient of the effect, or the *target object*. For the Boolean operation to work, both objects must be solids. You can't have an open face on the object or it will cause serious errors in most programs. The way Booleans are created varies from one program to another, but the effect stays the same. In some programs the two objects are on different layers, while in others they are on the same layer. You'll have to consult your user's manual to determine the method your program uses. To better understand Boolean operations, let's take a look at the most common types available in 3D programs: subtract, add, union, and intersect.

Working with Boolean Subtract

Boolean Subtract is the most commonly used Boolean operation, used to subtract the mass of one object from another, like cutting the core out of an apple. It carves out a hole in the shape of the effector object, leaving new polygons where the models overlapped. Let's take a look at how this Boolean operation works.

As you can see in Figure 2.7, we used an object representing the pumpkin's face to carve the holes in the pumpkin object. The wireframe views show the effector object in black and the target object in white. Notice how the newly created polygons inside the pumpkin have different surface attributes. When you Boolean Subtract or Intersect, the newly created polygons will have the surface name and attributes of the effector object. This can be very handy, particularly when creating complex objects. To carve out the interior of the pumpkin you would use an effector object with a name like *pumpkin interior* so you wouldn't have to manually select the polygons to rename them. Just imagine how much fun it would be to manually select all the polygons on the inside of the pumpkin. You'd be crazy to try!

Working with Boolean Add

Boolean Add is used to combine the mass of two objects. It doesn't remove the polygons where the objects overlap, but instead leaves them intact. It merely joins the two objects together. Let's take a look at how the Boolean Add operation works.

Figure 2.8 shows that the two objects were combined into a single object. This is obviously an undesirable thing for a jack-o-lantern, but you get the idea. This Boolean operation isn't used that often since it has little value when adding details to your objects.

Now let's look at a very useful Boolean operation, Boolean Intersect.

Working with Boolean Intersect

Boolean Intersect is used to create the difference between two objects. It cuts away everything except where the two objects overlapped. This operation creates new polygons, which retain the surface name and attributes of the effector object. Let's take a look at how this Boolean operation works.

In Figure 2.9 we used the effector object in black to cut away everything except the top of the pumpkin, which is the object in white. This is a very important Boolean operation to use when creating object details like the carved top of the pumpkin. When creating the carved look, you'll want to cut a hole and then fit the lid into the hole. This can be easily accomplished by using a Boolean Subtract operation to cut the hole. Then with another copy of the pumpkin, you use the Boolean Intersect operation to create the lid. Be sure that you scale down the effector object slightly so the lid fits in the hole, rather than seamlessly merging with it. Some tissue had to have been lost when the hole was cut.

Let's look at the last Boolean operation, Boolean Union.

Working with Boolean Union

The *Boolean Union* operation is similar to the Boolean Add except the polygons where the objects overlapped are removed. This is another very useful tool for

Figure 2.7 *The Boolean Subtract operation.*

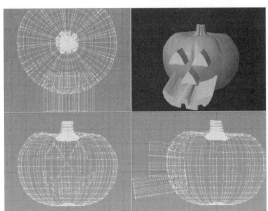

Figure 2.8 *The Boolean Add operation.*

Figure 2.9 *The Boolean Intersect operation.*

Figure 2.10 *The Boolean Union operation.*

adding details to objects. It also keeps the polygon count to a minimum. Let's take a look at how the Boolean Union operation works (see Figure 2.10).

It's not the best use for Boolean Union, but it does get the point across. Here you can see we added the effector object in black to the pumpkin, which is the object in white. All of the polygons where the two objects overlapped have been removed. This is a great Boolean operation for adding details to your objects like the rubber feet on a TV. You would want to literally weld these objects to the bottom of the TV, but you wouldn't want any extra polygons hanging around inside the TV since they wouldn't be seen. Simply use a Boolean Union operation where the feet are the effector object and the TV is the target object.

That does it for our study of Boolean operations. As you can see, they can be very powerful tools for creating photorealistic detail on your objects. Of course, nothing drives the concepts home like getting our hands dirty so why don't we actually add photorealistic detail to an object using the Boolean operations we just discussed?

Getting Our Hands Dirty with Boolean Operations

It's time to put those awesome Boolean operations to work. In the following exercise, we'll be using three of the Boolean operations to add photorealistic detail to a TV remote control. The final version will look like the model in Figure 2.11.

There are several model files that are included in the tutorial file for this chapter, which we need to create the detail on our exercise object. Check and make sure you have downloaded all of the following files listed here. You can

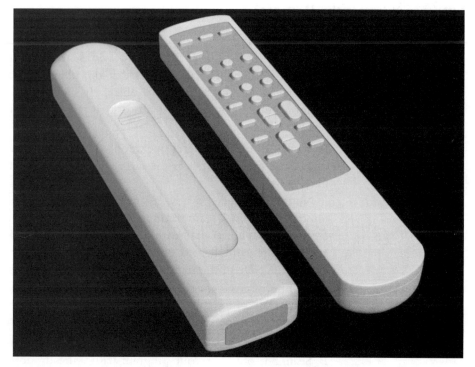

Figure 2.11 The remote control.

download them from the companion Web site at www.wiley.com/compbooks/fleming.

- Remote.3ds
- B_Arrow.3ds
- B_Beam.3ds
- B_Seam.3ds
- B_Buttn.3ds
- B_Dent.3ds
- B_Keypad.3ds
- Butons.3ds

In an effort to streamline this exercise the actual effector objects have already been created for you. As you'll see during the exercise, they are all simple objects that you can easily create using very basic modeling techniques. Before you begin the exercise, become familiar with how the Boolean operations in your program are performed, since this exercise is not software-specific. Let's get started.

Exercise: Where's the Remote?

1. Load the Remote.3ds file into your modeling program. Let's start adding the details. The first thing we'll do is create the battery door by adding a seam, which also shows that the object was assembled. Go ahead and load the B_Seam.3ds object. It should load in the proper position but if it doesn't, just move it so it lines up with the remote object as shown in Figure 2.12.

2. Perform a Boolean Subtract operation with B_Seam.3ds as the effector object and Remote.3DS as the target object. Your result should look like Figure 2.13.

   Notice how there is now a small seam running the length of the remote with a small seam running horizontally. The small floating piece created by the horizontal seam is the battery door. We could have created a more complicated effector object that actually cut a groove around the edge of the remote but that really isn't necessary unless you plan to put the camera right on the object. Normally you can just cut away portions of the model to create the seam since light won't make it far enough into the seam to show the interior.

3. It's time to add the hole for the infrared port. First, delete the B_Seam.3ds object if your program hasn't already done so, and then load the B_Beam.3ds object. This object will be used to cut a hole in

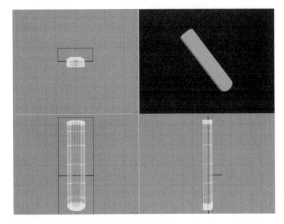

Figure 2.12 *The battery door seam effector.*

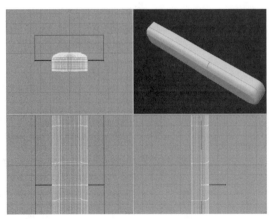

Figure 2.13 *The seam added to the TV remote model.*

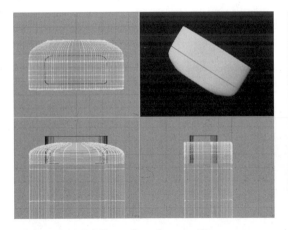

Figure 2.14 *The infrared port effector.*

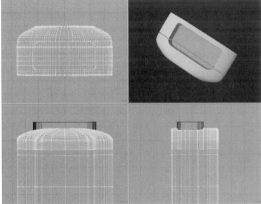

Figure 2.15 *The infrared port hole added to the TV remote model.*

the end of the remote. It should load in the proper position, but if it doesn't just move it so it lines up with the remote object as shown in Figure 2.14.

4. Now perform a Boolean Subtract operation with B_Beam.3ds as the effector object and Remote.3DS as the target object. Your result should look like Figure 2.15.

You should have a hole in the end of the remote object. This is where we will be placing the infrared port. We needed to create a hole since we want it to look manufactured and assembled. The next thing we need to do is create the actual infrared port.

5. First, save the Remote.3ds object with a new file name like TVre-mote.3ds. If you have multiple layers, load another copy of the Remote.3ds object on a new layer. If you have only one layer, delete the TVremote.3ds object and load a new one. If your program deleted the B_Beam.3ds object then load it again now.

6. Next, we slightly reduce the size of the B_Beam.3ds object so it fits in the hole and leaves a small seam. Scale the B_Beam.3ds object down so it's just slightly smaller as shown in Figure 2.16.

7. Great—now we need to perform a Boolean Intersect operation to give the infrared port the same shape as the remote. Perform a Boolean Intersect operation with B_Beam.3ds as the effector object and Remote.3DS as the target object. Your result should look like Figure 2.17.

8. You should have just the infrared port with the top rounded to the shape of the remote. Now load the TVremote.3ds you saved previously, or combine the remote and infrared port layers so you have an object like the one in Figure 2.18. Be sure to delete all other objects.

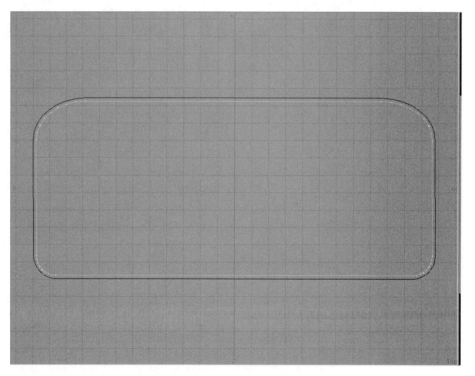

Figure 2.16 *Scaling down the infrared port effector.*

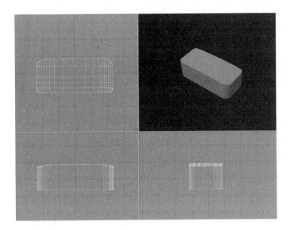

Figure 2.17 *The infrared port.*

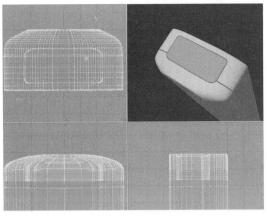

Figure 2.18 *The infrared port added to the remote.*

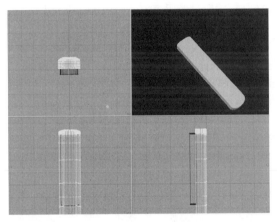

Figure 2.19 *The keypad effector.*

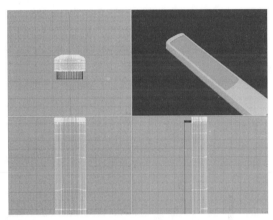

Figure 2.20 *The button panel added to the remote.*

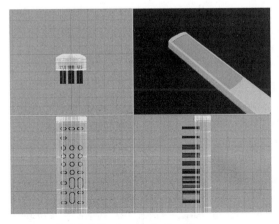

Figure 2.21 *The buttonhole effector.*

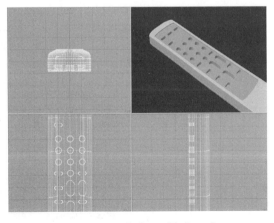

Figure 2.22 *Buttonholes added to the remote.*

9. Now we're starting to get somewhere. The next thing we need to do is add a panel on the front of the remote where the buttons will be located. Go ahead and load the B_Keypad.3ds and make sure it's positioned as shown in Figure 2.19.

10. Perform a Boolean Subtract operation with B_Keypad.3ds as the effector object and TVremote.3ds as the target object. Your result should look like Figure 2.20.

11. You can see where we'll be placing the buttons now. The next step is to create the holes for the buttons. Since we want the object to be photorealistic, we need to create buttonholes and ensure that they are slightly larger than the actual buttons so a minor is gap visible. If your program has left the B_Keypad.3ds object, go ahead and delete it now. The next step is to load the B_Buttn.3ds object and make sure it is lined up as shown in Figure 2.21.

12. Now perform a Boolean Subtract operation with B_Buttn.3ds as the effector object and TVremote.3ds as the target object. This operation might take a bit of time since there is a lot of geometry in the B_Buttn.3ds object. Some programs will allow you to select only the polygons that will be changed in the target object. This will greatly improve the Boolean speed. Go ahead and do this before you Boolean the objects if your program is capable. Your result should look like Figure 2.22.

We're more than halfway done with the model. Hang in there; it's almost over. Our next step is to add the thumb-grip detail to the back of the remote. This is actually a very complicated Boolean operation, which might fail with some software. If it does fail, just move the effector object slightly and try again. If it continues to fail, just skip this element. Unfortunately not all programs have stable Boolean operations.

13. If your program has left the B_Buttn.3ds object, go ahead and delete it now. The next step is to load the B_Dent.3ds object and make sure it is lined up as shown in Figure 2.23.

14. Alright, now perform a Boolean Subtract operation with B_Dent.3ds as the effector object and TVremote.3ds as the target object. This operation might take a bit of time since there is a lot of geometry in the B_Dent.3ds object. Your result should look like Figure 2.24.

15. We have just one more detail to add and we're done. It's time to put the direction indicator on the thumb grip. Before we do this, make sure the B_Dent.3ds object has been deleted. Now load the B_Arrow.3ds object and position it as shown in Figure 2.25.

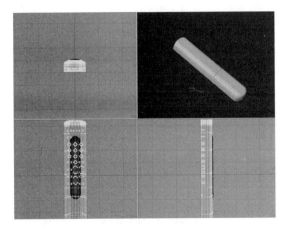

Figure 2.23 *The thump grip effector.*

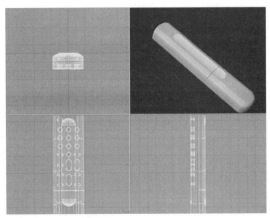

Figure 2.24 *The thump grip added to the remote.*

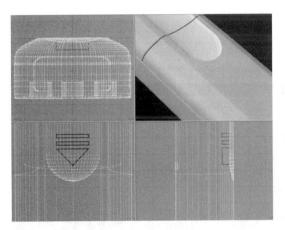

Figure 2.25 *The direction indicator effector.*

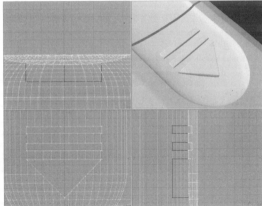

Figure 2.26 *The direction indicator added to the remote.*

16. Perform a Boolean Union operation with B_Arrow.3ds as the effector object and TVremote.3ds as the target object. This will add the arrow to the remote and remove the excess polygons. Your result should look like Figure 2.26.

17. We're done cutting up the remote control. Now remove all effector objects and load the Buttons.3ds object—make sure you position it over the buttonholes. Excellent, we just created a photorealistic TV remote control using three of the Boolean operations. Your completed model should look like Figure 2.27.

Well, that was fun. The Boolean operations are essential for adding photorealistic detail to your models. It would be difficult, if not impossible to create realistic details without them. Spend a little time adding more detail to the TV remote model to get the feel for Boolean operations. Try adding some gripping grooves down the side of the remote, or maybe the "Made In" box on the lower back. Add anything you want. Just get familiar with your Boolean operations because you'll be using them daily from this day forward.

More Modeling to Come

Well, we covered some interesting issues in this chapter. We now know that the viewers have certain expectations of objects, which we need to honor if we intend to make the object photorealistic. We also discovered that familiar details can make fantasy objects appear photorealistic. Ah yes, and we can't forget those wonderful nurnies, which are used to add high-tech details. And finally, we had fun with those marvelous Boolean operations.

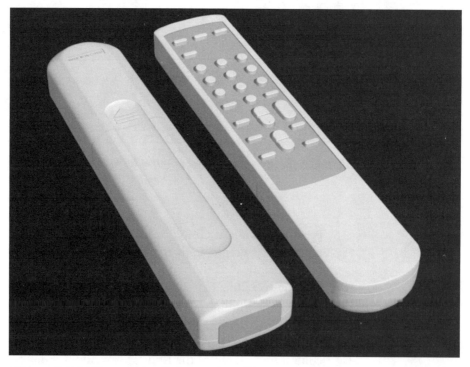

Figure 2.27 *The completed photorealistic TV remote.*

So with all that we have covered what can possibly be left? More fun, naturally. In the next chapter, we'll be taking a look at object construction and how we make 3D objects appear as if they are assembled like their real-world counterparts. But before we jump into this I suggest we take a break—I know I could use one.

I'll see you in Chapter 3.

3 *Material—What's It Made Of?*

Here's a question I repeatedly ask when viewing 3D images, "What is it made of?" Why do I ask? Simply because there is rarely a model that shows any sign of being manufactured. What I mean to say is that they never have seams, folds, or any other indicator that they were assembled. All manmade objects in reality are manufactured in one way or another. That's probably why we call them manmade, isn't it?

If we want our 3D models to be photorealistic they must show indications of being manufactured. For example: A plastic object can be molded as a single object or assembled from several molded parts. Either way it will have a seam somewhere on the object to show that it was manufactured.

Another great example is a simple cardboard box. How many times have you seen a 3D cardboard box that was merely a six-sided cube with image maps slapped on it? Yikes, I hate it when that happens. How exactly is someone supposed to get inside the box when there is no opening? You see the problem. Yes, it's the perfect childproof container but it also happens to be adult proof. There's just no way this object can be photorealistic unless it has the dimension of a real-world box. Without showing the folds, the object just won't appear realistic.

Before you begin modeling your next object, you need to determine the proper manufacturing method. Then you need to incorporate the visual signs of that manufacturing method somewhere on the model. This is actually quite a bit of fun. It's amazing just how critical these elements are in making the object photorealistic. Let's take a look at how we can add the manufactured look to our models.

Creating the Manufactured Look

There are several manufacturing methods you can use to make your objects photorealistic, which include seams, welds, glue, staples, and folds. There are other possibilities but these are used most frequently. You need to determine the manufacturing method you are going to use before you begin the modeling process. If you don't, you may not be able to add it later without a lot of unnecessary effort.

Let's examine the most common manufacturing methods and see how we can incorporate them into our models. We'll start with seams since they are seen most frequently.

Creating Recessed Seams

There are two types of seams: raised and recessed. Both are fairly easy to create as long as you plan the model properly. Let's consider recessed seams first.

Recessed seams are used to simulate objects that are created by joining two separate molded parts with screws or bolts. This technique is most often used when creating multimedia components and high-tech consumer products like the Personal Digital Assistant (PDA) shown in Figure 3.1.

On the back of the PDA we can see the battery door, which is an example of a recessed seam. Notice how it adds photorealistic credibility to the object. Naturally, the battery door can't be seamlessly connected to the body since it needs

Figure 3.1 *An example of recessed seams.*

to be removed. Therefore, we need to create a seam in the model. To make high-tech electronic objects photorealistic, you must use an abundance of recessed seams so they look manufactured.

How do we create recessed seams? It's actually fairly simple. There are two methods you can use and both of them involve the Boolean operations we discussed in Chapter 2. We'll start with the simple approach.

Exercise: Creating Simple Recessed Seams

1. The first thing you need to do is load your modeling program and create two simple six-sided cubes. Leave the first one intact, but scale the second slightly larger and then compress it along its z axis until it's about 1/20th the depth of the first cube.

2. Perform a Booloean Subtract with the thin box as the effector and the cube as the target object. You should have something similar to Figure 3.2.

You can see that we cut a small segment out of the cube, making a seam. This is the quick and dirty approach to creating recessed seams. Actually, it's not technically recessed since we actually cut a segment out of the cube, but unless you plan to shoot extreme close-ups there's no need to get more detailed. Yes, it's true, I actually condone skipping details when they are unnecessary—of course, only on rare occasions. You'll find that simple recessed seams work very well for distant shots since very little light actually gets into the seam.

So what if you are planning a close-up shot of the object and you want it to be extremely photorealistic? We need to create a more precise effector object. Let's do that now.

Exercise: Creating Complex Recessed Seams

1. The first thing you need to do is load your modeling program and create two simple six-sided cubes. Leave the first one intact, but scale the second slightly smaller as shown in Figure 3.3, and name it Effector.

2. You have just created the first of two objects we will use to create the complex effector object. Now create another cube, but this time scale it slightly larger than the first one and compress it along the z axis as shown in Figure 3.4. Then name it Target.

3. Now we have the two objects, which we need to create the effector object. Perform a Boolean Subtract operation where the Effector object is the effector and the Target object is the target . . . pretty obvious wasn't it? You should have an object that resembles the one in Figure 3.5.

4. You can see that we have to cut a hole in the effector object, making it look like a frame. This shape will leave a portion in the center of the tar-

Figure 3.2 *Creating simple recessed seams.*

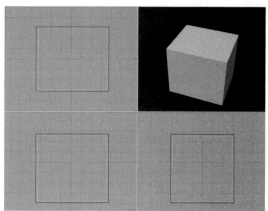

Figure 3.3 *Creating the first Boolean cube.*

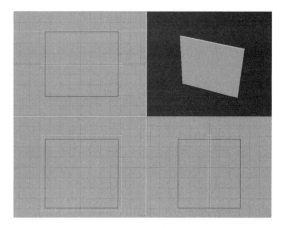

Figure 3.4 *Creating the second Boolean cube.*

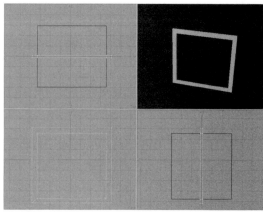

Figure 3.5 *The completed effector object.*

get object when we perform the Boolean operation. In fact, let's do it now. Perform a Boolean Subtract operation where the frame object is the effector and the cube object is the target. You should have something resembling the object in Figure 3.6.

Great; you can now see physical material in the recess, which makes the object perfect for close-up shots. This, of course, is a little more complicated when dealing with organic shapes but it still isn't terribly difficult to do. As you can see, recessed seams can make a significant difference in the photorealistic credibility of an object.

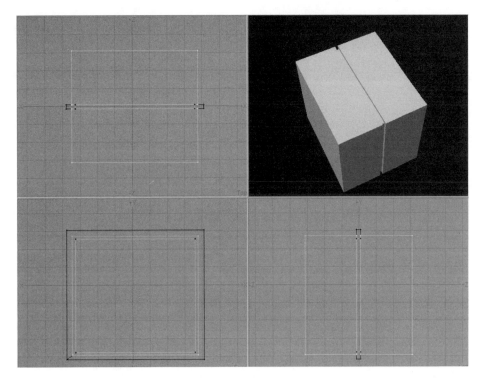

Figure 3.6 *A complex recessed seam.*

What about those raised seams that were mentioned earlier? Well, those are actually easier to create but they require more planning before you begin modeling.

Creating Raised Seams

Raised seams are usually found on plastic objects that were created with a single skin mold, like plastic bottles and toys. They are typically used because a recessed seam is either impractical or unsafe. You want to avoid using recessed seams on toys for small children since they will need screws, which are a choking hazard. And we all know that if there is a hazard, children will find it. In fact, I know a couple adults who are likely to choke on small objects, but that's another story.

Before we get into the creation of raised seams, let's take a look at a couple examples of objects that incorporate them. Figure 3.7 shows a typical laundry detergent bottle. The bottle on the right is the unsurfaced model and naturally the bottle on the left is the final surface version. Take a look at either model and you'll notice a seam that runs around the outside of the body. This is a great example of a raised seam, which adds tremendous credibility to the object. With-

Figure 3.7 *An example of raised seams.*

out this seam, the detergent bottle would look unnatural in spite of the great surfacing.

Now let's take a look at another example. Figure 3.8 shows a child's toy wrestling ring. Actually, I borrowed it from my nephew so I could model it. Well, I guess I sort of toynapped it. I'm planning to hold it ransom for some Halloween candy. I figure I'm doing his dentist a favor. Take a look at the large turnbuckle in the upper part of the image. You'll notice a raised seam that runs down the side as well as across the top. Nearly every toy is molded from plastic since they want to avoid using small parts like screws and such. Therefore, you need to create raised seams so they look properly manufactured.

All right, so we know raised seams are a large part of photorealism, but how do we create them? You'll need three edges on your object. This is much easier to show you so let's jump right into an exercise where we'll create a raised seam.

Exercise: Creating Raised Seams

1. The first thing we need to do is create a box with four segments on the *z* axis, as shown in Figure 3.9.

Figure 3.8 *Another example of raised seams.*

2. As you can see, there are three edges that run down the middle of the box. These are the edges we'll need to create the raised seam. Let's go ahead and start creating the seam by selecting the middle points and resizing them slightly as shown in Figure 3.10.

3. You can see that the difference is very slight. You don't want to make it too large or the seam will look way too big, and consequently unrealistic. Now select the points to either side of the center ones and stretch them so they are very close to the center points as shown in Figure 3.11.

There you have it. A simple raised seam and it took only a few steps to create. Now, obviously it's more difficult on complex objects but you can simplify the process if you plan the model properly by creating the three edges ahead of time. If you wait too long, it will be a nightmare to add them later and you'll find yourself taking a sabbatical at Bellevue Hospital . . . if you know what I mean. Trust me, I know from experience. I mean the agony, not the Bellevue vacation.

Well, that about does it for seams; now let's move on to a very rarely seen element on 3D objects: welds.

Creating Welds

How often have you seen welds on 3D objects? Well, I can tell you that I have yet to see a 3D model with welds. It seems that nearly every 3D metal object is miraculously held together by invisible welds. Sure, it sounds cool but it certainly doesn't look convincing since most people's imaginations aren't that creative.

You need to add welds to your metal objects to make them photorealistic. It requires a smoothing feature in your modeling program. They are often referred to as *SmoothMesh* or quite possibly *MetaForm*. Either way, they apply a smoothing to the mesh based on the tension between points. If the points are close the

Figure 3.9 *The foundation of a raised seam.*

Figure 3.10 *Resizing the center points.*

Figure 3.11 *The completed raised seam.*

smoothing is minimal, if they are distant the smoothing is severe. We can use this wonderful tool to our advantage when creating welds for our 3D models since we can build a basic shape and then smooth it to create the organic look of welds.

Let's take a look at a good example of using welds on 3D objects. Figure 3.12 shows the base of a fire hydrant. As you can see, we have a rather irregular shaped weld around the base. This really helps to make the object photorealistic since something needs to seal the seam where the base and top meet. You'll notice the weld bulges in places. This is important since the weld is laid in segments, which is what created the bumpy look. It you want the weld to be photorealistic, you need to mimic the real-world properties of the weld.

Normally viewers don't go out of their way to look for welds but they certainly will notice that something is wrong with the model if it doesn't have them. Of course, usually only heavy industrial items have welds, but you'll find they are used in a number of other places, such as joining the parts on art deco furniture.

I bet you're wondering how we go about creating the welds. Well, that's exactly what we're about to do. Let's get started.

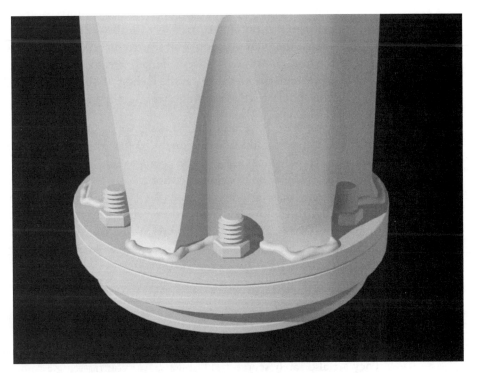

Figure 3.12 *Using welds on 3D objects.*

Exercise: Creating Welds

1. First, open your modeling program and create a cylinder. This will be the object we are creating the weld around. Now lay down a ring of joined polygons around the sphere, and then pull every other point on the outside of the mesh outward. This will help create the irregular shape of the weld. Now extrude the mesh as shown in Figure 3.13.

2. You should have a ring with an irregular shape on the outside. The mesh doesn't need to be neat since it's organic. In fact, you should probably add a little chaos to it like the one shown in Figure 3.13. Now we need to add vertical chaos to the weld so it looks natural. To do this, simply select every other point in the ring, both inside and out, and stretch them vertically as shown in Figure 3.14. In fact, you can add a little more chaos by skipping a couple points.

3. Now we need to soften the outer edge of the weld so it isn't too square. To do this select some of the outermost points and scale them down slightly as shown in Figure 3.15. We don't want to select all of the points since we want the shape to be chaotic.

4. We're almost there. Now we just need to perform a smoothing function and compress the mesh slightly so it looks more natural. Go ahead and perform a smoothing operation with the maximum value possible. Then stretch the mesh to about half its original size vertically. Now place it at the bottom of the tube we originally created and, for effect, you can add a box underneath so we get the feeling of objects being welded together. You should have something that resembles Figure 3.16.

There you have it, a rather convincing weld. Of course, if you want more detail you'll need to add more segments to the original ring. You can also randomly select polygons and extrude them to add the occasional severe bumps where the welder wasn't paying attention.

We're really making progress now. We have just a few more manufacturing methods left to explore. Let's slow things down by taking a brief look at some simple ones like staples and glue. We want to pace ourselves because we've got plenty more to look at and the folding exercise will definitely make your muscles sore. Particularly those finger muscles.

Creating Staples and Glue

Staples and glue are a couple of the more simplistic manufacturing methods. They are also rarely seen on 3D objects. Are you noticing a trend here? It seems that none of the manufacturing methods are incorporated into 3D models on a

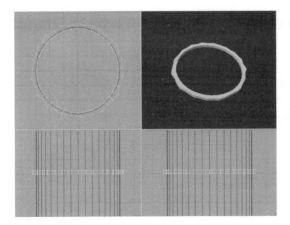

Figure 3.13 *Creating the basic weld shape.*

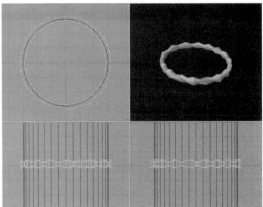

Figure 3.14 *Creating vertical chaos on the weld.*

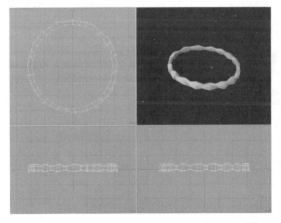

Figure 3.15 *Softening the edge of the weld.*

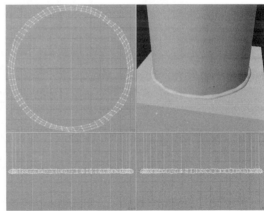

Figure 3.16 *The completed weld.*

regular basis. Hopefully this trend will change soon. In fact, if it's going to happen it's up to you to do it . . . no pressure.

Let's look at some uses for staples and glue. First we'll take a look at an object that uses staples. Figure 3.17 shows a simple magazine object, which has three staples that hold the pages together. I can't count the number of magazine objects I've seen in 3D images that lack the staples. If someone were to pick up the magazine in the scene, the pages would be everywhere. Nearly every paper publication under 100 pages is saddle stitched with staples. Staples are basically the easiest manufacturing method to simulate. You just need to create a tube with 90-degree corners on either end and suddenly, a staple is born.

Figure 3.17 *Using staples to create the manufactured look.*

Let's take a look at glue. There really aren't too many objects where glue is used to join the parts. Well, not ones where you can see the glue anyway. Of course, there are some abstract uses for glue, such as the silicon caulking used to seal the crack where the tub meets the tiled floor. In fact, let's take a look at an image that shows 3D caulking being used.

In Figure 3.18 we can see that 3D silicon caulking was added to the base of the tub where it meets the tiles. Notice how this gives the scene a more realistic look. It's a subtle detail but it adds tremendous credibility to the scene. Also notice that the caulking has a very irregular shape, which adds photorealistic credibility. You should never overlook the small details since they are the ones that make the scene photorealistic.

So how do we create glue? Well, I'm sure you noticed the similarity between glue and welds. In fact, creating glue is done the same way one would create a weld. Just make a simple polygon mesh in the shape of the glue and start pulling points to add chaos. Then apply smoothing to give it the organic look. It's really very simple.

Just one more manufacturing method to go and it's my personal favorite—folds.

Figure 3.18 *Using glue/caulking to create the manufactured look.*

Creating Folds

Here I am back on my mission to create detailed 3D boxes. It seems that very few 3D artists actually go to the effort of adding photorealistic detail to boxes. They think that merely placing image maps on the surface will give it all the photorealistic credibility it needs. It would be great if this were true, but unfortunately it's not. The viewer can easily pick up on the fact that the box has no opening, particularly if you have intrigued them about the contents inside.

There have been occasions where I have seen 3D boxes that actually had the flaps, which show that it can be opened, but they were lacking another critical feature of photorealistic objects: object material depth. There's something unnatural about cardboard that's paper thin. You can't just simply add single-depth polygon flaps to a box and expect it to be realistic. The cardboard needs depth. In fact, cardboard is usually corrugated, which means it actually has layers visible to the human eye. Let's take a look at a photorealistic model of a cardboard box shown in Figure 3.19.

Now this is a realistic box. Notice the folded flaps. In fact, there is even a small tab inside the box where it was glued—just like real boxes. This is a level of detail that you'll likely never see in another 3D box. At least not until you start putting your photorealistic creations out for the world to see. Now let's take a look at the other end to see how the flaps come together to make the object appear natural.

Take a look at Figure 3.20. Notice how the flaps don't meet perfectly in the middle. This is paramount to the success of the model. The odds of the box being folded perfectly are slim to none. In fact, take a look at the top edge and you'll see that the flaps are not lined up with each other. This, too, is an important element of chaos that makes the object realistic. Take a look at Figure 3.21.

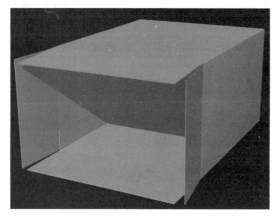

Figure 3.19 A photorealistic cardboard box.

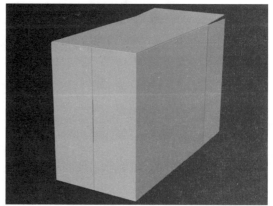

Figure 3.20 Photorealistic folding of box flaps.

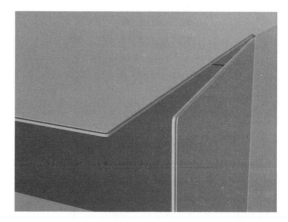

Figure 3.21 The layers of corrugated cardboard.

Here we have an extreme close-up of the cardboard's material depth. Figure 3.21 shows there are actually two layers of material that make up the cardboard. This may seem like nit-picking but you'll need to create both layers if you plan to shoot the object in close-ups. Besides, it really blows the viewer's mind to see this kind of detail.

We know that boxes need folds and material depth, now we just need to figure out how to do it. That's where we can thank the designers of actual product boxes. They've gone through the effort of creating the template for us. Have you ever unfolded a box before? If you had, you would have noticed that it's a single piece of cardboard that has been die-cut to create the sides and flaps. There's no better way to create a 3D cardboard box that using the real-world technique. That's right. We'll need to create a die-cut template to make our cardboard box. Box templates are very easy to create since they are all around us. Just unfold a box and start taking measurements.

Personally, I like to scan the unfolded box and bring the image in as a background template. Then I just start building the polygon mesh over the box template. For our exercise we'll use a box template image to make it easier to create the initial foundation. In fact, we'll be creating the same box we just saw in the last three images. You'll need to make sure you have downloaded the tutorial files from the companion Web site at www.wiley.com/compbooks/fleming before we begin the exercise. You'll need to have the Template.jpg for the exercise. Check to see if you have it.

Now that we have our template file, we are ready to jump right in and start making our box.

Exercise: Creating a Cardboard Box

1. The first thing we need to do is load the template image into our modeling program as the background image. If your program cannot do this, you should take measurements from the Template.jpg image to use as guidelines. Once you have the image loaded, begin to create joined polygons that cover the template. Create a single polygon for all the sides and flaps, then join them with three polygons along the seam. This can be a bit confusing, so let's take a look at what this means. Take a look at Figure 3.22.

   You can see that the template is fairly simple. All of the sides and flaps are created with a single polygon. Then they are joined with three polygons along the seam, which give us the geometry to make the folds. You see, we will be creating the folds with the polygons we used to join the segments. Let's take a close look at the seams in Figure 3.23.

2. As you can see, the seams were created by joining the sides and flaps with three polygons. We're almost ready to start folding, but first we

need to create some material depth. To do this, simply extrude the box template. Of course, we have to make the extrusion very small if it's to look like cardboard. You should extrude it to 1/16 of an inch. This will create the first layer of the cardboard. Since we are making corrugated cardboard we'll need to add another layer. This is relatively simple; make a copy of the template and paste it so you have a 1/33 of an inch gap between the two templates. Yes, I know it's small but we're basically working with paper here. Now scale the top layer so it is 1/32 of an inch thick. Whew, that was some seriously small detail work, but we now have a very detailed cardboard box template. Now comes the fun part—the folding.

3. This is a bit tricky so try to follow along closely. You may have to read this segment a couple times to catch all the details—I know I did, and I wrote the thing. The first folds we want to make are the flaps that will be on the interior of the box. These would be the top and bottom flaps on the narrow sides of the box. The best way is to fold all the flaps on each side at the same time. This will save you a great deal of repetitive work. To fold the flaps, select all the points that don't connect to the side panel of the box. For a visual reference take a look at Figure 3.24.

4. You can see the highlighted points in blue and the actual polygons that we'll be moving in black. You don't want to select the points that are connected to the side panel because we want it to be stationary. Now the trick is to rotate these polygons toward the center of the box, stopping when they are at a 90-degree angle. Of course, we can't just rotate all of them at the same angle since this will give us a hard edge. Instead, we need to rotate each of the seam polygons at 30 degrees to create a rounded edge. This will be easier to see in an image so let's look at how it's done. Take a look at Figure 3.25.

5. This is the first 30-degree rotation we need to make. The narrow white arrow shows the direction you want to rotate the polygons, and the wide red arrow shows the direction you want to move the points. You see, we need to move the points closer together as we rotate the flap so we create a tight fold. Otherwise the box will look very unusual. Now we are ready to make the second 30-degree rotation. Before we do this you need to deselect the polygon that's closest to the fold so we don't rotate it again. Now rotate the remaining polygons another 30 degrees as shown in Figure 3.26.

6. Here you can see the polygons were rotated another 30 degrees and moved closer to the seam. The only polygons that you should have edited are indicated in black. Be sure that you move the polygons closer to the seam so the fold is nice and tight. Now deselect the polygon

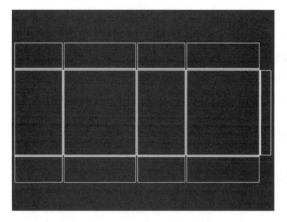

Figure 3.22 *The cardboard template made with polygons.*

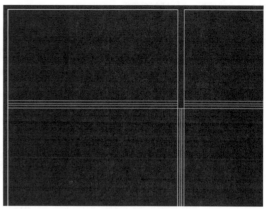

Figure 3.23 *The box template seams.*

Figure 3.24 *Selecting the points to fold the flap.*

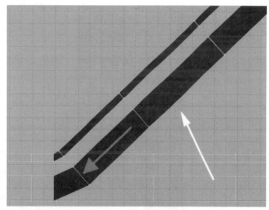

Figure 3.25 *The first 30-degree rotation.*

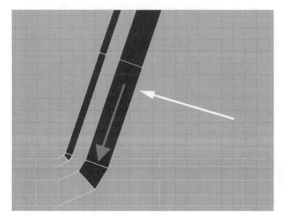

Figure 3.26 *The second 30-degree rotation.*

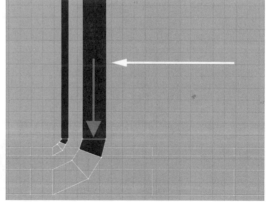

Figure 3.27 *The final 30-degree rotation.*

that's closest to the seam and rotate the remaining polygons another 30 degrees as shown in Figure 3.27.

7. You should have the flap folded at a 90-degree angle. Don't forget to move the selected polygons closer to the seam, as shown in Figure 3.27, to make the fold tight. (Admittedly, that was complicated to explain, in spite of the fact that it's really a fairly simple procedure.) This is the method you should use to fold all of the flaps.

8. Repeat the same folding procedure until all the folds are made. Of course, there is a proper order to fold them, so we'll continue with the exercise. Let's repeat the same procedure we just did for the flaps on the other side so we have a model that looks like Figure 3.28.

9. Now we need to fold another set of flaps. This time we'll fold the larger flaps that will cover the small ones when we close the box. You will need to repeat the same folding procedure, but with one exception. Make sure there is enough room in the fold for the big flaps to overlap the smaller ones, as shown in Figure 3.29.

10. As you can see, when you create the first rotation, you need to move the polygons farther out so they will rest on the smaller flaps when the

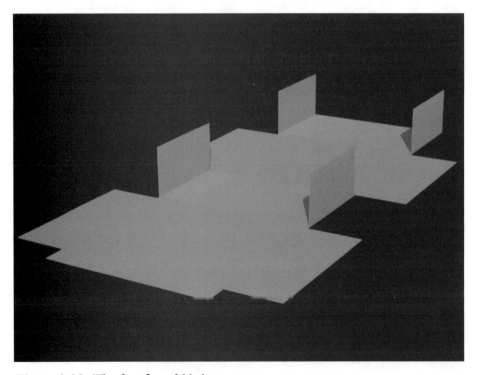

Figure 3.28 *The first flaps folded.*

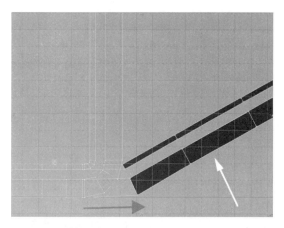

Figure 3.29 *Allowing room for the flaps to overlap.*

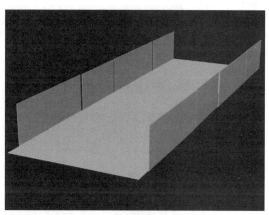

Figure 3.30 *The larger flaps folded.*

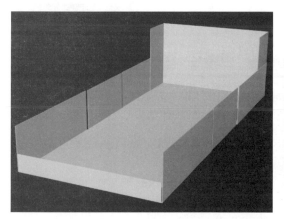

Figure 3.31 *Folding the first side and tab.*

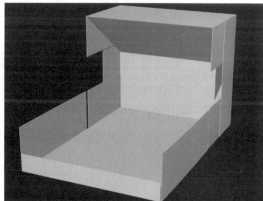

Figure 3.32 *Folding the large side.*

fold is complete. Complete the fold for the larger flaps. When you are finished, your model should look like the one in Figure 3.30.

11. Now that we understand how to rotate the flaps, and we are aware that the flaps must overlap properly, we can complete the rest of the folds very easily. The next thing we need to do is fold the tab and the small side on the opposite end inward at a 90-degree angle. Go ahead and do this now. Your model should look like Figure 3.31 when you are finished.

12. Great—now the box is really starting to take shape. Now we have just two more folds to make and we're done. I bet you thought it would

Figure 3.33 *The completed cardboard box.*

never end. Okay, now fold the large side on the left upward 90 degrees
as shown in Figure 3.32.

13. Well, it's the moment we've all been waiting for. The last fold to complete our photorealistic cardboard box. Simply fold the large side on the
left upward 90 degrees as shown in Figure 3.33.

Well, that was certainly a bit more effort than the other manufacturing methods.
But, as you can see, the effort was well worth it. In fact, you now have a box that
can be easily resized to fit any box need you have. You'll likely never have to fold
another cardboard box again. That should make you happy. Well, that is until the
next time you move to a new home. Ugh, nothing is more painful than moving.

There's More to Come . . .

There you have it, the most commonly used manufacturing methods and some
very simple techniques for recreating their details on your models. That wasn't so
bad. Well, not too bad, anyway.

We're about halfway through the photorealistic modeling segment of the book. We're really starting to make some progress now. We have a firm handle on creating the manufacturing look, but we still need to actually add the elements that hold the objects together. We could neglect them, like so many others seem to do, but where's the fun in that? Of course, many of the manufacturing methods we discussed actually do hold the objects together, like welds, staples, glue, and raised seams. That really leaves only one to discuss, and of course, it's the most popular one—recessed seams.

All right, let's get out those screwdrivers, wrenches, and power tools because we're about to get cracking on Chapter 4, "Construction—How's It Assembled?"

4 Construction—How's It Assembled?

How many multimedia components do you have in your home? Well, if you're anything like me you have plenty of them. How many of them are lying around in pieces? None, you say? Well, I would certainly hope they weren't lying around in pieces; it kind of defeats their purpose. So if they are still assembled, what is actually holding them together? Probably screws for most of them. Of course, I've seen them held together with duct tape before, but that had something to do with children running amuck.

So if real-world objects are held together with screws and such, why aren't the 3D objects? Are we getting lazy? Well, that might have something to do with it. Yes, it can be tiresome to create 3D models but adding the elements that hold the pieces together is really very simple. And it certainly does a lot for making the object appear photorealistic. Attention to detail is very important when you are creating photorealistic models. You have to capture every subtle detail you find in real objects. What is the impact of adding screws to 3D models?

The Credibility of Screws

Although screws may be a small factor in the development of the model, they pack a big punch when it comes to photorealistic credibility. That's right. Something as simple as a screw can make a tremendous difference in the realism of an object. How is this possible? Well, it's easier to explain while looking at an object, so let's take a look at Figure 4.1.

Here we can see the bottom of a personal CD player. Notice the five screws that hold the unit's parts together. Obviously this isn't a surfaced model but it actually looks real because of the high level of detail. The screws serve to anchor the photorealistic credibility of the model because they are a smaller detail, which tends to have more leverage in making the object photorealistic. What? Small objects are better leverage for making objects appear photorealistic? How is this possible?

73

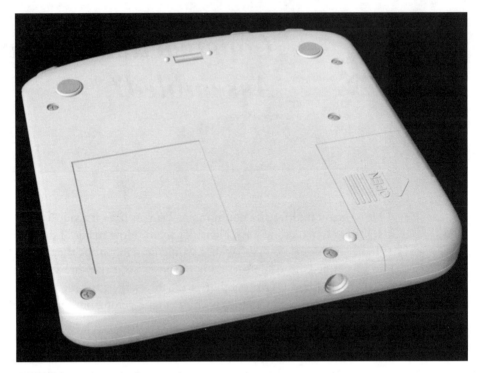

Figure 4.1 *Joining parts with screws.*

It's simple really. We expect the large details but rarely do we expect the small ones. When we encounter a 3D object with small details we are more easily convinced it's real. This actually happens for two reasons. The first is that the details make the object more chaotic, which is what we expect from real objects. The second is that most viewers have been conditioned to expect a much lower level of detail from 3D objects. This is mainly because they are not used to seeing detail in 3D models, but on the other hand, they are used to seeing plenty of detail in real objects. So when they see a highly detailed 3D object they are easily convinced it's real. This, of course, explains why screws make excellent photorealistic detail.

ALWAYS CREATE RECESSES FOR SCREWS.

You should always create a recess for a screw since you don't want it to be surface mounted. This would be a flaw in the design because the screw would be a serious scratching hazard. Your object would end up destroying the surface of whatever it sat upon. Those engineers who design products have really done their research to find the best ergonomic designs. We can learn a lot from them.

You probably noticed that all the screws are sitting in recesses. This is another critical element when using screws. You must create a recess so the screw head doesn't protrude from the surface of the object. This would obviously be a nasty hazard in reality for any surface that scratches easily. You should always try to create very ergonomic designs, which are both user and environment safe. Speaking of safe: Just who came up with the idea of creating glass coffee tables, where the glass extends a foot beyond the legs? That guy must have had two wooden legs because I must hit that thing with my shins at least once a week. I guess you can't predict all the hazards when creating your objects.

As you can see, screws are great for making objects appear photorealistic, particularly objects with recessed seams, but they have many other uses that are equally as effective. They can also be used to attach elements to other objects. I know this is painfully obvious but you don't see too many 3D models that incorporate screws. For example, when was the last time you saw a 3D door where the doorknob was actually attached with screws? I don't think I've ever seen one, which is strange since every doorknob you'll see in reality is attached with visible screws. Let's take a look at an example of screws being used with a doorknob to see the impact they make on its realism. Take a look at Figure 4.2.

As you can see, this is a rather nice photorealistic scene but we want to focus our attention on the doorknob. Notice how it has a screw located in the center of its base, which holds it to the door, unlike those other 3D doorknobs that are apparently attached with super glue. While super glue might actually work for

Figure 4.2 *More uses for screws.*

attaching a doorknob, I find it much better for gluing hard hats to I beams—and certainly a lot more fun.

Now take a look at the door latch. Notice how it has a couple screws holding it in place. This is another thing you'll rarely see on 3D doors. They will often put the latch on the door but they usually forget to include the screws. In reality, these 3D scenes should be rendered with the latch lying on the floor since there were no screws holding it in place. Say, that might actually be fun to do.

I'm sure you noticed that both the doorknob and latch were very nicely surfaced with a reflective brass finish. While this is a great surface, the real photorealistic credibility comes from the details, which in this case are the screws. Man, those screws really get around. Without the screws, the objects would have looked nice but they definitely wouldn't have been photorealistic. Even the best surfacing can't make up for poor model quality.

ALWAYS ADD ELEMENTS THAT MAKE YOUR OBJECTS APPEAR ASSEMBLED.

All objects that are manmade have something holding them together. Sometimes it will be hidden but more often than not they are clearly visible. You should always try to add elements like screws and bolts to your manufactured objects to make them photorealistic. Just don't get carried away.

Even though screws are tiny objects, they have a tremendous amount of impact on the photorealistic credibility of the model. Of course, it isn't just screws that can leverage the credibility of the object, it can also be nuts, bolts, and even nails. In fact, it can simply be a hole in the object. Yes, it doesn't sound like a convincing detail but it is. Why don't we take a look at holes and a few other details that dramatically improve the photorealistic quality of a model?

Holes, Latches, and Other Common Assembly Items

Screws are great for creating photorealistic details but you don't necessarily always have to use them. There are many cases where you can imply that a screw is used by simply creating holes. That's right, holes. Let's take a look at an example so can see what I'm talking about. Take a look at Figure 4.3.

Here we have the back of a portable radio. I'm sure you noticed the screws on the back but what I want you to take a look at is the large holes on either side of the screws. They are recesses that go rather deep into the radio. They are designed

Figure 4.3 *Creating photorealistic credibility with screw holes.*

for screws, and while they do actually have screws in them, you wouldn't necessarily have to include one since it's very unlikely anyone will ever see them. Light doesn't get that far into the holes unless you're shining it directly in the hole. Besides, the shadows are guaranteed to cover them even if they are there.

You'll find these screw holes on a large number of electronic items around your home or office. They are a simple and convenient way to make your 3D objects more photorealistic without having to create a bunch of screws. They are also particularly useful if you are concerned about the polygon count of the object.

USE SCREW HOLES TO QUICKLY ADD PHOTOREALISTIC CREDIBILITY TO YOUR RECESS-SEAMED OBJECTS.

When recessed seams are present we assume that the object is held together with screws. This isn't always true but it is in most cases. You can quickly add photorealistic detail to these objects by adding screw holes, which make the object appear assembled. Usually you won't need to actually add the screw since the hole will be too deep for the light to penetrate.

Of course, screw holes are very easy to create. All you need to do is Boolean a few holes in your object. Just make sure you're putting them in an appropriate place. Putting deep holes in the narrow part of an object wouldn't make a great deal of sense. You should always put them in the deepest part of the object where they will make the most sense.

Okay, so creating screw holes is an easy way to add photorealistic credibility but what are some others? Well, I'm glad you asked. There are actually a number of very unique assembly features that you can add to make your object photorealistic. Let's take a look at a unique one that lends tremendous photorealistic credibility to objects—latches.

Using Latches to Create Photorealistic Details

I've seen 3D objects assembled in a variety of ways but I have yet to see very many latches used. Latches are wonderful detailed features that make objects pop off the screen. Any level of detail you can add to a model will greatly improve its photorealistic credibility, but latches do it extremely well because they are rather detailed themselves.

There are, of course, proper places to use latches. You can't just stick them to any old object. The most popular types of latches would be found on lunchboxes and toolboxes. These latches are also some of the most detailed in appearance.

Let's take a look at the effect a latch has on the photorealistic credibility of an object. In Figure 4.4 we have a simple lunchbox. You can see that the object doesn't have a lot of detail but the latch really does a nice job of making it realistic. Admittedly, the handle plays a major role in photorealistic credibility, too, since it is very detailed. A lunchbox is an obvious use for a latch. In fact, it's even the most common type of latch. Now what are the other kinds of latches and where are they used? Well, there is a very common latch used to keep the battery doors of electronic equipment closed. Let's take another look at that portable radio we saw earlier. The new version is shown in Figure 4.5.

You can see that the battery door on the lower part of the radio is secured with two plastic latches. These aren't extremely detailed features but they sure help to add photorealistic credibility to the object. It's critical that your object design makes sense based upon its function and use. It wouldn't be very logical to attach a battery door with screws on an object where the batteries will be frequently changed. This is a relatively simple and common latch, so how about something more extraordinary? Take a look at Figure 4.6.

Now this is a nice latch. Actually, it serves two purposes. It's a latch and a locking mechanism. Both actually perform the same function—they keep the battery door closed. This is a very unique detail that, once again, makes the object appear realistic. Keep in mind, the more unique and complicated the latch, the more realistic the object will appear. Viewers are suckers for high-tech details. I know I am. Tell me you don't get mesmerized by the plethora of flashing lights on the front of stereo amplifiers and receivers? We all do. That's why they make them that way. Well, the viewers of your 3D images are just the same. They are literally hypnotized by details.

Of course, high-tech features are always great photorealistic details, but just about any small item on the model can be a powerful tool for creating photorealistic credibility. In fact, let's digress slightly for a moment and examine this theory. Take a look at Figure 4.7.

Figure 4.4 *Using latches to add photorealistic credibility.*

Figure 4.5 *A simple battery door latch.*

Figure 4.6 *A complex latch/locking mechanism.*

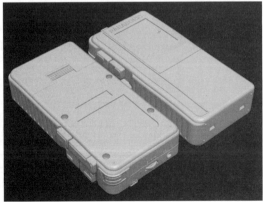

Figure 4.7 *Tiny details that anchor the photorealistic credibility of a model.*

Take a close look at the bottom of the model and you'll see some very tiny bumps in the corners. These are the actual feet of the minirecorder. They keep the plastic body from getting scratched on tabletop surfaces. Now take a look at the back of the minirecorder and you'll find those same little bumps. These are tiny little features but what a difference they make. It's elements like these that make an object undeniably realistic in the eyes of the viewer.

>> ALWAYS ENDEAVOR TO ADD SMALL DETAILS TO YOUR MODELS.

Small details are the photorealistic anchors of a model, particularly if it is a manufactured object. We have been conditioned to expect a lot of small detail in these items. If you fail to add the details, the object will likely appear unnatural.

How many times have you seen this level of detail in a model? I'll bet not very often. It's very important that you understand the object you are creating. I know it sounds weird but you have to realize that manufacturers spend millions designing their products. They have tried to think of everything. If we fall short of this ideal, we'll end up creating an object that isn't photorealistic.

Oh yes, before we return to adding the assembly details to our objects, did you notice the screws? They're everywhere.

Let's have some fun by taking a look at working with abstract assembly methods.

Working with Uncommon Assembly Methods

So what are uncommon assembly methods? They are the less frequently seen, but readily recognized methods of attaching objects. These methods include cables, magnets, and even force. It's always nice to get creative when assembling your objects; of course, you can't get too creative or the object won't be believable. For instance, you can't assemble a VCR with wooden dowels. Sure, it would look interesting but not very practical, and therefore unrealistic. When working with creative assembly methods, you need to ensure that they make sense based on the use of the item.

Let's take a look at a very common, yet unusual assembly method—force. Yep, that's right, pure unadulterated force can be a great assembly method. Take a pickax for example. The wooden handle is just stuck in the head by force. While the head has been tightly molded to the wooden handle, they are still just stuck together. Sure, there may be some glue added in cases but not usually.

There are some things to consider when using this type of assembly method. You can't just stick a wooden handle on an object. You must physically create the hole in your 3D object so the handle can be naturally inserted. Let's take a look at an example (see Figure 4.8).

Here we have a typical ballpeen hammer. You'll notice that the handle is inserted in the head of the hammer. Now take a close look and you'll see that there is a very distinct hole where the handle enters the head. This is a critical feature to include if you want to make the object photorealistic. If you just performed a simple Boolean Union operation on the two objects they wouldn't look assembled. In fact, they would look like they were created from the same material since there would be no seam. Now take a look at the top of the hammer shown in Figure 4.9.

Notice how the handle goes all the way through the hammer. This is how nearly all forced assembly objects appear. The handle usually comes out the top of the object to which it is attached. Now take a closer look and you'll notice the seam around the wooden handle, which is very important since you want the two objects to look as if they are made from separate materials. Obviously the surfacing will help, but it can't make up for the lack of details in the model. That's why we need to create the detailed hole. What we have here is a very photorealistic model of a hammer, which was assembled with the force method.

Let's take a look at another uncommon assembly method. How about something with cables? Go ahead and take a look at Figure 4.10.

Here we have a nice photorealistic living room scene. Let's examine the assembly of the coffee table. Take a look at the middle of the table and you'll notice

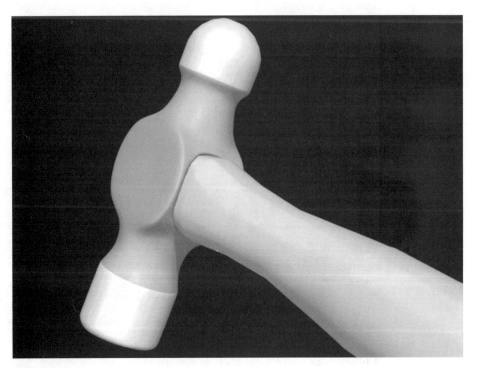

Figure 4.8 *An example of force assembly.*

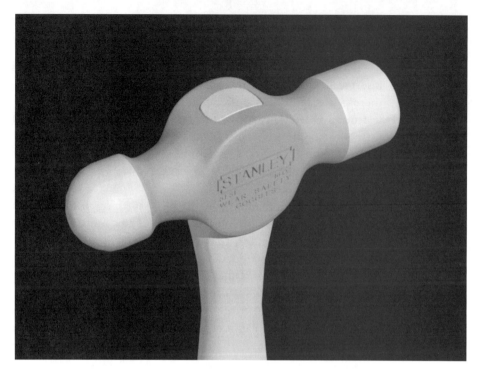

Figure 4.9 *Making objects appear assembled.*

Figure 4.10 *An example of cable assembly.*

two cables. These are used to reinforce the frame of the table so it doesn't flex. These cables are very common in modern and art deco furniture. It's definitely nice to break away from the same old wooden furniture and do something interesting so the image stands out in the crowd.

Okay, just one more uncommon assembly method to look at and we'll move on to more exciting stuff. Take another look at the table and you'll notice a little black knob at the end of the metal bar that runs down the middle of the table. This is another very nice subtle detail that makes the object photorealistic. The knob is actually the head of a hex screw, which was used to attach the legs to the stabilizing bars. It's just another form of assembly that you should consider when creating your objects.

Well, that does it for assembly methods. There are literally thousands of them to consider but we just don't have the space to cover them all. There are a number of techniques you can use to simulate your object's assembly. It really doesn't matter which one you use as long as it makes sense based on the use of the object. Remember, no VCRs with wooden dowels.

Let's take a look at a topic that's related to assembly—mounting features.

What's Holding It Up?

This isn't a long, drawn-out topic. It's just an overview of how to create photorealistic credibility by providing the necessary mounting features on your models. For instance: If you plan to hang a phone on the wall, you'll need some sort of mounting feature on the back. In fact, take a look at Figure 4.11.

Here we just happen to have an example of a kitchen wall phone with the appropriate mounting features on the back. Typically you'll never see the backs of most objects but I like to model them anyway since you never know when you'll want to shoot the back. You may just want to render a scene where the phone has fallen off the wall, or maybe it was knocked off in a struggle to give the winning Phrase that Pays to a radio station disc jockey. At any rate, it's always easier to add the details when you first create the model than going back after some time to retrofit it with additional features.

How about a mounting feature that is much more common, like hinges? How often do you see hinges on 3D models? It's pretty rare that a 3D object has hinges, in spite of the fact that they have doors. Now, I've seen hinges on regular doors but I rarely see them on cabinet doors. So what exactly is holding the doors to the cabinets? It must be that super glue again. Boy, that's got to make it tough to get inside. You should always create hinges for your cabinet doors as shown in Figure 4.12.

Here we have a hinge on the door to a credenza. I know, it's pretty obvious that doors need hinges, but so many 3D artists will try to shortcut their work by

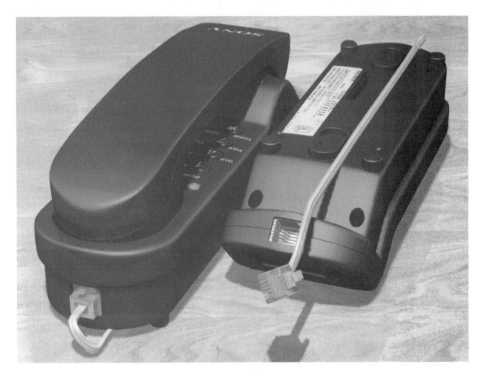

Figure 4.11 *Creating detailed mounting features.*

skipping them. Sure, they'll get the image done faster but will they captivate their viewers? Probably not since they don't have enough detail to keep the viewer's interest. Your scenes need to be visual smorgasbords of detail. There should be something there for everyone. Of course, I'm getting ahead of myself. We'll be talking about staging scenes in Part IV, "Photorealistic Staging Techniques."

We have time to squeeze in one last plug for mounting features. Always be sure to include mounting features when creating photorealistic scenes. All too often you'll find that 3D artists have included items in their scene that have no mounting features, yet they are mounted. This just doesn't look right. No, you don't need to worry about the mounting features on the back of the objects, but there are cases where the mounting features will be on the front as shown in Figure 4.13.

Take a look at the drainpipe and you'll see a mounting bracket, which is holding it to the wall. You'll see several drainpipes in 3D scenes but rarely will you see a mounting bracket. In fact, you'll see plenty of 3D industrial images, but where are the mounting brackets? They're probably in the imaginations of the viewers. You should always justify the presence of mounted objects by providing visible mounting features whenever possible.

As you can see, mounting features are pretty obvious but in our rush to complete the image we often overlook them. Try to live by this creed: "We'll render

Figure 4.12 *Using hinges to add photorealistic credibility.*

Figure 4.13 *An example of a front-mounting feature.*

no image before its time," and you won't go wrong. Slow down and take a few extra moments to make your image photorealistic. The result is definitely worth the investment.

Time for a Little Mechanics

Well, that was a completely bizarre chapter. We've covered quite a bit of information on assembly. You can probably assemble just about anything now. Just think, you'll have a tremendous edge at Christmas, where assembly skills are critical for putting together those easy-to-assemble toys.

I'd say it's a good time to take a break before we dive into a little mechanical fun with Chapter 5, "Movement—What Are the Mechanics of Objects?" Why don't you stretch your legs a bit while I figure out what I'm going to cover in the next chapter?

5 Movement—What Are the Mechanics of Objects?

Movement is a frequently overlooked subject in regard to photorealistic 3D images. Not too many people actually consider the mechanical feasibility of their creations. Even when they clone a real-world object they typically neglect to add the subtle details of motion mechanics. We may be working in a virtual world but our creations are founded in reality, so they need to be logically assembled and most definitely need to apply to the laws of physics.

I can't count the number of 3D creatures I've seen that couldn't possibly exist in reality. Alien or not, they still need to conform to the laws of physics . . . nobody is above the law! I know it's fun to create new life forms but if you want the viewer to believe in it you are going to have to play by the rules. You'd be surprised at how mechanical creatures are. Think about it: They all have some sort of skeletal structure or at least something very similar, which means they have motion mechanics. Why don't we take a look at a great example of creature motion mechanics, shown in Figure 5.1.

Here we have a marvelous example of creature motion mechanics. This is a model of a Madagascar hissing cockroach, which happens to be the largest and most intimidating of the roach species. They can reach three inches in length! You'll need something a bit larger than a Roach Hotel to snag these guys— maybe something along the lines of a Roach Resort would work. Did you know there are actually more than 3000 species of cockroach? I wonder who counted all of them?

Let's take a look at the actual creature mechanics of the roach model in Figure 5.1. The first thing we notice is that the body is segmented, which is an absolute must since insect bodies are basically armor plating and are not flexible. If we made the body a single piece, it would be impossible for the roach to bend. In other words, it would cripple the mechanics of motion. Now take a look at the legs. You can see they are all jointed which gives them a broad range of movement. Insects have an exoskeleton so they look very jointed. If we hadn't made the legs jointed, well, the roach wouldn't be able to move, which is probably not a bad thing when I think about it.

Figure 5.1 *Creature mechanics.*

All right, now take a look at where the legs meet the body. Here we can see some very detailed sockets for the hind legs but the front legs have a joint. This means the motion for the hind legs is rather limited while the front legs are very flexible. Why is the range of motion limited for the rear legs? What we have here is something to the effect of rear wheel drive. The hind legs propel the roach while the front legs are used for steering. Therefore the front legs need to have a broader range of motion to guide the body while the hind legs are limited in range to provide stability. Pretty impressive design for an insect isn't it?

As you can see, there are a lot of motion mechanics to consider when creating photorealistic creature models. Of course, it's not just creatures that need to conform to the laws of physics, it's machines too. If you are planning to include mechanical objects in your photorealistic scenes, you need to ensure that they are mechanically sound, whether the object is real or not.

It's not that difficult to create logical mechanical objects. More often than not you are merely cloning real-world objects that provide you with plenty of mechanical source material. When creating 3D objects that are based on real-world objects you need to pay close attention to the mechanical details. This applies to more than just machines; it's anything that has moving parts. In fact, let's take a look at a great example of nonmechanical motion mechanics. It sounds contradictory but mechanics actually means the science of motion. So anything that moves has motion mechanics, regardless if it's a machine or not. Let's get back to our example. Take a look at Figure 5.2.

Here we can see three books. I'll bet you never thought of a book as being mechanical. Well, they definitely are, so we need to design them properly if we want them to be photorealistic. Take a look at the book on the far left. This model represents just about 90 percent of the books you'll see in 3D images. In fact, it's probably more detailed than most. The problem is that the book doesn't have any motion mechanics. Currently, there is no way to open the book. Well, no reasonable method anyway. You see, hardbound book covers are made of thick material, which doesn't bend easily. In order for a hardbound book to be opened, you need to create a literal paper hinge. Basically, you need to crease the cover so it has an inherent weak spot where it will bend.

Now take a look at the book in the middle. This book has the proper motion mechanics for a hardbound book cover. Notice the crease that runs the length of the spine. The material in this area has been curved to make it flexible, and it's also thinner than the rest of the cover so it will flex easier. What we have here is a paper hinge, which provides the motion mechanics for opening the book. The book model in the middle is photorealistic, whereas the one on the left is not.

Now take a look at the paperback book on the right. You'll notice this book doesn't have any motion mechanics. Since the cover is very thin and pliable there

Figure 5.2 *Nonmechanical object mechanics.*

is no need to create the hinge. Well, at least no need to put one on the model. You will find that a paperback book usually has a very small crease, which runs the length of the book. It's a subtle detail that is best created with a bump map. This is a case where there is no need for the model to have motion mechanics since it will be easier to do with image maps.

NOT ALL MOTION MECHANICS ARE BASED ON MACHINERY.

Although it's true that the overwhelming majority of motion mechanics is based on machinery, there are cases where it isn't. Take books for example. They have a cover that has motion mechanics so you can open it. Sure, it's only a simple crease next to the spine, but it's motion mechanics just the same. If we didn't include the crease, the book would look unnatural since we would have no way to open it. Well, without destroying the cover anyway.

As you can see, motion mechanics isn't limited to just machinery. There are literally thousands of nonmechanical items that have a need for motion mechanics. Just try opening a cardboard box without it. In fact, you'd be hard pressed to get that Cuban cigar out of the cigar box without motion mechanics. Let's not forget your favorite 3D magazine, which can't be opened without motion mechanics either.

We've covered every form of motion mechanics except the machine-based type, so I guess we should look at it for a moment. Working with truly mechanical objects can get tricky. It usually involves a plethora of moving parts, which can get rather complicated to assemble in a 3D environment. You need to consider the motion mechanics of the model carefully before you begin creating it since it will have a major impact on the way you develop the model. Sometimes the motion mechanics of an object are very subliminal so you have to look closely to find them. You might think that if you have to look to find them they aren't necessary but this isn't the case. While you may not pick up on them immediately, viewers definitely will since they are looking at the image from a different perspective. You need to capture the subtle details of motion mechanics in order to make your object convincingly photorealistic. Let's take a look at an example of subtle motion mechanics, shown in Figure 5.3.

Can you see the subtle motion mechanics on the jeep? They are actually well camouflaged. Take a look at the leading edge of the passenger door and you'll see a couple of hinges. Now these aren't normally visible on a car but this is a unique case, so therefore we need to ensure that we include them. Now take a look at the base of the windshield and you'll find a couple more hinges, which allow the windshield to fold forward. These are elements that you will find on every jeep but rarely on their 3D counterparts. Although they may be small elements on the

Figure 5.3 *Finding the subliminal motion mechanics.*

car, they definitely need to be there or the jeep won't have the proper motion mechanics to be photorealistic.

Now let's take a look at a very subliminal example of motion mechanics. Did you see the detail under the jeep, behind the rear wheels? I'll bet you didn't even think twice about it. Why? Because we fully expect this kind of detail on a real jeep, or any other automobile for that matter. You see, it's subtle details like this that anchor the photorealistic credibility of an object. If we had left out the motion mechanics details under the jeep, it would have looked unnatural for obvious reasons. It's a little difficult to get around without a drive train. In fact, quite often you'll see 3D vehicles that have no motion mechanics at all, which makes them great paperweights but lousy transportation.

APPLY MOTION MECHANICS ONLY WHERE THEY WILL BE CLEARLY VISIBLE.

Don't make the mistake of getting too carried away with adding detail to your models. Motion mechanics are important but only where they are clearly visible from normal camera angles. You need to determine the use of your model before you add the motion mechan-

ics so you don't do a lot of work for nothing. It doesn't make any sense to invest a lot of time adding details that nobody will ever see.

While it may sound like a lot of work to create motion mechanics it really isn't all that bad. Usually it's just a matter of adding some mechanical looking parts to the object. In fact, take a look at Figure 5.4.

Here we have the unsurfaced jeep model. You'll notice that the jeep on the left has no motion mechanics whereas the jeep on the right has plenty. You can see that the detail under the jeep on the right isn't completely accurate. In fact, the axle is merely jammed into the wheels. This is a good example of knowing when to limit the motion mechanics details. You see, there will never be a time where you will be able to see the point where the axle meets the wheel, so it's unnecessary to add any more detail at this point. Of course we can see this area now but our camera is literally lying on the ground. If you plan to shoot camera angles like this, well, then you would need more detail, but typically you'll never use this camera angle. You definitely don't want to get carried away with the motion mechanics of an object. Before you start modeling your object, consider just how much of its detail will be visible. While details are important, there is a point where they become unnecessary.

Let's have a little fun by examining a motion mechanics case study.

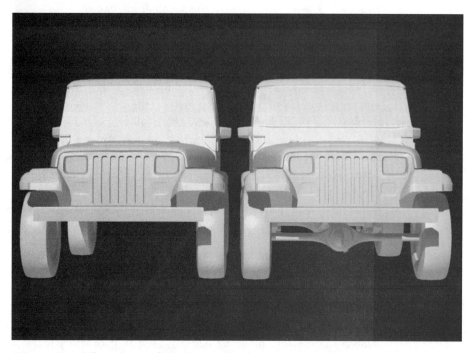

Figure 5.4 *The impact of motion mechanics.*

Gizmo—A Study of Motion Mechanics

Creating motion mechanics for real-world objects, which you are cloning, is relatively simple since you have a logical model to work from. What about those times when you want to create a fantasy object that needs motion mechanics? You really need to be careful to ensure that the motion mechanics you are creating make sense. Sure, very few of your viewers will actually be certified mechanical engineers but even the most uneducated individual can still identify flaws in motion mechanics. For example, we all know that a square wheel doesn't roll. That example was a little too obvious. How about cabinet doors? I'm sure we all know that they need hinges, just like we all know that automobiles need axles for their wheels to turn. I'll bet you've never seen a human knee bend forward. Well, it's possible but it would definitely hurt.

Before you start modeling your fantasy creation, you should spend a little time studying its motion mechanics to ensure that it makes sense and is actually feasible. Speaking of original creations, let's get to our case study of Gizmo, the robot from the Dwellers short film. Take a look at Figures 5.5 and 5.6.

Here we have a couple images of Gizmo, which show the detailed motion mechanics that were used to make him realistic. This character presented a particular challenge because he needed to have logical motion mechanics, but all of the parts had to be common, and recognizable by nearly everyone. Talk about tricky!

It's very important that you create motion mechanics that make sense. You need to justify all of the elements of your motion mechanics so the viewer is convinced the object is real. For example, you can't have a robot that doesn't have some form of energy source for its mechanical parts. It just wouldn't be convincing to the viewer. Ah yes, so now you're wondering where Gizmo gets his energy. Well, maybe we should take a look at what's behind door number one. Take a look at Figure 5.7.

There you have it. Gizmo runs on a single C cell battery. Now that we have a logical energy source we need to justify his motion mechanics. We need to determine just exactly how he gets around. Since we've got him opened up we might as well start here. If you look at the bottom of the can you'll notice a couple of servomotors, which appear to have come from a radio-controlled car. These are high-torque motors, which are capable of reversing direction quickly, and with great force, making them perfect for moving Gizmo's legs back and forth. In fact, let's take a close look at how Gizmo's legs actually work. Take a look at Figure 5.8.

Here we have a close-up of Gizmo's legs. Sure, they're not the sexiest robot legs around but they get him from place to place well enough. Look at his hip joint. You'll see that he has a clamp attached to the rotor that comes out of the

Figure 5.5 *Gizmo, a fantasy object with proper motion mechanics.*

Figure 5.6 *Another look at Gizmo.*

Figure 5.7 *Gizmo's energy source.*

Figure 5.8 *Gizmo's leg motion mechanics.*

servomotor. This makes perfect sense. Now take a look at the bottom of the clamp and you'll see that we have a furniture hinge, which is attached to the earpiece of my favorite headphones. Man, I've been looking for them everywhere.

The furniture hinge plays an important role in the motion mechanics of the leg. You see, it has a limited range of motion, much like that of a human knee. It can rotate backward but not forward, which gives Gizmo great stability when he's standing still. It also keeps him from falling forward when he reaches out to grab something.

Now take a look at those big feet, which provide him with great weight distribution and balance. In fact, they also make him a silent runner since they are padded. You'll notice that the headphone earpiece has a bracket attached to it, which allows it to rotate through a wide range of motion, just like a human ankle joint. When the leg rotates forward, the earpiece will rotate upward from the momentum as shown by his right foot. Then, when the leg is rotated backward, the earpiece will rotate downward from the momentum, thus placing the hypothetical ball of his foot on the ground as shown by his left foot. You can see that he has very similar motion mechanics to that of a human. We'll let's make it even easier to make the comparison by taking a look at Figure 5.9.

Here we have a direct comparison of the similarities between Gizmo's leg and a human leg. The arrows indicate the similar joints between the models. As you can see, the human leg served as the perfect model to create the motion mechanics for Gizmo's legs. The great thing about reality if that it is full of great source material for creating logical motion mechanics. For example, when creating biped motion mechanics for robots, you simply study the motion mechanics of humans. In fact, you can also determine the animation sequences by studying the human walk cycle. Take a look at Figure 5.10 and you'll see a frame from Gizmo's walk cycle.

As you can see, Gizmo has a very natural looking walk cycle. This is because his motion mechanics were modeled after a human. Okay, so the motion mechanics of his legs make perfect sense but what's telling them to move? That's a good question. You see, when creating automated motion mechanics you have to also create the brain that drives them. This could be as simple as an on/off switch or it could even be a complex computer system like you find in car engines. Why don't we take a look at the computer that drives Gizmo's motion mechanics? Take a look at Figure 5.11.

Here we have Gizmo with all of his surfacing stripped away so we easily identify his parts. Take a look at the model on the right and you'll see that he has a circuit board attached to his back, which is the brain that drives his motion mechanics. In fact, why don't we take a moment to explore the many uses for Gizmo's brain?

The circuit board does far more than just control his motion mechanics; it's also the source of his personality. You see, Gizmo is a cognitive thinking creature, which means he's basically alive. To bring Gizmo to life, a learning chip was installed on the circuit board that allows him to expand his knowledge and make intelligent decisions. In addition to adding creative thought, it also controls his communications network. If you take a look at the top of his body you'll see a cellular antenna, which he uses to communicate with the other Dwellers and occasionally browse the Internet. You'll be pleased to know that he's a big fan of 3D graphics.

Ah yes, the circuit board also controls his audio output, which he used to communicate with carbon-based life forms. Of course, it's also used to intimidate potential predators. How, you ask? Well, it's actually quite ingenious. Since Gizmo is only a foot tall, he isn't very intimidating. In fact, he looks like a very appealing toy to children. In order to scare off predators, like children, he plays really loud RoboCop-style servo sounds through his speaker. This way he sounds like he's ten feet tall as he approaches. Pretty cool, isn't it?

Let's look at one more example of Gizmo's motion mechanics before we move on to the next chapter. Take a look at Figure 5.12.

This is a great example of complex motion mechanics. What we have here is a close-up of Gizmo's right hand, which happens to be a Swiss Army knife. You can see that there is plenty of detail on the knife. This is of particular importance since the motion mechanics of knife blades are rather complex. You see, each blade has a spring-loaded locking mechanism that keeps it from folding back once you've opened it. In order for Gizmo's hand to look realistic, we needed to add those locking mechanisms. If you take a look at the base of the saw blade,

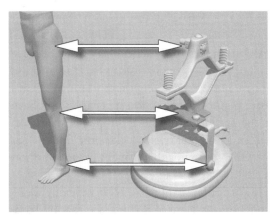

Figure 5.9 *The similarities of motion mechanics.*

Figure 5.10 *Gizmo's walk cycle.*

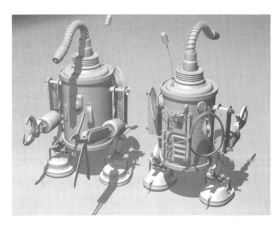

Figure 5.11 *Gizmo's brain.*

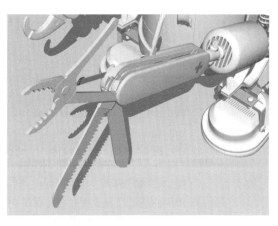

Figure 5.12 *Complex motion mechanics.*

where it meets the body of the knife, you'll see the locking mechanism, which is being pushed up by the saw blade. Yes, this is a seriously neurotic detail, which probably could have been skipped, but you must admit it makes the image really impressive. If you want to truly captivate your viewers you'll need to be very detailed with the motion mechanics.

We could go on for hours discussing the motion mechanics of Gizmo, but I think you get the idea. Making the motion dynamics for Gizmo took a lot of planning and study of mechanical motion, but you can see that the results were well worth the time invested. Proper use of motion mechanics has made this fantasy character more believable, and subsequently photorealistic.

Don't be in such a rush to finish your model that you sacrifice its photorealistic credibility. Take your time to ensure it makes proper use of motion mechanics. I know you'll be pleased with the results.

Wrapping It Up

Well, as you can see, it's of paramount importance that you take the time to properly develop motion mechanics for your objects. It's an essential element of photorealistic credibility. It's also a lot of fun to explore. Before you start your next model, take a moment to consider its movement. Remember, it doesn't matter if it's a machine or not. If it has moving parts, it's got motion mechanics.

Now we're ready for a little more fun. It's time to take a look at secular reality, which is just another of the many elements that make an object photorealistic. What are you waiting for? Flip the page and let's get started.

6

Beveling—The Key to Specular Reality

How many hard right angles edges are there in reality? Actually, there are very few because most edges are beveled. Well, the manufactured objects are anyway. Oddly though, beveling is one element that is rarely seen in most 3D models, even though it is critical for creating photorealistic objects.

What is a bevel? It can take many forms but to put it simply, a *bevel* is a dampening of right angle edges. In the real world, bevels are done to remove the harsh right-angle edge on manufactured objects, which makes them safer to handle. Quite often, right-angle edges can be hazardous since they are rather sharp. They are also a great deal more painful on impact.

If you have toured any new homes lately you'll notice that, in some homes, the corners of the walls have rounded edges. This may look like it was done to prevent damage to the wall but it's actually to keep small children from injuring themselves when they hit the wall. Basically, the corners were beveled to prevent the injuries that come from hitting a right-angle edge—well, they prevent severe injury anyway.

Bevels can be many shapes, such as flat, round, or even very ornamentally detailed. Their shape depends on where they are used. It's important that you always make an effort to add bevels to your objects so they will appear photorealistic. A lack of bevels can be the enemy of detail. If you don't use them on your details, the model will look artificial because the edges will be too harsh.

Of course, there is another, and more important, reason for using bevels—specular reality.

Creating Specular Reality with Bevels

Specularity is best described as the reflection of the light source on the object. It's basically the white highlights we see on surfaces. Specularity is an essential aspect of 3D photorealism because the human eye uses it to determine the hardness of the surface. A soft object would have a wide specular highlight, whereas a hard object would have a small specular highlight. Without specularity, surfaces would appear soft and dull.

Specular reality is the effect that is created by seeing small specular highlights on the surfaces of objects. To be direct, it's the specular highlights we see on beveled edges. Beveled edges will typically show a small specular highlight, even when the rest of the object doesn't, because they are at a different angle to the light source, usually about 45 degrees off from the rest of the surfaces. All real-world objects that are manufactured have beveled edges, so they are literally covered with tiny specular highlights on their bevels. We have become accustomed to seeing these specular highlights in real-world objects, so a 3D model must also have them to be photorealistic. Therefore, we must put bevels on all the right-angle edges of our 3D models.

ALWAYS ADD BEVELED EDGES TO YOUR MODELS.

You should always try to add beveled edges to your models because they create specular reality. In other words, they create specular highlights, which emphasize the details on the model.

The effect of specular reality is incredible. It makes a tremendous difference in the depth of the object. It makes the object appear more three-dimensional. For example, take an object that has the same surface color for all of its details. If the object was created without beveled edges there would be no specular highlights to separate the details from the main surface. They would just blend together, making the object less dimensional. Bevels are of paramount importance when working with dark-colored objects, where details can be lost if there are no specular highlights. Let's take a look at how specular highlights bring out the details on dark objects. Take a look at Figure 6.1.

Here we have a mini cassette recorder that is literally all black. The button and the body are the same color. Take a look at the tape buttons on the front of the recorder. Notice the subtle highlights on the tops of the buttons. These are great indicators of the plastic's hardness. *You can tell* this is a relatively soft plastic *because the highlights are rather small.* Now take a close look at the buttons and you'll see some diagonal specular highlights. These are the direction indicator arrows on the buttons. They are very common details on tape players, which the viewer expects, but more important is the fact that you can actually see them due to the specular highlight. If we didn't bevel the arrows, they wouldn't be visible at all.

They would just blend in with the button color. The same thing applies for the microphone on the corner of the recorder. You can see specular highlights, which indicate that there are a couple grooves in the microphone. Without the beveling, these would disappear. In fact, let's remove the beveling from the arrows and the microphone to see what happens. Take a look at Figure 6.2.

The arrows and microphone grooves have literally disappeared. They are actually still there but they just don't have any bevels to create specular highlights. Specular highlights are critical when you are dealing with details on dark objects. They are critical all the time but definitely under these conditions.

Figure 6.1 *Adding depth to dark-colored objects with bevels.*

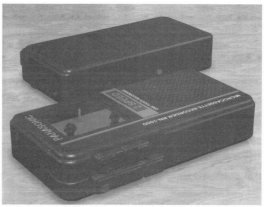

Figure 6.2 *What happens when you don't bevel details on dark objects.*

Figure 6.3 *Identifying specular reality.*

Figure 6.4 *The downside of having no beveled edges.*

IT'S IMPORTANT TO INCLUDE BEVELS ON DARK-COLORED OBJECTS.

Dark-colored objects tend to hide their features. Therefore we need to add bevels so there will be specular highlights to emphasize the details on the model. If you don't add bevels the model will end up looking very flat when rendered because the details will bleed in with the body of the object.

You probably noticed that specular highlights call our attention to the details of the object. This is a very important function of bevels. In fact, let's take a moment to explore several examples of specular reality, which was achieved by using bevels. Take a look at Figure 6.3.

Here we have a typical answering machine, which also happens to be a photorealistic 3D model. Take a close look at the corner closest to you and you'll see a number of small specular highlights. The largest one on the top edge of the answering machine body is a very obvious specular highlight, but it isn't the most important one on the object. Actually, it's the small specular highlights that call our attention to the details in the objects. Now take a look at the small specular highlight just below the big one. This is a very critical highlight since it adds depth to the object by bringing out the detail in the seam. If the specular highlight weren't there, we wouldn't really notice the seam, which happens to be an important detail for photorealistic credibility. In fact, let's take a look at what happens when we remove a few bevels from the answering machine (see Figure 6.4).

Ouch! What happened to the model? Suddenly we have a very dull and unappealing object. It lacks the luster of the answering machine with bevels. In fact, this one looks like it's made out of chalk, in spite of the fact that the model's surface attributes haven't changed. Due to the angle of the light source, the surfaces don't show specularity, which is why the bevels were so critical. Bevels will always show specular highlights, which are required to make the surface appear to be plastic. As we discussed earlier, we use the specular highlight to determine the hardness of the surface, so with no highlights the surface appears dull like chalk. We are accustomed to seeing specular reality, which means the model doesn't look natural without it.

Let's treat our eyes to something truly spectacular. Take a look at Figure 6.5.

Here we have the Personal Digital Assistant (PDA) we discussed in Chapter 3, "Material—What's It Made Of?" This object is a literal smorgasbord of specular reality. Let's start by looking at the buttons. Notice how every button has a small specular highlight on its front right corner. You can see how the tiny highlight makes the keys appear as if they are made out of hard material. In fact, the keys are rather hard since they need to withstand the pummeling of barbaric fingers,

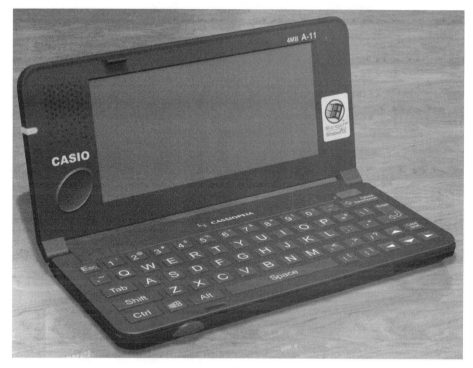

Figure 6.5 *The photorealistic influence of bevels.*

day in and day out. Now let's take a look at the base of the PDA. Did you notice the nice specular highlight on the front edge? This highlight isn't nearly as crisp as the keys so it implies that the case is actually made out of a softer material, which is correct.

Just below that specular highlight you'll find another, which is much smaller. This is a great detail that helps to make the object photorealistic. In Chapter 3, we discussed the importance of adding manufacturing details to your 3D objects. This tiny specular highlight shows the seam in the case, which indicates that it was manufactured. Bevels create specular highlights that bring out the manufacturing details, which are paramount to the photorealistic credibility of the object.

You can see that no one element stands on its own. You need to make sure you apply all the rules of photorealistic 3D we discussed in Chapter 1 or the object just won't appear realistic. Yes, there are occasional exceptions to the rule but these are rare. When creating details on your objects you also need to create bevels so they will be distinguishable on the object's surface. Without the bevels, they can be very difficult to see.

Beveled edges make a huge impact on the believability of the objects. They also add depth to the object and make it possible to distinguish the details. In general, they are necessary or the object won't be photorealistic. How do we create them? We're just about to explore this question.

Creating and Planning Your Beveled Edges

Creating bevels can be a snap or it can be a bit of work. It all depends on how your program handles them. Some programs can't create bevels so you'll have to do them manually, which isn't a lot of fun, but it can be done relatively quickly. We're going to explore both the automated and manual methods for creating bevels, but first we need to discuss the requirements for creating them.

You can usually bevel only a single polygon. Sure, you can select a group and then bevel them but each polygon will end up having its own bevel, which looks cool but is rather unrealistic in most cases. It all depends on the capabilities of your program. For the sake of this discussion, we cover the most common beveling features available.

ALWAYS PLAN YOUR BEVELS BEFORE YOU START MODELING THE OBJECT.

Beveling edges can be tricky. If you don't plan them out before you start modeling the object you can get into a situation where adding the bevels can be very difficult if not impossible. Try to think of every possible detail in the model before you start building it. It can take a bit of time to get used to doing this but believe me, it will save you countless hours you'd spend trying to retrofit the model with bevels.

It's important to note that we can't start adding the bevels randomly or we'll get ourselves in trouble. We need to plan them out carefully so we don't end up spending a lot of time creating them. It's paramount that you plan the beveled edges before you begin to model your object. If you wait until after you have added the details, you may not be able to create the bevels, or at least not without a lot of added work. In fact, why don't we take a look at why planning is important.

In Figure 6.6 we have the model of the PDA we examined earlier. You can see that the buttons have very nice recesses around them, which are beveled on the edges. This creates a very clean look and provides a lot of specular reality for the model. We're going to re-create these recesses, which will require some planning since we will want to bevel the edges around the recesses.

In order to make the recesses we'll need to use a Boolean Subtract operation. Here's where we start to run into planning issues. If we just jumped right in and started adding the bevels as we develop the model, we might run into a problem

Figure 6.6 *Planning your bevels.*

adding the bevels where we need them. In fact, let's have a little fun and test this theory by jumping in and adding the bevels with no regard to planning. (This is the last time we're going to do this. I don't want you to make a habit out of bad planning.) Take a look at Figure 6.7.

You can see that a nice bevel was added to the top of the PDA base. This, of course, is what we wanted but what happens when we add the key recesses by performing a Boolean Subtract operation? Let's take a look at Figure 6.8 and see for ourselves.

Here we have the result of our Boolean operation. Take a look at the shaded view in the upper right corner and you'll see that we have a bevel on the outer edge of the target object, but we don't have one on the edge of the recesses. This happened because we did the beveling first, which, of course, was bad planning. You always want to perform the Boolean operations before you bevel the surface. This way, when you create the bevel it will react with the holes in the polygon, which will create bevels on the recess edges. Use some proper planning and perform the Boolean operation first. Take a look at Figure 6.9.

Here you can see the effector object in black and the target object in white. Performing a Boolean Subtract with these two objects will create the recesses in the PDA base. Once this has been done, we can select the top polygon of the PDA base and create a small bevel as shown in Figure 6.10.

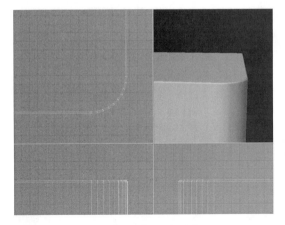

Figure 6.7 Beveling the PDA base.

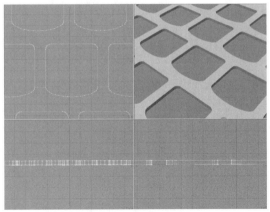

Figure 6.8 The result of not planning the bevels.

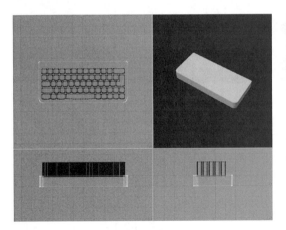

Figure 6.9 Creating the recesses.

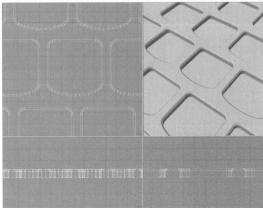

Figure 6.10 The result of proper bevel planning.

That's more like it. Now we have a bevel on the outside of the PDA top and around the recesses. You can see how proper planning is critical to the success of your bevels. How do we actually create the bevels?

Creating Bevels

There are two ways to create bevels: automatically and manually. Obviously the automatic method is best since the computer does all of the work for you. All you have to do is select the polygon and enter a bevel value. It doesn't get any easier than this. In fact, let's take a look at how it is actually done.

In Figure 6.11 we have two simple objects. The one on the left shows the object before the bevel and the one on the right shows the result of the bevel operation. To automatically create the bevel, select the polygon you want to bevel, as shown in the object to the left, and then perform the bevel operation. When you chose the bevel operation you will be asked to enter a value which represents the size of the bevel. Usually you will be prompted for two values: the amount of shift and inset. The *Shift* represents the distance the new polygon will move away from the object and the *Inset* controls the depth of the bevel. Let's take a look at a visual representation of these values before we get too confused.

You can clearly see in Figure 6.12 how the shift and inset values work. Now, your program may refer to these values by different names but their functions will remain the same. Many programs refer to the inset value as bevel and the shift value as height. Once again, the functions are the same, only the names have changed.

As you can see, the automatic method is a very fast and simple method for creating bevels. Let's look at how effectively it creates complex bevels. In Figure 6.13 we have the same two objects as before, but now they have a hole in the center. Notice how the bevel operation is the same but this time we have a bevel on the outer edge of the object and around the edge of the hole. It's a great effect and provides a lot of visual detail on the model. Creating bevels with the automatic method is easy when you are working with single polygons, but what happens when there is more than one polygon on the surface? We need to do a little beveling trickery.

Creating Automatic Bevels with Multiple Polygons

There will be many occasions where you'll need to create a bevel on a surface that has several polygons. Since automatic beveling operations usually work only with single polygons, we need to be creative to find a solution. We can't just select all the polygons or we'll end up with something that resembles the image in Figure 6.14.

While the effect certainly looks cool, it's not what we were trying to accomplish. The problem is that the automatic bevel operation created a bevel for every polygon selected. There are a few programs that will allow you to bevel groups of polygons as a single bevel, but this is rare. How do we get around this problem? There are a couple of ways.

The first method is to merge the polygons into a single polygon; you can bevel it as shown in Figure 6.15.

As you can see, it was simple to bevel the polygons once they were merged. If you needed the top polygon to be divided into segments, all you need to do is manually split it up after you've beveled it, which is relatively simple using basic polygon editing tools.

Creating Bevels Manually

The second beveling technique is manual beveling. The manual method isn't as simple as the automatic method since it requires a bit more effort to perform and a completely different way of looking at bevels. Sometimes you'll find that even if you can do automatic bevels, you'll still need to do them manually because the surface is too complex for an automatic bevel, as is the case when you need to bevel details into a group of polygons.

Manual bevels are created in two different ways. They can be created using the Boolean or Extrude operations. We'll take a look at the Boolean method first.

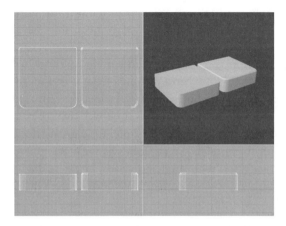

Figure 6.11 *Using the automatic method to create bevels.*

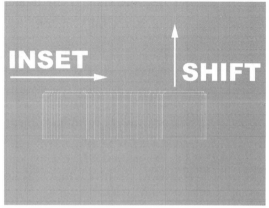

Figure 6.12 *The beveling values.*

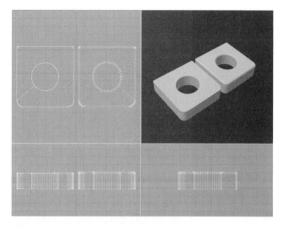

Figure 6.13 *Creating complex bevels with the automatic beveling method.*

Figure 6.14 *Using the automatic bevel operation with multiple polygons.*

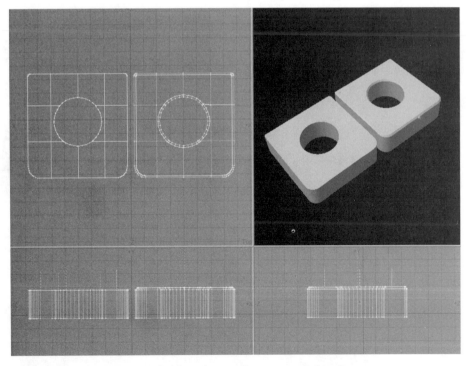

Figure 6.15 *Merging multiple polygons for automatic beveling.*

109

Creating Bevels with Boolean Operations

Let's assume for a moment that you have a complex model and you need to add a hole with a beveled edge. Let's also assume that you have already done a beveled edge on the surface some time ago, and to make things worse, the surface has several polygons. Well, this certainly rules out using automatic beveling, doesn't it?

This is when it's time to employ a little beveling trickery using the Boolean Subtract operation. The key to the Boolean beveling method is the shape of the effector object. It's actually kind of simple when you think about it. Just create a negative version of the beveled edge on the effector object as shown in Figure 6.16.

You can see that the effector object has been created with the negative version of the bevel so it will create a positive bevel in the target object. Now all we need to do is perform a Boolean Subtract operation and we'll have a perfect beveled hole as shown in Figure 6.17.

Looks great doesn't it? You can see how this method is very effective for creating beveled edges on complex shapes. You'll find there will be many occasions where you need to use this method to create details with bevels. For instance, you might need to put a few controls on a portable CD player, which happens to be a very organic shape. You can't just Boolean a hole and use the automatic bevel

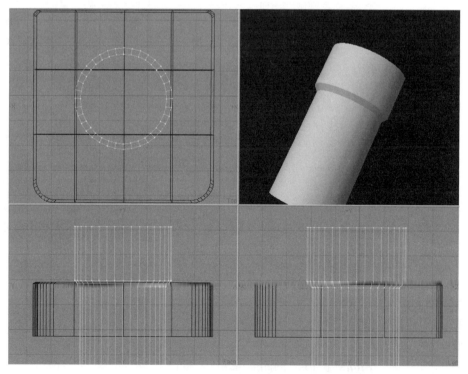

Figure 6.16 *Creating the beveling effector object.*

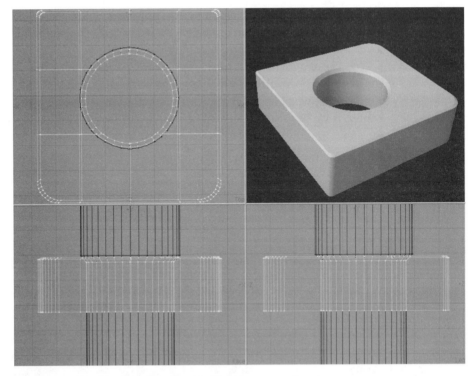

Figure 6.17 *Creating bevels with Boolean operations.*

operation since the shape is organic. To be specific, the body of the CD player doesn't have bevels, or need them, since it's an organic shape. Instead you want just the hole where you are placing the controls to be beveled. You'll have to use Boolean beveling.

As you can see, the Boolean method of creating bevels can be extremely effective where an automatic bevel just wouldn't work. I use this technique more often than any other since it's very effective for creating bevels on organic shapes.

Creating Bevels with Extrude Operations

Using Extrude operations is by far the least desirable method for creating bevels, but there are times when it's the only method that works, especially if you don't have automatic beveling tools. Actually it's not all that bad, it just requires a bit more patience. It's important to note that your program may have another name for the Extrude operation, such as Sweep or Smooth Shift. Either of these will create a new layer of polygons from the ones selected. In fact, it might have both the Extrude function and a Smooth Shift or Sweep feature. In these cases you'll want to use the later options since they are more reliable and cause less potential errors when extruding multiple polygons at the same time.

Let's jump right in and take a look at how we create bevels with Extrude operations. The first thing you'll need to do is select the polygons and extrude them a very short distance as shown in Figure 6.18.

You can see that a new layer of polygons has been added to the object. Now the trick is to shrink these polygons to create the beveled edges. I'm sure you noticed that we have a slight problem when doing this since there is a hole in the center. If we just scale the new polygons as a group, the hole will have an inverted bevel because the points around it will shrink. What we need to do is enlarge the points around the hole to create the bevel. This means we'll have to create the bevels in two steps.

First, select all of the points on the outer edge of the surface and scale them down to create the outer bevel as shown in Figure 6.19.

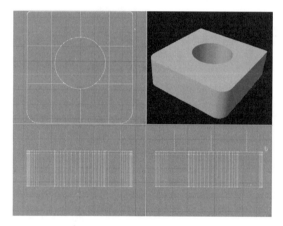

Figure 6.18 *Extruding the polygons to create a bevel.*

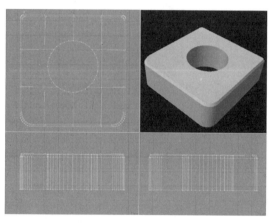

Figure 6.19 *Creating the outer bevel.*

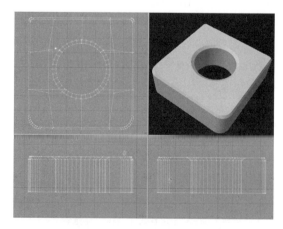

Figure 6.20 *Creating the inner bevel.*

We now have a very nice outer bevel on the object. Next, select all the points on the interior of the surface and scale them up so they create the inner bevel as shown in Figure 6.20.

There you have it, a very nice beveling job done the hard way. It wasn't that difficult. It's important that you become familiar with all of the beveling methods since you will encounter situations where you will need to use all of them to make your object photorealistic.

We know that beveled edges are necessary but where and when do we use them? That's a great question. Why don't we take a look at how we determine where bevels should be used?

When to Use Bevels

It's actually very easy to determine where bevels are necessary since they are designed to soften harsh edges that would be safety hazards. This means that you need to bevel any edge that will be encountered when handling the object. I told you it was easy. The good news is that it's completely unnecessary to bevel edges that can't be reached since they aren't a safety hazard. In fact, real-world objects

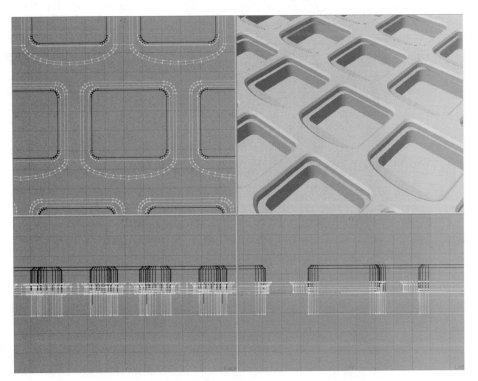

Figure 6.21 *Edges that don't require bevels.*

don't have bevels on edges that you can't touch. Let's take a look at an example of edges that don't need to be beveled (see Figure 6.21).

❯❯ YOU NEED TO ADD BEVELS ONLY TO EDGES THAT CAN BE TOUCHED.

Don't get carried away adding bevels. They were originally designed to protect against hazardous sharp edges so you only need to add them to edges that can be touched while handling the object. You don't need to bevel the untouchables, like button/key holes and even recessed seams.

Here we have the key recesses on the PDA. You'll notice that there isn't a beveled edge on the inside recess. That is because your finger will never touch it since the key doesn't go down that far. In fact, let's look at the same image with the keys in place.

Figure 6.22 shows that the keys prevent you from being able to touch the edge of the inside recess, so there is no point in beveling their edges. I'll bet you're glad there are actually edges that you don't have to bevel. In fact, there are other cases

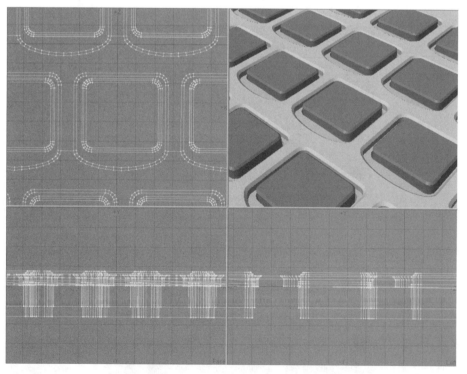

Figure 6.22 *The recess edge being hidden by the keys.*

where beveling isn't necessary. You'll find that recessed seams are very rarely beveled either since they are too small to be a hazard. It would be unlikely that you could get your finger far enough into the seam to hurt yourself, and if you did you probably deserved it for horsing around with the seam.

You should definitely try to avoid overdoing it with bevels. They are critical for photorealistic credibility but they need to be used only in areas where you can physically touch the edges. I should say where the average finger can physically touch the edge, since if you had "gorilla" fingers there would be a whole lot of edges you couldn't touch.

Get Ready for a Little Demolition

Well, that was fun. You now know a number of ways to create bevels. In fact, you won't find a situation where at least one of these methods won't do the job. Just make sure that you always include bevels on your objects to create specular reality. They go a long way toward creating photorealistic credibility since the viewer is used to seeing bevels on real-world objects and, conversely, not used to seeing them on 3D objects.

I'm sure you have some tension to release after all the modeling tutorials you've done, so now it's time to take out some of your aggression by demolishing your models. Maybe that would be a bit much. How about if we just age them a bit? Great; then let's continue on to Chapter 7, "Dents and Dings—Aging Your Models."

7 Dents and Dings—Aging Your Models

It's time for a little damage! It's about time someone wreaked havoc on their 3D models. I'm sure you've seen literally hundreds of 3D images by now. So tell me, just how many of them had aging on the models? One? Two? Maybe three? I've seen a couple but it's generally been rather disappointing. I want to see more damage! Perfect objects just aren't natural—especially in my home.

So, how many new things do you own? I mean objects that have no dents or dings. How polished and clean is the world around you? Well, if your world is anything like mine, it's a complete mess. Sure, it's likely that the objects in our homes are relatively unscathed but step outside your home and it's a literal disaster area. One of the best things about reality is that nothing is perfect. It gives our environment character. A perfect world would be boring, much like the current offering of 3D images.

ALWAYS TRY TO AGE YOUR OBJECTS IF THEY ARE FREQUENTLY HANDLED.

Frequently handled objects are likely to have some form of damage. You should always add a little aging to your models that are frequently handled, such as cell phones, watches, and even sidewalks.

I don't mean to make it sound like all 3D images lack depth, but when you view an image your eyes scan it for details. If you can't find enough detail in the image you'll quickly lose interest. Of course, we've already discussed detail on many levels but now it's time to make our 3D objects look like they've experienced reality. The fact is that reality can be quite destructive. How many times have you seen a car accident on your way to work? If you live in Los Angeles I'm sure you see them daily. Car accidents are an extreme form of damage, but how about the sidewalk you walk upon daily? Have you ever looked down? Maybe to snatch that lucky penny? If you have, I'm sure you noticed that the sidewalk isn't perfect. It probably has plenty of dents, dings, and gouges, which were created by years of wear and tear from foot traffic. In fact, it probably looks a little something like Figure 7.1.

Now that's what I call a sidewalk! Notice the chunks that have been chipped away from the edges of the concrete. This is exactly what happens to sidewalks over the years. Think about it. Thousands of people have walked on the sidewalk, which means you've got to see some damage. I'm sure you noticed that this scene is very photorealistic but it's actually the chipped sidewalk that provides the most photorealistic leverage. It's a detail that is rarely found in 3D scenes but nearly always found in reality. You'd be surprised at how influential damage can be in convincing your audience that the image is photorealistic.

I'm sure you recall our frequent discussion on how detail is what makes an object realistic. Aging is just another detail that lends credibility to your objects. It's the details that make your models photorealistic. Of course there are other types of details that impact the photorealistic credibility of a model, but nothing makes it appear more natural than a little aging. Aging makes the model appear lived-in. (Obviously nobody lives in the models, unless it's a house, but you get the idea.) Aging tells us that the model has been around a while and has probably been frequently handled. Damage doesn't happen on its own, you know.

Figure 7.1 *An example of an aged sidewalk.*

Aging our models is important, but how exactly is it accomplished? Well I'm glad you asked because we're getting ready to create some damage.

Applying Damage to Your Models

Applying damage to your models separates them from the currently sterile crowd of 3D models. Nearly all objects you'll see in 3D scenes are flawless. Sure, they might be a little dirty but where's the damage? Consider this for a moment: One out of every three households in the United States has a child living under its roof. Of course, we all know that children are basically walking disaster areas. Nearly everything they touch is decimated. They quite literally leave a wake of havoc as they pass through the house.

You know, if Samsonite Luggage really wanted to impress us they would get rid of that silly gorilla and let a child play with the luggage. If it lasted more than a minute I would buy it. Have I mentioned that damage is important? Okay, I'll stop nagging now.

How do we do it? There are a number of methods you can use. The most popular methods include Boolean operations, magnet tools, and point manipulation. We covered Boolean operations in Chapter 3, so I guess we need to cover the magnet tool and point manipulation next.

A *magnet tool* does exactly what it says. It pulls polygons and points just like a real magnet. Magnet tools are extremely flexible since you can control the strength and range of the magnetic effect to create precise deformations. In fact, several programs actually let you change the shape of the magnet effect for even greater control, though this is actually undesirable when aging your models since you want the effect to be chaotic. In fact, the less precise the better. I'm sure you can see how the magnet tool is an indispensable asset when creating aged models.

Point manipulation is no more than moving and dragging point the old-fashioned way. That's all there is to it.

Now that we're familiar with the aging methods, let's jump right in and explore the different ways you can apply them to your models.

Aging Your Models with Booleans

The Boolean Subtract operation is an essential tool when creating damaged objects. It offers you a high degree of control because you can use literally any shape for the effector object, which makes the aging process a lot easier. In fact, why don't we see if we can re-create the chipped cement that we saw in Figure 7.1?

First, let's take a look at the actual unsurfaced model that was used in the scene, so we can determine the best approach for aging our sidewalk. You can see that the model in Figure 7.2 is actually very simple. Now that we've seen the model, it becomes obvious that a Boolean Subtract operation will do the job nicely. The first thing we need to do is create our effector object, which is actually quite simple since all you need to do is create a box with a jagged edge, as shown in Figure 7.3.

As you can see, the object really isn't all that complicated. In fact, to create this object you merely need to lay down a few points, create a polygon, and extrude it. It doesn't get much easier than this. Once you have created the effector you need to load your sidewalk object and perform a Boolean Subtract operation. Of course, making the gouges look right is the trick, so before we perform the Boolean operation we need to give our effector object a unique surface name. This is necessary since we want the actual gouges in the cement to be a different surface than the sidewalk. Why? It's simple really; chipped cement is very rough and jagged, whereas finished cement is rather smooth and porous. Therefore, to make the object photorealistic, we need to create separate surfaces for the sidewalk and gouges.

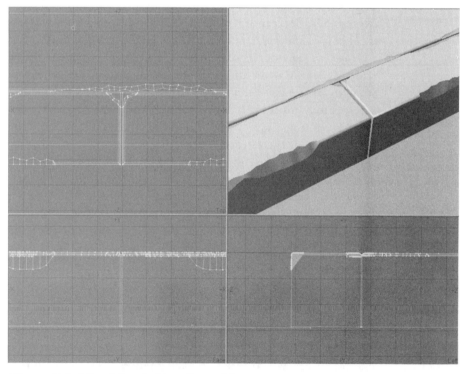

Figure 7.2 The chipped sidewalk model.

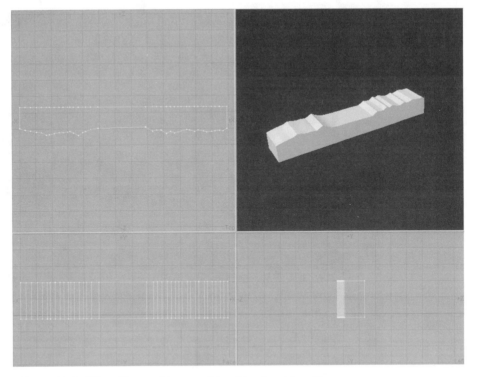

Figure 7.3 *The effector object used to chip the sidewalk.*

Now that we have given the effector a unique surface name, we need to position it properly so we have a realistic gouge in the sidewalk. This requires rotating the effector object so it's at roughly a 45-degree angle as shown in Figure 7.4.

Once you have rotated the effector you can move it into position and perform the Boolean Subtract operation as shown in Figure 7.4. You can see that it was very simple to create gouges and chips in the cement with the Boolean Subtract operation. If you wanted to make the object truly photorealistic, you would need to create several effector objects so the gouges would all be unique. In addition, you would want to rotate them all at different angles to add a little more chaos so the effect appears more natural.

That was a very simple technique for creating a chipped sidewalk but the effect was awesome in the final render. The aging doesn't have to be very complicated to create photorealistic credibility. It just needs to be applied correctly. It's important that you add the aging in logical places or it will make the object appear unnatural. For instance, you wouldn't normally put gouges in the middle of the sidewalk since it's a flat surface, which resists gouges. If you did gouge the cement in the middle you would need to justify it with an object in the scene that was

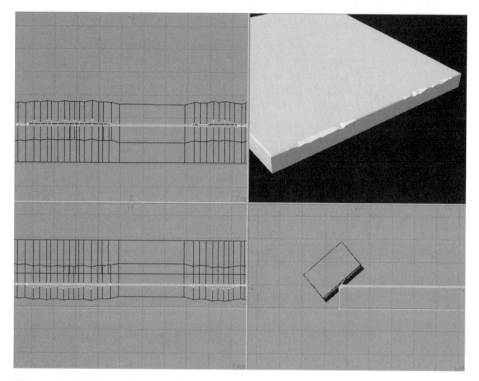

Figure 7.4 *The Boolean Subtract operation done to add gouges to the sidewalk.*

responsible for the damage. We'll talk more about object justification in Chapter 12, "Adding Chaos—Creating Clutter."

Let's create some very simple aging by using the most basic aging method—pulling points.

Aging Your Models with Point Manipulation

Sometimes all it takes to age your object is pulling a few points. This is particularly effective when the object is made of a paper product or some other pliable material. Obviously, using Boolean operations on paper products wouldn't make much sense since they can't be chipped or gouged. Of course, they can be dented, but now that I think about it, it's actually more like a crease or fold, which we would create by dragging points.

Let's take a look at how easily aging can be applied by pulling points. Figure 7.5 shows a very photorealistic roll of duct tape, with a variety of aging techniques applied. No doubt you noticed the wonderful surface aging that was applied with image maps. Surface aging is also very important but it's usually used to support the model aging. We'll be covering surface aging in Chapter 8, "Photorealistic Surfacing Fundamentals." Right now let's focus on the aging that was applied to the model. You can see that the model isn't perfectly round like most 3D models of tape. This model actually has a very realistic, irregular shape, which is common for objects like tape because they are pliable. It's very easy to change their shape by grabbing them or even dropping them on the floor.

Let's take a look at how the aging was applied to the duct tape. First take a look at the basic model in Figure 7.6 to determine where we need to apply the aging.

We can see that the model is fairly basic but has some nice detail on the center cardboard core. The only problem is that the tape is too round, which makes it look artificial. There isn't a single roll of tape in our universe that's perfectly round. (There may be one floating around in a UFO somewhere, but you'll have to consult the *X Files* on that one.) It's obvious that we need to apply some minor distortion to the general shape of the tape. But we have to be careful to avoid distorting the area around the core since this region is unaffected by being handled or dropped. To age the tape we'll need to pull a few of the outer points to create some valleys and bulges as shown in Figure 7.7.

You can see that the tape now has an irregular shape. The actual points that were manipulated are highlighted in blue. Notice how nearly all of the points were slightly altered to give the tape a nice organic shape. This chaos is important for establishing photorealistic credibility.

We could call it quits now but we haven't quite added enough aging yet. What's missing? We can assume that the tape was dropped, which is why it is slightly deformed. If this is the case, it's highly unlikely that it landed flat on its side. It's more likely that it landed at an odd angle, which would create some depressions on the edge of the tape at the point of impact. Once again, this is a matter of pulling a few points as illustrated in Figure 7.8.

Here you can see that a couple of things were done to create the flattened edges of the tape. The first thing we did was to move the center points closer to the top. This was done because we needed to drag some of the points on the top edge inward to create the flattened spots. If we had left the points in the middle of the tape, the flattened spots would have been too large. We want them to be small so it looks like the tape landed on its edge.

The second thing we did was to pull a few points inward, which created the flattened spots. The actual points that were moved are highlighted in blue. As you can see, it was very simple to add photorealistic aging details to the tape by merely pulling a few points. You can use similar methods to add photorealistic aging to all your models that are made with paper products or other pliable materials.

Speaking of pliable materials, let's take a look at that wonderful magnet tool.

Figure 7.5 *Object aging that was created by point manipulation.*

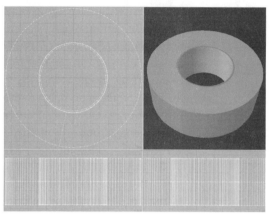

Figure 7.6 *The basic duct tape model.*

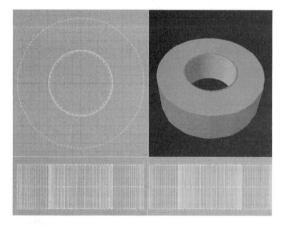

Figure 7.7 *Applying aging to the duct tape model.*

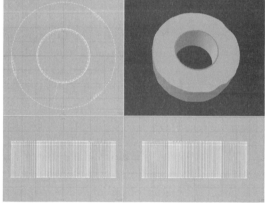

Figure 7.8 *Creating points of impact by pulling points.*

Aging Your Models with the Magnet Tool

The magnet tool is a very useful tool in creating organic aging. So what is organic aging? In many cases the aging that occurs on real-world objects is very free flowing, which makes using Boolean operations impossible and point manipulation undesirable. Instead, you want to be able to influence portions of the mesh simultaneously—somewhat like dragging multiple points at the same time, but slightly different because merely dragging the points would move all of them to the same distance, which is undesirable. What you want to do is create a curved deformation in the points. Basically, you want the effect to be like a magnet, where the strength of the effect tapers off as you get further away from the center of the magnet. This is exactly what the magnet tool does: Just like a real magnet, it has a limited range of influence.

How do we create aging with the magnet tool? Let's take a look at an excellent use for the magnet tool. Let's add the aging that occurs at the top of hardbound book covers—you know, the sort of folded and smashed look that comes from being set down on its edge. Before we can use the magnet tool we need to prep the model. The first step is to ensure that we have enough polygons to create the effect. Take a look at Figure 7.9.

If you look at the top of the book, you'll see three rows of polygons, which we will be using to add the aging details. It's important that you have these polygons or you won't be able to apply the aging. You should always plan for aging when you create your models because adding polygons to the finished object can be difficult and downright annoying. Fortunately, many programs have a knife tool, which makes it simple to add polygons by dividing a current polygon along a particular axis.

►► ALWAYS CONSIDER AGING BEFORE YOU START MODELING YOUR OBJECT.

You should always plan for aging when you create your models because adding polygons to the finished object can be difficult if not downright annoying. Most of the aging details require a solid polygon mesh so the effect isn't jagged. You should try to plan your models so they have the proper mesh density in the areas where aging would occur.

Now that we have enough polygons we are ready to start adding the aging. The first thing we need to do is select the points at the outer edge of the spine as shown in Figure 7.9, and then rotate them slightly as shown in Figure 7.10.

You can see that we are starting to deform the shape of the spine. Next, use the magnet tool to drag these points out and down to create the fold as shown in Figure 7.11.

You can see that we now have a slight curvature to the spine's top edge, which was created by selecting the outermost points, which are highlighted in blue, and then dragging them with the magnet tool. The magnet effect is limited to the points that we have selected. Doing this allows us to control the impact of the magnet tool.

We need to add the final detail, which makes the fold more prominent. Select the points at the base of the fold and pull them inward as shown in Figure 7.12.

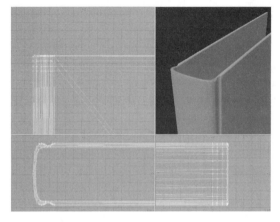

Figure 7.9 *Building the foundation for aging the book.*

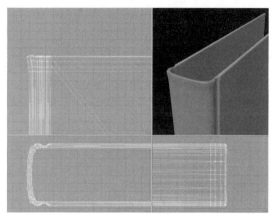

Figure 7.10 *Rotating the points at the top of the spine.*

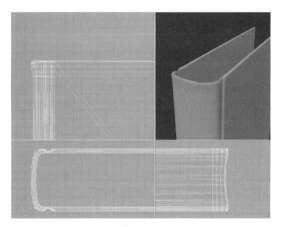

Figure 7.11 *Bending the spine's edge with the magnet tool.*

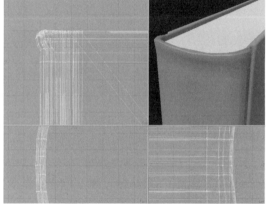

Figure 7.12 *Making the fold more prominent by dragging points.*

Now we have very realistic aging applied to our book. The next step would be to create some nice bump image maps that will add fine wrinkles to the fold. We explore image maps in Chapter 9, "Image Map Surfaces."

As you can see, the magnet tool is very useful for creating organic aging details. In fact, all three tools are great for creating aging details. There are literally thousands of aging effects that can be created with these tools. The possibilities are truly unlimited. Just remember to plan for aging when you create your models so you don't kill yourself trying to modify them later.

That Does It for Modeling!

Well, that about does it for the photorealistic modeling techniques. We've covered a lot of information in a mere few pages. I don't know about you, but I think my head is going to explode. Well, it's swelling at any rate.

Now it's time to take a look at the photorealistic surfacing principles. But first, I think we've earned a break. Why don't you take some time off and let the concepts you've just learned sink in before you pummel your brain with more information? Believe me, the surfacing chapters are filled with awesome techniques and principles for making your objects appear realistic so you'll want a clear head before you dive in.

PART III
Photorealistic Surfacing Techniques

How many of you have seen a 3D image where you could see stretching in the image maps? You know, the wood surface that stretches over the end of the board, or maybe the pinching of the texture at the top of a basketball? I'm sure you all have seen this problem. Surfacing photorealistic objects can be very challenging. It's by far the most complicated aspect of the photorealistic process. Not because of the work, but more the level of detail required for creating photorealistic surfaces.

Surfaces in reality are very unique. They have subtle, and often not so subtle, details that make them complicated to mimic. The goal of photorealistic surfacing is to mimic the chaos of real-world object surfaces. This chaos takes on two forms: visual and physical. Simply put, they are visually chaotic with detail and also physically chaotic with texture you can feel. It's important to capture these details in the surfaces you create for your 3D objects.

3D programs have given us a number of tools for re-creating the surfaces of reality. The most common tools are procedural textures and image maps. The goal of Part III is to give you a complete understanding of these tools and where they are best used. There are many factors to consider when creating your object's surfaces. The surfaces we see in reality have a number of attributes, which make up their appearance. There are many ways to re-create these attributes using procedural textures and image maps, which we will cover in detail. So sit back, relax, and get ready for a wild ride into the world of photo-realistic surfacing.

VISIT THE COMPANION WEB SITE FOR TUTORIAL FILES.

Before you begin Part III, go to Appendix F and learn about the companion Web site. All of the TUTORIAL FILES referenced in this part are located on the companion Web site, which is located at www.wiley.com/compbooks/fleming. You should also download the color figures from the companion Web site since they will be easier to review than the grayscale images printed in this book.

8 *Photorealistic Surfacing Fundamentals*

Creating photorealistic surfaces can be challenging, but it can also be a lot of fun. Surfacing is the most important aspect of the model's photorealistic development. While the modeling of an object is important, it won't make the object appear photorealistic. It's a good foundation, but you need to add surface attributes to make the object appear realistic. For example: A product that is a simple four-sided box with scanned image maps will look photorealistic at first but it won't hold up under close scrutiny. On the other hand, a perfectly modeled box with poor surfaces will immediately appear unrealistic. You need to place an equal amount of energy on both the model and surfaces to make the object realistic.

There are many elements that make a surface photorealistic. These elements can best be described as the *Rules of Photorealistic Surfacing,* which serve as guidelines for surfacing your objects. I know what you're thinking: "Not more rules!" (If you think this is bad, wait until you get to Chapter 12.) All kidding aside, these rules make it easy to analyze the surfacing on your objects to ensure they are photorealistic, so let's jump right in and take a look at them.

Every Surface Must Have a Bump Texture

All real-world objects have a surface texture. While they may not be as obvious as tree bark or rusted metal, they are definitely present. One of the most common problems in 3D images is the lack of surface texture. Completely smooth objects look unrealistic. They just don't have the surface chaos that we expect from real objects. Even smooth objects like glass and mirrors have very subtle surface textures. You may not be able to feel them, or even see them, but they play a major role in the photorealistic credibility of the object. Surface texture is particularly important when the object is reflective. Even a minor surface texture will have a clearly visible effect on the surface's reflectivity. Without a surface texture, the reflection will be too perfect. Let's take a look at an example of how a bump map impacts the reality of reflections.

Take a look at Figure 8.1. Here we have two of my favorite insects, Madagascar hissing cockroaches, which are snacking on some crackers that fell to my kitchen floor. Okay, so I put them there to feed the roaches. No, I don't have giant roaches running around my house; they are pets that get to occasionally come out of their terrarium for exercise. Now that you're convinced I should be institutionalized, let's get back to the image. Take a look at the bottom image.

Figure 8.1 *The impact of bump textures on reflections.*

Notice how the reflection on the floor is irregular, following the contours of the bump map on the floor. This is very important for making the surface realistic. A perfect reflection would suggest that the floor was smooth, which wouldn't make sense based on the visual chaos we've seen on the floor tiles.

Speaking of not making sense, take a look at the top of Figure 8.1. Here we have the same scene, but no bump map texture has been added to the floor. Notice how the reflection is very clear and smooth. The floor looks like a mirror. This doesn't look natural because the floor tiles look like they have a surface texture, which would make the reflection irregular. The lack of irregularity in the reflection has undermined the photorealistic credibility of the scene. You want to make sure that all your surfaces have a bump texture.

➤➤ ALWAYS ADD BUMP MAPS TO YOUR REFLECTIVE SURFACES.

A bump map will create subtle distortions in the reflection on a surface. If you neglect to add the bump, the reflection will be too clean, which makes the surface seem artificial. A metal surface with perfect reflections just can't exist since the process of making metals isn't pure. The only place we are used to seeing clean reflections is in a mirror, which happens to have an extremely minor bump that has little impact on the reflection.

Another reason to add surface texture is to create specular reality. The surface texture on an object breaks up the specular highlight. If there is no texture, the highlight is too consistent and looks artificial. Let's take a look at an example of how surface texture makes an object more realistic.

Take a look at Figure 8.2. Here we have two pagers. The farthest one has no surface bump, whereas the one in the foreground does. Notice how the one in the foreground looks convincingly realistic. That's because it has a minor surface bump texture. Pagers are made of plastic, which we expect to have a rough surface texture. Without this texture, the pager looks artificial.

Now let's take a look at the impact the surface bump has on the specularity of the object. You can see that the specularity on the pager in the foreground is more intense than the one in the background. Both pagers have the same value of specularity but the bump texture makes the pager in the foreground appear harder, which is what we expect from a plastic pager. The specular highlight on the pager without a bump texture is softer, making the object appear soft, which is unrealistic for a pager.

You can see how a surface bump plays a major role in making an object photorealistic. Since we're on the subject of specularity, let's take a look at the next rule of photorealistic surfacing: All surfaces must have specularity.

Figure 8.2 *The relationship between bump textures and specularity.*

All Surfaces Must Have Specularity

I regularly see objects that lack specularity, particularly ones like natural wood or fabrics. In reality, all surfaces have specularity. Remember that *specularity* is the reflection of the light source on the object. Specularity is an essential aspect of 3D photorealism because the human eye uses it to determine the hardness of the surface. A soft object would have a wide specular highlight, whereas a hard object would have a small specular highlight. Without specularity, surfaces would appear soft and dull. In fact, even the most dull and porous objects have a minor level of specularity. Let's take a look at how specularity helps to make an object photorealistic.

APPLY SPECULARITY TO EVERY OBJECT TO CREATE A VISUAL CUE FOR HARDNESS.

The human eye uses specularity to determine the hardness of a surface. If you fail to add specularity, it will be impossible to determine the hardness of the surface.

Take a look at Figure 8.3. Here we have the same two pagers, but this time the farthest one has a bump texture and no specularity. Notice how dull it appears. In fact, it looks like it's made of chalk. I'm sure there is some use for a chalk pager but I can't imagine what it would be. Even though it now has a realistic bump texture, it lacks the specularity that makes the pager in the foreground photorealistic. It's the same model, but it lacks depth because there are no specular highlights. Specularity adds depth to an object, particularly when there is a bump texture.

As you can see, your models need to conform to all of the rules of photorealistic surfacing. If you are missing just one, the object will appear unnatural. Speaking of unnatural, let's take a look at a common problem in most 3D images: 100 percent diffusion levels.

Never Use 100 Percent Diffusion

This is the rule that is most often abused. I can't count the number of 3D images I've seen that have 100 percent diffusion for all of their objects. *Diffusion* is best described as the amount of the object's color that it shows on its own surface. For

Figure 8.3 *The value of specularity.*

example: A metal object is reflective so it shows a small portion of its own color because it is also showing its environment. The more reflective, the lower the level of diffusion. Metals typically have a diffusion level of 25 to 45 percent. On the other hand, a mirror would have a diffusion of 0 percent since it's 100 percent reflective.

There are only a few surfaces in reality that show 100 percent of their own color. These would be matte surfaces such as flat paint. Usually, using 100 percent diffusion will make your objects too crisp, almost as if they are too new. While it's a subtle element in the scene, it definitely undermines the realism. You'd be surprised how easily the human eye picks up these subtle details. I'm sure you've seen many scenes that looked great but there was something that didn't feel right about it. It was probably the level of diffusion on the surfaces. Typically, you'll want to set your diffusion levels to around 90 percent on objects that aren't reflective. Of course, metals and plastics have even lower diffusion levels since they are reflective. Just make sure that you don't exceed 90 percent diffusion on your surfaces.

AVOID USING A DIFFUSION LEVEL THAT IS GREATER THAN 90 PERCENT.

There are very few objects in reality that display 100 percent of their surface color. If you use values of 100 percent, your models will appear too crisp and bright, making them appear unnatural. A good rule of thumb is to avoid using diffusion values that are greater than 90 percent.

Let's take a look at the difference between 100 percent diffusion and a proper setting of 90 percent. Take a look at the two books in Figure 8.4. Actually, they happen to be one of my favorite source books. Now take a close look and you'll notice that the book in the background has a sharp, crisp color. In fact, the surface is a bit washed out by the light. This is because the surface has 100 percent diffusion. Take a look at any book in your studio and you'll notice that they aren't bright, shiny, and new. In fact, if they're anything like mine, they are rather dull from being handled frequently. There are very few surfaces in reality that show 100 percent of their color. This book is an excellent example of an object that would make a photorealistic scene appear unnatural. We discuss more on surface source material in Chapter 9, "Image Map Surfaces."

Now take a look at the book in the foreground. Notice how it has a more subdued coloration. This is a very natural level of diffusion. It doesn't get washed out by a specular highlight because it shows only 90 percent of its own surface color. Light-colored objects can easily become washed out by specularity, so it's necessary to lower their diffusion level to soften the specular highlight.

Figure 8.4 *Using less than 100 percent diffusion to make surfaces realistic.*

Even though the difference in diffusion levels is minor, it plays a major role in the credibility of a photorealistic scene. Since we're on the subject of diffusion, let's take a look at how we can modify a surface's diffusion level to make it appear wet.

Creating Wet Surfaces with Diffusion

Creating wet surfaces is one of the most challenging 3D effects. In fact, it's a regular pain in the neck, but the results, if done correctly, are definitely well worth the effort. Adding water to a scene requires a number of changes to the surface attributes of existing objects. When you cover an object with moisture, it becomes reflective and more specular, which are the attributes of water. You'll find that most 3D scenes with wet surfaces have these attributes, but they almost always lack the most important attribute of wet surfaces: lowered diffusion. Water is basically transparent, with no color of its own. This means it has a very low diffusion level. When you place water over another surface, the diffusion level of the water effectively lowers the diffusion of the surface below it.

The diffusion level will vary depending on what type of surface the water is covering. Basically there are two types of surfaces: absorbent and nonabsorbent.

Absorbent surfaces become darker when they are wet because the water soaks in and lowers the diffusion level, making the surface darker. I'm sure you've noticed that tree bark is significantly darker when it's wet. That's because bark is absorbent. The wood of the tree also gets darker, but this depends on the type of wood. Oak is very hard wood so it doesn't get much darker, while balsa is a softer wood so it gets significantly darker. When making absorbent surfaces wet, you need to lower the diffusion level, usually by at least 35 percent.

▶▶ LOWER THE DIFFUSION LEVEL BY 35 PERCENT WHEN MAKING ABSORBENT SURFACES WET.

Water has a low diffusion level because it's transparent and shows very little of its own color. When water is placed on an absorbent surface it soaks in and actually changes the surface, lowering the diffusion level. When making absorbent surfaces wet, you need to lower the diffusion level—usually by at least 35 percent.

What if the surface is nonabsorbent? The diffusion levels of these surfaces don't change because the water won't be absorbed by the surface. On the other hand, they will appear lighter in color when rendered because the water has a high level of specularity, which makes the surface lighter. For example: Try placing some water in a stainless steel spoon. Then hold it under a light. You'll notice that the surface with the water covering it is now lighter in color because of the water's specularity. Actually, it's not the surface, but in fact the water that's lighter. Fortunately, you don't need to make any changes to the object's diffusion level to create this effect.

Now that we know when and where to apply changes in diffusion to create the wet look, let's take a look at the theory in practice. First, we need to start with a dry scene like the one in Figure 8.5. Here we have a scene from the Dwellers film. This scene represents a dimly lit sidewalk in a rundown part of town. We see that Gizmo is on his way to collect some discarded parts that were discovered by another Dweller. Let's make it look like it has recently rained. We'll do this by adding some water puddles on the sidewalk and a little water pouring from the drain spout. We'll also need to make the surfaces in the scene reflective and specular to make them appear wet. Let's see what the scene looks like after these modifications have been made. Take a look at Figure 8.6.

Here we have the same scene with a few modifications to its surface attributes. Notice how there are a bunch of little puddles near the ledge. If you look closely, you'll notice that the sidewalk surface under the water is darker. In fact, the dark parts are feathered on the edges, which shows the water is evaporating. It looks really nice but there is something wrong with this scene, something that under-

Figure 8.5 *A dry scene with normal diffusion.*

Figure 8.6 *A wet scene with typical diffusion levels.*

Figure 8.7 *A wet scene with proper rust diffusion levels.*

Figure 8.8 *A wet scene with correct water diffusion levels.*

mines its photorealistic credibility. I wonder what it is? Ah yes, you probably noticed that the rusty metal wall, drain pipe, and can are now brighter. This makes sense because the moisture is reflecting the environment but what is the common element of all these surfaces? They are all absorbent surfaces. Rust is very grainy, and therefore absorbent. This means that the water would soak into the surfaces and lower their diffusion levels. Let's reduce the diffusion levels of these surfaces by 35 percent and see what happens. Take a look at Figure 8.7.

Now that's more like it. You can see that the rusted surfaces are now darker, which makes them appear more natural. The scene is now photorealistic . . . or is it? Now that I look at it, there seems to be something wrong with the water puddles. While the surface under the water seems to be properly darkened, the water itself appears too light on top. This is because the image map for the cement was manually darkened in Photoshop. While this is the correct way to create isolated water spots, you also need to apply an actual diffusion map to the surface so it reacts with the water in the scene. The diffusion map will prevent the water from reflecting a large amount of the pavement's surface color. The water is now light because it's reflecting the surface of the pavement, which doesn't have a lowered diffusion level. You can't fake diffusion by simply adding darkened spots to the image map. You need to create diffusion maps, which will properly diffuse the surface when rendered. We explore diffusion maps in more detail in Chapter 9, "Image Map Surfaces." Let's apply a diffusion map to the sidewalk and see what happens. Take a look at Figure 8.8.

YOU MUST USE AN ACTUAL DIFFUSION MAP TO CREATE REALISTIC WATER EFFECTS.

When creating water puddles, you can't fake diffusion by simply adding darkened spots to an image map. While it's important to create the altered color image map, you still need to create an actual diffusion map, which will properly diffuse the surface when rendered. Diffusion is computed mathematically in memory; if you simply color the image map, there will be no diffusion values computed during the render.

At last, we finally have a truly photorealistic scene. You can see how the surface of the water is now darker. This is the natural effect of water on an absorbent surface. You've probably noticed that water effects are complicated to create. While this may be true, the results are definitely worth the effort. Being able to create convincing water effects gives you great leverage when seeking contract work or employment. It will make you stand out from the crowd.

Let's get back on track and continue with the rules of photorealistic surfacing. It's time to take a look at the most obvious problem with 3D images: image map stretching.

No Image Map Stretching!

Don't you just hate it when you see a great 3D image but right there in the middle is a glaring example of image map stretching? I hate it when that happens. It takes all the glory away from the image. The unfortunate thing is that this is a common problem in nearly every 3D image.

It can be difficult to properly surface objects with image maps—particularly if they are organically shaped. Photorealistic surfacing requires a complete understanding of the pros and cons of the image mapping methods. Once you understand the mapping methods and their limitations, you can properly define the surfaces on the model so the image maps won't stretch. I know you've probably seen a hundred descriptions of the image mapping methods and now you're going to see number 101. I promise to keep it brief.

Let's take a look at the four most common image map methods: planar, spherical, cylindrical, and cubic.

Understanding Planar Image Maps

Planar image maps are the most frequently used image mapping method since the majority of objects have relatively flat surfaces. A *planar image map* projects the image onto the surface of the object the same way a movie projector displays an image on the screen. For this reason, it's best to use planar image maps on flat surfaces such as TV screens, boxes, walls, floors, or any other relatively flat surface. Let's see how a planar image map works. Take a look at Figure 8.9.

This image illustrates how a planar image map is applied in each of the three axes—*x, y,* and *z.* You can see that planar image maps are great for flat surfaces

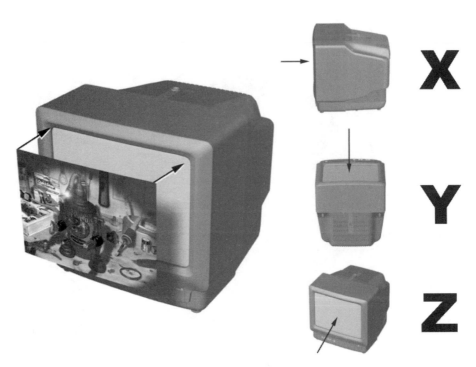

Figure 8.9 *The planar image map.*

but what if you need to surface a round object? You would use spherical image maps.

Understanding Spherical Image Maps

Spherical image maps are probably the least frequently used image mapping method. This is mainly because they tend to pinch the image map at the top and bottom of the surface. This is a by-product of the way they are mapped. A *spherical image map* wraps a flat image around the object in similar fashion to gift wrapping a basketball. Have you ever tried to giftwrap something that was round? Somehow I seem to get the task of doing this every Christmas. It's just doesn't work that well because you always have too much paper at the top and bottom. The package ends up looking like a giant candy wrapper. Well, this problem doesn't happen with a spherical image map because it pinches the image at the top and bottom, so you don't have any excess material. Take a look at Figure 8.10. Here you'll see an image that illustrates the spherical image mapping method along the *x, y,* and *z* axes.

The pinching of the image at the top and bottom of the surface can also be a problem. It works fine if your image map has a solid color in these areas like a

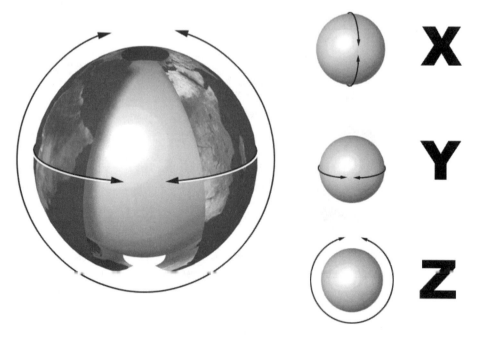

Figure 8.10 *The spherical image map.*

pool ball or marble. But what if you have a detailed texture, like the surface of a basketball? The result is less than photorealistic. If you have an image map with a detailed texture, like that of a basketball, the texture will pinch at the top and bottom of the ball as shown in Figure 8.11.

Here you can see the basketball texture is pinched at the top of the ball, making it very unrealistic. There are methods you can use to correct this problem, which we discuss later in this chapter in the segment on Defining Surfaces. For the most part, you want to avoid using a spherical image map to wrap images that are highly detailed.

Understanding Cylindrical Image Maps

Cylindrical image maps are frequently used to surface tube-shaped objects. A *cylindrical image map* wraps the image around an axis the same way toilet paper is wrapped around the cardboard tube. I know it's not the most glamorous comparison but it works. Well, maybe not the exact same way but you get the idea. Cylindrical image maps are great for surfacing objects such as soda cans, batteries, tree trunks, baseball bats, or any other cylindrical object. Let's take a look at

Figure 8.11 *Spherical image map pinching.*

Figure 8.12, which illustrates the cylindrical image-mapping method along the *x*, *y*, and *z* axes.

You can see how cylindrical mapping is very effective for mapping tubular objects like batteries. Of course, as with all image-mapping methods, there is a drawback to using cylindrical image maps. Cylindrical image maps are great for tube-shaped surfaces that don't have ends, but what happens when they do have ends? Well, the result is undesirable stretching of the image around the axis, as shown in Figure 8.13.

As you can see, the watermelon image has pinched around the axis that we used to map the image. As with the spherical image map, there are ways to prevent this problem, which we discuss later in the segment on Defining Surfaces.

Now we have just one more image mapping method to cover—cubic image maps. Hang in there, we're almost done with the boring stuff.

Understanding Cubic Image Maps

Cubic image maps are probably the most versatile image-mapping method. It's great for mapping images to organically shaped objects. A *cubic image map* is

Figure 8.12 *The cylindrical image map.*

Figure 8.13 *Cylindrical image map pinching.*

essentially a planar image map times three. It projects the image from all three axes at the same time, as shown in Figure 8.14.

As you can see, cubic image maps can be useful for quickly surfacing objects that have the same image map on all sides, which makes it a great alternative to planar mapping each of the sides individually.

Well, that was fun. Now that we are all on the same wavelength in regard to the pros and cons of the image-mapping methods, we can explore the problem of image map stretching.

Take a look at Figure 8.15. Here we have a typical wooden board. The board on the top illustrates the usual mapping method we see in 3D images. Notice how the image map is stretched over the end and sides. This is because the board was planar mapped from the top, or y axis. As we learned earlier, a planar image map is best used for flat surfaces, which worked well for the top of the board, but the end and sides are a mess. To correct this problem you need to planar map these with separate image maps, along the appropriate axis.

Now take a look at the board on the bottom. This board has been correctly image mapped. Three image maps were used to surface the board. A small image was planar mapped along the z axis to make the end of the board realistic. Notice how the grain matches the top of the board, and is slightly pinched toward the center. The pinching is the proper effect since the grain of a tree is circular. If the

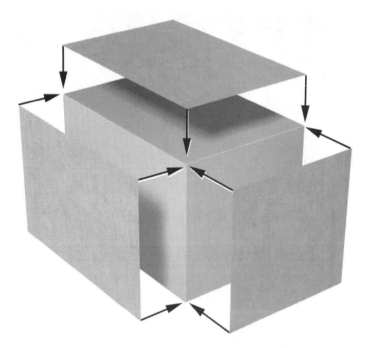

Figure 8.14 *The cubic image map.*

surface had straight lines, it would have appeared unnatural since it's impossible for the grain in the tree to be straight. You'll notice that a different image map was used to create the grain that runs down the side of the board. This image was planar mapped along the *x* axis to prevent image map stretching. The result of proper image mapping is a very realistic wooden board.

All right, we've seen the results of proper image mapping but how did we determine the right mapping method to use? It's a matter of properly defining the surfaces, which we're about to explore.

Defining Surfaces

The first step in surfacing your models is to define the surfaces and their surface-mapping method. The way you select your surfaces can have a profound impact on the quality of your finished model. We've already seen that improper surface definition results in undesirable image map stretching. Before you begin to surface your object, you need to define the actual surfaces. This is a critical step in creating photorealistic surfacing.

Determine the image-mapping method you plan to use. Once this has been determined, you can proceed to define the surfaces on the model. Let's take a look at a model and see if we can determine the proper image-mapping method to use. Take a look at Figure 8.16.

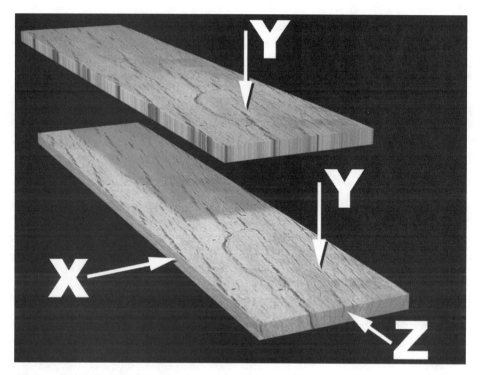

Figure 8.15 *Preventing image map stretching.*

Here we have a hamburger bun model. You'll notice that while it's a simple object, it has a complex organic shape. It's definitely not a sphere and clearly not a tube. This makes photorealistic surfacing of the bun rather tricky. Here's where we need to get creative. You can see that the base of the bun is relatively cylindrical. This means we can use a cylindrical image map to surface it. Now take a look at the top of the bun. It's definitely not flat, so we can't use a planar image map without stretching the image over the edges. A spherical map definitely won't work since it will pinch at the top. Our only option left is to use a cubic image map. Let's take a look at what the surface selection will look like for a cylindrical map on the sides and a cubic map on the top. Take a look at Figure 8.17.

You can see that the top of the bun has been selected to create a new surface, which is represented by the lighter color in the shaded view window. We now have two separate surfaces for the hamburger bun. I'm sure you're wondering about the interior of the bun. Since it's flat we'll use a planar image map to apply its surfacing. Now we have three surfaces for the hamburger bun that use three different mapping methods. How do we keep track of which mapping method to apply to these surfaces? The answer is simple: Include the mapping method in the surface name. For example: The hamburger bun top surface would be named Bun Top (cubic). If you are on an operating system with limited character capa-

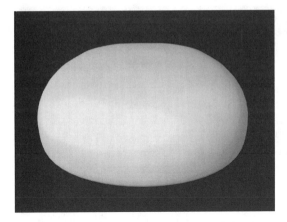

Figure 8.16 *Properly defining a model's surfaces.*

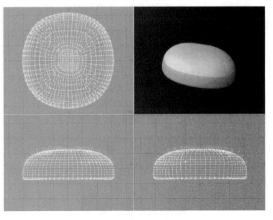

Figure 8.17 *Proper surface selection for the organically shaped hamburger bun.*

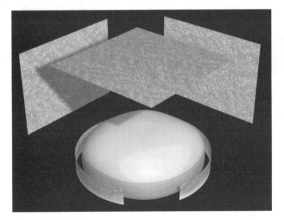

Figure 8.18 *Correct application of image maps.*

Figure 8.19 *The completed photorealistic hamburger bun, with no image map stretching.*

bilities you could have named the surface buntop_c. Either way, you now have a great means for keeping track of the image-mapping method.

❯❯ INCLUDE THE MAPPING METHOD IN THE SURFACE NAME.

You should always include the mapping method in the surface name so you don't lose track of which mapping method to use. For example: A surface with a cubic image map would be named surface name (cubic).

Now it's time to apply the image maps. Take a look at Figure 8.18. Here we have a visual representation of the image-mapping method for the hamburger bun surfaces. We have applied a cubic image map to the top of the bun and a cylindrical image map to the sides. Notice how the cylindrical image map fades to a lighter color at the base. This is the natural look for a hamburger bun. You see, the top and bottom of the bun get browned because it's glazed with butter before it goes through the toaster. The heat sources in the toaster are at the top and bottom so they lightly toast these parts of the bun, while the sides stay relatively unchanged since there isn't a heat source on the sides of the toaster. (Say, you're now qualified to work the bun machine in a fast food restaurant.)

As you can see, adding this detail to the image map goes a long way toward making the surface photorealistic. (All this talk about hamburgers is making me hungry. I'll have to render myself some lunch.) I'll bet you're wondering what the hamburger bun looks like when it's fully surfaced. Well, you're in luck. I just happen to have a picture of the completed bun. Take a look at Figure 8.19.

Here we have the completed hamburger bun sitting on top of my lunch. I'm sure you're wondering why that funny little guy is sitting on the hamburger. Well, everyone knows that only a rendered character can eat a rendered hamburger, so I had to render myself to eat it. . . . Well, anyway.

Taking the time to properly define surfaces can have a tremendous impact on the photorealistic credibility of an image. It can take some experimentation to find the right combination of mapping methods but the results are well worth the time.

Now let's take a look at a very frequently overlooked aspect of photorealistic surfacing: aging.

Apply Aging to All Surfaces

Now we're going to have some fun. Aging objects is my favorite part of the photorealistic 3D process. How often do you get to trash objects without having to clean them up? Not often enough.

Have you noticed that nearly every object, in a typical 3D scene, is perfectly clean and free of blemishes? That Mr. Clean guy must be as ominous as Santa Claus to find the time to tidy up everyone's 3D images. Nothing makes a 3D scene appear more unnatural than perfect surfaces. Reality is messy. My cleaning person can testify to this fact.

You'd be surprised how a little bit of aging can make your scene appear incredibly realistic. Very few surfaces in reality are 100 percent clean. About the only place we expect to find clean surfaces are in hospitals and laboratories, and even they have their dirty places. When creating your surface you'll want to apply a little natural aging. The amount of aging really depends on the story behind the scene. If your scene takes place in a grungy city street alley, you'll want to apply a severe amount of aging. It's likely that the metal elements in the scene will be heavily coated in rust, and there are probably oil stains and grease marks on the pavement. In fact, I'll guarantee there's some graffiti on the walls. Your level of aging needs to support the scene.

On the other hand, if your scene takes place in the living room of a typical family dwelling, you'll want to limit the aging to dust and scratches. Dust is something I have yet to see in a 3D scene. It covers nearly everything in existence, yet nobody bothers to include this element in their surfacing. Of course, adding dust can be a bit tricky but it really adds an awesome amount of depth to a scene. Let's take a look at how we can add dust to 3D surfaces.

Creating Dusty Surfaces

Adding dust to your 3D objects really separates them from the pack. It's an unparalleled and subtle detail of realism that is absent from nearly every 3D image produced. The ironic thing is that it takes only a few minutes to add dust.

Dust is created with image maps. There are a few possibilities using procedural textures but the effect isn't as realistic as when image maps are used. To create dust with image maps, your program needs to have the ability to use alpha image maps. This is a relatively new feature in the 3D industry. An *alpha image map* is basically a transparency map for the image you are mapping to the surface. It's used to filter out portions of the image so they won't be seen. In the case of dust, you'll use an alpha image map to filter out the majority of the color image map so only a fraction of the dust is visible on the surface.

Adding dust to objects requires the use of three image maps. To make this discussion easier, let's take a look at the image maps we'll be using. Take a look at Figure 8.20.

The image in the upper left corner is the color image map. Dust is gray, but the color of the particles varies, so you should create a color map that periodically shifts from a dark to light gray. The cloud filter in Photoshop is perfect for creating this subtle color shifting. Now take a look at the image in the upper right. This is the alpha image map. The white areas in the image will be transparent, while the gray areas will be semitransparent. You can see that there are varying levels of transparency, which help to make the dust a little chaotic. Since dust is a 3D element, you'll need a bump map to give it some depth. The image in the lower left corner is the bump map, which was created by simply reversing the colors in the alpha image map. The white, or transparent areas, are now black and represent zero altitude. The gray areas will vary the altitude of the dust particles to make them appear more realistic. You'll find all three of these image

Figure 8.20 *The image maps for creating dust.*

maps in the tutorial file you downloaded for this chapter from the companion Web site at www.wiley.com/compbooks/fleming. The images are: dust.jpg, dustbump.jpg and dustfilter.jpg

The next step is to map these images to the surfaces of our object. The best way to map dust to an object is with a cubic image map. Since the dust is very small, it's nearly impossible for any image map stretching to occur. The cubic image map will easily wrap the dust around the entire objects as shown in the lower right corner of Figure 8.20. Now let's take a look at the finished product.

In Figure 8.21, we have two televisions. The one on the left is your typical clean surface, while the one on the right has the dust image maps applied. Notice how natural the TV on the right appears. TVs are literal dust magnets because

Figure 8.21 *The visual difference between clean and dusty surfaces.*

they produce a great deal of static electricity. For a TV to appear completely pho-torealistic, it needs to be dusty.

You probably noticed that the tabletop on the right half of the image is dusty. We couldn't make the TV dusty without making the table it's sitting on dusty as well. Nothing looks more out of place than a dusty object on a clean surface. Be sure that when you apply dust to your objects, you also apply dust to whatever they are sitting upon.

►► ADD DUST TO YOUR OBJECTS TO MAKE THEM EYE-POPPINGLY PHOTOREALISTIC.

Nothing says reality like a dusty surface. Very few 3D images have dusty objects, which is a direct contradiction of reality. Dust permeates everything in reality. To create eye-poppingly photorealistic surfaces you need to add dust.

It looks like we've covered dust fairly well but it's not the only type of surface aging we can apply to objects. We can also apply scratches, dents, and dings, so get ready to have a little more destructive fun.

Applying Scratches, Dents, and Dings to Your Surfaces

As hard as we may try to keep our possessions blemish free, they ultimately fall prey to chaos. Nearly every object has its own distinguishing blemishes. The more the object is handled, the more blemishes you'll find. While I have seen blemished objects in 3D scenes, it's usually done only in industrial images. Obviously, we expect industrial objects to be dented and dinged, but we can't forget about the everyday objects. Take a look around your house and I'm sure you'll find that nearly every object has some level of aging. More often than not it's in the form of scratches.

Applying dents and dings to surfaces is a great deal easier than adding dust. It requires only one image map to do the job. All you need is a simple chaotic bump map to add surface details. Let's take a look at my favorite aging bump map, which is shown in Figure 8.22.

You can see how this bump map would wreak havoc on the surface of an object. It has a variety of dark and light spots, which represent scratches and dings. The great thing about this image is that it can be used to apply unlimited levels of aging. You can resize the image on your surface to create large dents or tiny

Figure 8.22 *A general aging bump map.*

scratches. You'll find this bump map image in the tutorial files you downloaded for this chapter. The file is called 'Peened.jpg'. Now, let's take a look at several examples of aging created with this bump map. Take a look at Figure 8.23.

You can see we have a variety of different objects in this image. Each of them has a different level of aging based on their use and how frequently they are handled. Let's take a look at the aging of each object, starting with the laser pointer.

Take a close look at the laser pointer and you'll see several minor dents around the base. This is a very subtle form of aging. The pointer is made of thin, pliable aluminum, which is easily deformed if you handle it aggressively. It looks like maybe the presentation didn't go so well. Even though this is minor aging, it breaks up the uniformity of the surface so it doesn't look too new. Let's take a look at the CASSIOPEIA PDA. Since this is a palmtop computer we can assume it's handled regularly. As you can see, there are subtle dents and dings covering the surface of the object. These were likely created when the PDA was bounced around in the briefcase, where it collided with other objects such as pens, cellular phones, videotapes, and so forth. It's a more obvious level of aging than the laser pointer but still not terribly obvious, particularly from a distance.

Figure 8.23 *A variety of aging examples created with a dent and ding bump map.*

Now take a look at the cellular phone. This too is a frequently handled object but it's likely to have more severe aging since it's probably been dropped several times on the sidewalk when someone bumped into the owner. If you take a look at the bottom of the phone you'll see several deep dents that were created when the phone hit a tiny rock on the pavement. There are also several less apparent dings on the side and top. These were created when the phone bounced around when it was dropped. If you could zoom in even closer you would notice that the display screen is also aged with the addition of little scratches. As you can see, it helps to get into character with the object to understand the hazards it encounters throughout the day.

All right, on to the last and most obviously aged object—the crescent wrench. Here we have a typical auto mechanic's shop tool. This poor wrench has been bounced off and rammed into every possible hazard in a car engine. For this reason, it's heavily aged with serious dents, dings, and gouges. It probably earned several of those blemishes while being bounced around in the toolbox when the mechanic came to fix my chronically ill car for the fifth time this month. But I digress.

EXPLORE THE HISTORY BEHIND OBJECTS BEFORE YOU AGE THEM.

All too often 3D artists will jump right in and carelessly surface their objects with no regard to its history. You can't effectively age your object until you know where it has been and the hazards it may have encountered along the way. Before you surface your next object, consider where it has been.

Aging plays a major role in the believability of an object. Nobody would expect a mechanic's tools to be perfectly spotless. You might get away with a perfectly clean cell phone but it wouldn't be the most photorealistic portrayal of this item either. You should spend some time exploring the history of your objects before you begin surfacing them. It takes only a few moments and it's actually a lot of fun.

That about does it for rule number 5. Just one more rule to go, and it's an easy one too. Let's take a look at one of the most frequently abused rules of photorealistic surfacing, no repeating patterns!

No Repeating Patterns!

This is one of the most abused of photorealistic surfacing rules. It's just too easy to create repeating patterns in our images. How many times have you seen a great image that was undermined by a painfully obvious repeating pattern? Probably too often. I often find myself battling repeating patterns in my images. Seamless image maps are wonderful for creating photorealistic images but they have the shortcoming of being far too repeating.

Repeating patterns usually aren't a problem with images that are shot fairly close to the objects, but when the camera is pulled back, yeow—major repeating! This usually happens because the seamless tiles that are readily available are typically too small. They often max out at 512×512 pixels, which really doesn't help much when you are rendering a large environment, particularly if the image is rendered to print resolutions. So what's the solution?

It's easy enough to fix the repeating pattern by importing the image into Photoshop, or any other paint program, and editing out the patterns. If the image is 512×512, simply create a new image that is 1024×1024 and tile the image map four times. Then use the clone tool to remove the repeating areas by sampling the source from another area in the image map. Now you have a seamless image map that's twice as large as the original and no longer has the repeating pattern. What's the downside? You will need more RAM to load the larger image maps into memory. Of course, with the prices of RAM plummeting on a daily basis, this isn't much of a downside.

Of course, the patterns may not always be so obvious. Sometimes it can be difficult to spot the repeating patterns so you'll really need to take a close look. You're probably wondering why you should bother with removing the patterns that are not obvious. They aren't obvious to you because you have been staring at the scene for hours, but they are obvious to people who are viewing your image. Let me put it this way: I'm sure you have all written something that included spelling errors, which someone else found when reading it. Somehow you missed the error, even though you knew the proper spelling, but they found it immediately. That's because you had a preconceived perception of how the word was supposed to be spelled, so your eyes did the error correction in real time when you proofread it. The amazing thing about our perception is that we will autocorrect things that we know to be an error, particularly if we created it. We will quickly spot errors in words we don't know how to spell, but rarely catch the errors in words we can spell because we already have a preconceived perception of the correct spelling.

This translates directly to working with patterns in your images. You won't recognize subtle patterns because your eye does the error correction for you. On the other hand, people who are viewing your image don't have a preconceived perception of the surface, so they pick up patterns very easily. Let's take a look at an example of a subtle repeating pattern in an image in Figure 8.24.

Here we have a very photorealistic scene that just happens to have a couple of subtle repeating patterns, which tell us that the image is rendered. Take a look at the top edge of the stucco wall. You'll see a dark spot that repeats three times. Now follow those spots downward and you'll see them again toward the bottom

Figure 8.24 *An example of subtle repeating patterns.*

of the wall. While it's not a very obvious pattern, it definitely undermines the photorealistic credibility of the scene. There are no repeating patterns in nature. While the wall is manmade, it would be impossible for repeating patterns to have been created, particularly since stucco is applied from scratch. It's not as if tiles were applied to the wall.

Now take a look at the cement on the leading edge of the doormat. You'll notice a dark spot that repeats twice, once on the bottom edge of the scene and again at the end of the doormat. This, again, undermines the photorealistic credibility of the scene. Of course, these are relatively simple errors to correct. Let's take a look at the corrected scene to see the impact of making the changes. Take a look at Figure 8.25.

Now that's better. Notice how the stucco and cement appear more natural. We made a minor change but the impact was significant. The scene now looks very photorealistic and will hold up under close scrutiny.

Removing the repeating patterns is a necessary step in making your images photorealistic. Although there will be some cases where repeating patterns are desirable, such as floor tiles, it's usually something you want to avoid. When you have finished your image, take a step back and try to view it objectively so you can spot the repeating patterns. I usually have someone else take a look at my

Figure 8.25 *The same scene with repeating patterns removed.*

image so I get an untainted perspective from someone with no preconceived perception of the image.

There you have it, the six rules of photorealistic surfacing. If you carefully abide by these rules your images will become strikingly photorealistic. I know what you're thinking: "Rules stink!" Sure they do, but in this case I think you'll agree they can be a lot of fun. The rules may take a bit of getting used to, but in time they will become second nature.

Now let's put all these rules to work by surfacing the photorealistic pumpkin we just saw in the last image. We'll use the precarved pumpkin to make things a bit easier. I'll let you carve it yourself.

Putting the Rules of Photorealistic Surfacing to Work

Now we're going to have some fun. I'll bet you were wondering when you would finally get to use the tutorial files you downloaded from the Web site? Well, there's no time like the present.

You'll find a file named pumpkin.3DS in the files you downloaded from the companion Web site at www.wiley.com/compbooks/fleming. This is the pumpkin model we'll be surfacing. First we're going to start with a simple pumpkin model, then we'll determine the proper surface definitions, and finally, we'll apply image maps to make the pumpkin photorealistic. This tutorial is designed for programs that can use multiple image maps on a single surface. If your program can't do this, you'll need to make some modifications to the image maps to perform the tutorial. Combine the multiple bump map images into a single image.

Let's get started. Take a look at Figure 8.26.

Here we have a simple shaded image of the pumpkin model. Since it's an organic model, we'll need to be creative with our surfacing efforts. As with the hamburger bun we surfaced earlier, the pumpkin isn't round or flat, but parts of it are, so we'll have to break the model into several surfaces. Take a look at the sides of the pumpkin. They are basically cylindrical so we can use a cylindrical image map for this surface. Now take a look at the top of the pumpkin. It's relatively flat so we can use a planar image map for its surfacing. Let's take a look at how we should define the surface for the top of the pumpkin. Take a look at Figure 8.27.

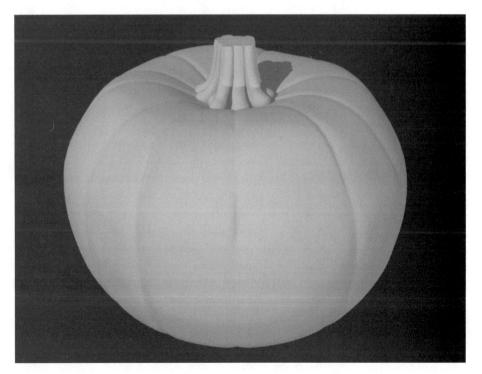

Figure 8.26 *The pumpkin model.*

Figure 8.27 Defining the pumpkin surfaces.

Notice how the selection was made up to the point where the shape of the pumpkin starts to fall off. This was done to prevent image map stretching. The image for the top of the pumpkin will be planar mapped on the y axis so you don't want to select any polygons that are parallel to the x or z axis. If you do, the image map will be stretched over these polygons. You don't need to worry about defining these surfaces on your model since they've already been done for you.

Now take a look at the shaded view in the upper right corner. You'll notice that each surface is represented with a different color. This makes it easier to distinguish them when working on the model. Take a look at the stem and you'll notice the sides and top are two different colors. A cylindrical image map makes perfect sense for the sides of the stem, but it would be pinched at the top so a planar image map will be used to surface this portion of the model. Now we're ready to start surfacing our pumpkin. There are several JPG files that were included in the files you downloaded, which we will use to surface the pumpkin. It's a good time to check and make sure you have all of the following files:

- Branch.jpg
- Bumps.jpg

- Pores.jpg
- PumpkinBump.jpg
- PumpkinColor.jpg
- PumpkinDiff.jpg
- PumpkinTop.jpg

As you can see, the photorealistic surfacing of a pumpkin requires an abundance of image maps. Now that we've confirmed we have the image map files, let's begin surfacing the pumpkin. We'll start with the fourth rule of photorealistic surfacing—no image map stretching—since it will make it easier to visualize that we are creating a pumpkin. Before we surface the pumpkin the correct way, let's take a look at what we are avoiding by using multiple surfaces. Take a look at Figure 8.28.

You can see that the pumpkin skin and stem were both cylindrically image mapped, which caused severe pinching at the top of these surfaces. Although this may not be visible from a distance, it certainly undermines the photorealistic credibility when viewed at close range. Now let's apply the image maps to the pumpkin skin on our model, which has the surfaces properly defined.

The following exercises are generalized so you'll have to fill in the blanks when necessary. I won't be making specific references on how to map images in your program. You'll need to explore this yourself. Let's get started.

Exercise: Applying the Pumpkin Skin Image Maps

1. Load the model into your rendering program. Make sure that you load all of the images in the previous list. We'll be using all of these images to surface the pumpkin. The next thing you need to do is light the pumpkin so you can clearly see the surfaces. Take a look at Figure 8.29. This image shows how we will be mapping the images to the pumpkin skin surfaces. Let's get started on the surfacing.

2. Select the SKNSIDE_C surface. You'll notice we've added a C at the end of the name, which tells us that we need to use a cylindrical image map for this surface. Go ahead and cylindrically map the PumpkinColor.jpg image along the y axis. Be sure to wrap the image only once.

3. Now select the SKNTOP_P surface. You'll notice we've added a P at the end of the name, which tells us that we need to use a planar image map for this surface. Go ahead and planar map the PumpkinTop.jpg image on the y axis. Make sure that you size the image to cover the whole surface.

4. Now render the pumpkin. You should have something that resembles the image in Figure 8.30. You can see that the pumpkin skin is very naturally surfaced, with no signs of image map stretching. Now let's surface the pumpkin stem.

Figure 8.28 *Image map stretching caused by using a single surface for the pumpkin skin.*

Figure 8.29 *Applying the pumpkin skin image maps.*

Figure 8.30 *Image maps applied to the pumpkin skin surface.*

Figure 8.31 *Image maps applied to the pumpkin stem surface.*

5. Select the BRANCH_C surface. As with the previous surfaces, the letter at the end of the name tells us which image mapping method to use. In this case, we'll be using a cylindrical image map. Go ahead and cylindrically map the Branch.jpg image along the y axis. Be sure to wrap the image only once.

6. Now select the BRNCHT_P surface. In this case, we'll be using a planar image map. Go ahead and planar map the Branch.jpg image on the y axis. Make sure that you size the image to cover the whole surface.

7. Now render the pumpkin. You should have something that resembles the image in Figure 8.31. You can see that the pumpkin stem is very naturally surfaced, with no signs of image map stretching.

It's starting to look like a real pumpkin. Now that we have image maps on the surfaces, we need to apply the first rule of photorealistic surfacing: Every surface must have a bump map texture. This is where we start to breathe life into the object. The bump maps will give the surface realistic texture and depth. This process will take a bit of time to complete since we will be using several bump map images on each surface. Let's get started.

Exercise: Applying Bump Maps to Our Pumpkin

1. Select the SKNSIDE_C surface, open the bump layer, and cylindrically map the PumpkinBump.jpg image along the y axis. Be sure to wrap the image only once. Now set the bump value to 100 percent. This bump map will add subtle creases around the surface of the skin.

2. Now select the SKNTOP_P surface, open the bump layer, and cylindrically map the PumpkinBump.jpg image along the y axis. Be sure to wrap the image only once. Set the bump value to 100 percent. This will create the subtle creases at the top of the pumpkin, which will line up with the creases you created on the side of the pumpkin. The cylindrical image map works great for this surface since we actually want the creases to pinch at the top, which is what happens on a real pumpkin.

3. Now we have the subtle creases mapped to our pumpkin skin. The next thing we need to do is create a little surface texture. Pumpkins, like all fruits and vegetables, have small pores in their skin. These details are critical for making the object photorealistic, particularly when shooting close-ups. To create the surface texture, we'll use the color image maps. This saves on having to load another image in memory. We don't need a separate bump map since the skin pores aren't very deep.

4. Select the SKNSIDE_C surface, create a new bump layer, and cylindrically map the PumpkinColor.jpg image along the y axis. Be sure to wrap the image only once. Now set the bump value to 100 percent. (If your program is capable of exaggerated setting, I recommend that you set this value to 150 percent for the best effect.) This will create small pores in the pumpkin skin.

5. Now select the SKNTOP_P surface, create a new bump layer, and planar map the PumpkinColor.jpg image on the y axis. Make sure that you size the image to cover the whole surface. Then set the bump value to 100 percent. (If your program is capable of exaggerated setting, I recom-

mend that you set this value to 150 percent for the best effect.) We have some detailed texture on the skin. The next thing we need to do is add a surface texture to the stem. Let's get to it.

6. Select the BRANCH_C surface, open the bump layer, and cylindrically map the Branch.jpg image along the y axis. Be sure to wrap the image only once. Now set the bump value to 100 percent. We're using the color image to create the bump texture because it saves on memory and does the job very well. This image will create vertical cracks in the surface of the stem.

7. Now select the BRNCHT_P surface, open the bump layer, and planar map the Branch.jpg image on the y axis. Make sure that you size the image to cover the whole surface and then set the bump value to 100 percent. Now we need to add an important detail to the stem. The pumpkin stem has tubular pores that run its length. These pores carry moisture to the pumpkin. We need to simulate these pores by adding an additional bump map to the top of the stem. Let's do this now.

8. Now select the BRNCHT_P surface, add a new bump layer, and planar map the Pores.jpg image on the y axis. Make sure that you size the image to cover the whole surface and then set the bump value to 100 percent.

9. Great; now we have several layers of detail bump textures added to the pumpkin. Let's see what they look like. Go ahead and render the pumpkin. You should have something that resembles the image in Figure 8.32. You can see that the bump maps have literally brought the pumpkin to life. It now has a very natural surface texture.

We're about halfway there now. The next thing we need to do is apply the second and third rules of photorealistic surfacing: All surfaces must have specularity and never use 100 percent diffusion. These are relatively simple changes so let's do them now.

Exercise: Setting the Specularity and Diffusion Levels for Our Pumpkin

1. The first thing we need to do is set all of the diffusion levels to 90 percent. Go ahead and do this for all four surfaces. Now we need to modify the diffusion in the creases of the pumpkin, which we created in the previous exercise. Since they are created with a bump map, we'll need to add depth to them by lowering the diffusion levels at the lowest point of the crease. A bump map really only simulates altitude changes. To make the simulation more convincing, we need to darken the lowest point of the crease. We'll do this by applying a diffusion image map. Let's add the diffusion image maps now.

Figure 8.32 *Bump maps applied to the pumpkin stem surface.*

2. Select the SKNSIDE_C surface, open the diffusion layer, and cylindrically map the PumpkinDiff.jpg image along the y axis. Be sure to wrap the image only once. This diffusion map will slightly darken the lowest point of the creases to make them appear natural. If you take a look at a pumpkin, you'll notice that the skin color is slightly darker in the lowest point of the creases.

3. Now select the SKNTOP_P surface, open the diffusion layer, and cylindrically map the PumpkinDiff.jpg image along the y axis. Be sure to wrap the image only once.

4. We're ready to modify the specularity of the pumpkin skin. Start by setting the specularity of the two pumpkin skin surfaces to 35 percent, and then set the two pumpkin stem surfaces to 5 percent. Now we need to add the second part of the specularity formula, glossiness. *Glossiness* is used to determine the size of the specular highlight. Since we know the specular highlight is used to determine the hardness of the object, we'll want to set the pumpkin's glossiness very low. Go ahead and set the glossiness/hardness to a value of 16 percent. This will make the specular highlight spread out over the surface, making it appear soft and porous.

5. Now render the pumpkin. You should have something that resembles the image in Figure 8.33. You can see that the pumpkin skin looks soft and porous, and the creases are more apparent.

Wow, the pumpkin is really starting to look photorealistic. Now we're just about done with the surfacing. We have only two more rules to go. Since the image maps were created with no visible repeating textures, we don't need to worry about the sixth rule of photorealistic surfacing—no repeating patterns. This leaves us with only one remaining rule: Apply aging to all surfaces.

How do we age a pumpkin? Part of our work has already been done for us. Take another look at Figure 8.32 and you'll notice a few scars on the top and right side of the pumpkin. These are very typical features on a pumpkin, which make our 3D pumpkin appear very believable. They are extremely effective aging elements. Since this is only part of the aging we need to do, what else is needed? We're in need of a little surface texture chaos.

Currently the surface is too perfect. It lacks the subtle, chaotic irregularities that make an organic object believable. These are very subtle changes, but they have an effect on the specularity of the surface, which can be easily detected. If the specularity is too consistent, the object will appear too perfect. To create these irregularities all we need to do is apply a bump map that has periodic and

Figure 8.33 *Diffusion and specularity levels modified.*

chaotic changes in altitude. This adds a large bumpiness to the surface, which makes it appear more organic. Let's add a little surface chaos now.

Exercise: Creating Surface Texture Chaos

1. Select the SKNSIDE_C surface, open a new bump layer, and cubic map the Bumps.jpg image. Now set the size of all three axes to 14 cm. This is important because we will need to apply the bump map to the top as well, and we want to make sure the textures are seamless. Making the size the same on both surfaces will ensure the texture is seamless. Now set the bump value to 100 percent.

2. Now select the SKNTOP_P surface, open a new bump layer, and cubic map the Bumps.jpg image. Then set the size of all three axes to 14 cm, and the bump value to 100 percent. This will ensure the texture seamlessly merges with the one we applied on the sides of the pumpkin.

3. Render the pumpkin. You should have something that resembles the image in Figure 8.34. You should see that the pumpkin skin texture is more chaotic, which makes it appear very photorealistic.

Figure 8.34 *The completed, photorealistic pumpkin—ready for carving.*

Boy, that was a bit of work. I'll bet you thought surfacing a pumpkin would be easy. You can see that photorealistic surfacing requires a lot of attention to detail. In fact, we could have added a couple more bump maps to bring out some detail in the scars but we have to draw the line somewhere. It's important that you adhere to all six rules of photorealistic surfacing if you want your objects to be truly realistic. If you skip just one, it's likely your object will lose its photorealistic credibility.

The good news is that you are now prepared for Halloween! All you need to do is carve the pumpkin and you're done. Well, there is the matter of lighting the pumpkin, but that's a whole other topic. I couldn't resist taking the pumpkin to the next level so I carved it and placed it on my digital doorstep, which you saw in Figure 8.25.

That pretty much does it for the rules of photorealistic surfacing. Before we move on to Chapter 9, I thought we'd cover just one more surfacing topic, photorealistic water and glass.

Creating Photorealistic Water and Glass

Photorealistic water and glass are elements that will make your images pop. I've seen a great number of glass and water objects in 3D scenes but I've rarely seen any that were photorealistic. Water and glass are relatively simple effects to create but it seems most 3D artists only do half the work required to make these surfaces photorealistic.

To create realistic glass and water you need to mimic the properties of these surfaces in reality. These surfaces are both refractive, causing the light to bend as it passes through them. The thing most 3D artists fail to realize is that light is bent as it exits the object and enters the surrounding air. This is better illustrated by looking at Figure 8.35.

The light passes through glass as it enters the object, but then passes through air as it exits the object. If you only give an object a glass surface you will be bending the light for glass, but you won't be bending it for air. This won't be a problem if you have a flat piece of glass, but what if you have an object like the ashtray in Figure 8.35, or maybe a drinking glass? In these objects, light will pass through the glass on one side, travel through the air in the middle, and then pass through the glass on the other side. If you don't bend the light as it passes through the air, you'll end up refracting the light at twice its value when it passes through the glass on the other side. Since the index of refraction for glass is 1.6, you'll end up with an effective refraction of 3.2 in the glass on the other side. Needless to say, the result is less than desirable.

To create photorealistic glass, you need to have two surfaces. One for glass and the other for air. The trick is that the air surface must face the opposite direction of the glass surface. Otherwise you'll be passing light through glass and air at the same time. What you need to do is make a copy of the glass polygons, paste them in a new layer and flip the surface normals so they face the other direction. At this point your object should look inside out, like the ashtray in Figure 8.36.

Here you can see that the polygons are facing the opposite direction, making the object appear inside out. Once you have flipped the polygons, you need to rename them to something like AIR. Then you need to paste them on the original glass polygons so you have a complete object. Now you have both a glass and air surface on your model.

The next step is to apply the proper surface attributes. The proper surface attributes for glass and air are presented as follows:

Surface Attributes for Glass and Air

	GLASS	AIR
Surface color	128, 128, 128	128, 128, 128
Luminosity	0	0
Diffusion	0	0
Specularity	80%	75%
Glossiness	64	64
Reflectivity	10%	0
Transparency	90%	95%
Refractive index	1.6	1.0

You'll notice that neither the glass nor air is completely transparent. All too often 3D artists will surface these items with 100 percent transparency, which just isn't possible in reality. There is always some minor level of noise in the surface that prevents it from being 100 percent transparent. Even air isn't 100 percent transparent, particularly if you live in an industrial town where there is an abundance of smog. If you wanted to be regionally accurate, you might want to lower the transparency of the air surface to compensate for the smog. In case you're wondering, smoggy air has a transparency of 83 percent and a surface color of 141, 131, 114.

Now take a look at the refractive index levels. As you can see, the light will be refracted at a value of 1.6 as it enters the glass and then at 1.0 as it enters air. Let's take a look at Figure 8.37, which illustrates the index of refraction values for light as it passes through the glass ashtray.

You can see how skipping the air surfaces would result in a dramatically different index of refraction. You must include the air surface for the light to be refracted properly. Of course, this sounds nice but what is the real difference?

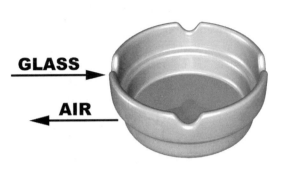

Figure 8.35 *The surfaces that light passes through.*

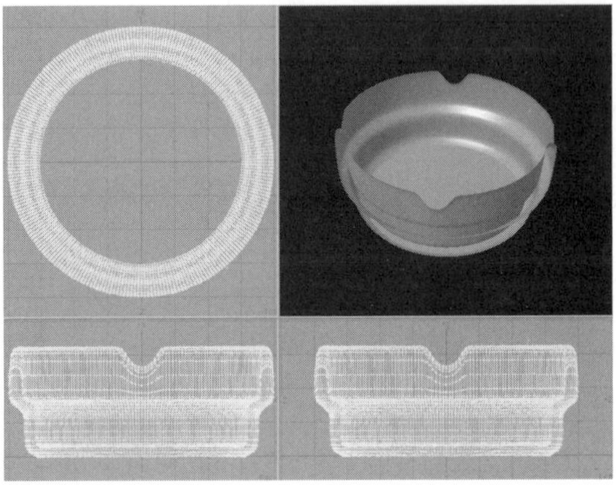

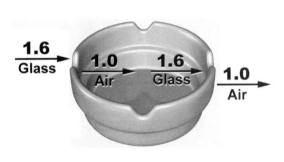

Figure 8.36 *The air surface for an ashtray.*

Figure 8.37 *The index of refraction values for light as it passes through a glass ashtray.*

Figure 8.38 *Glass with an air surface and glass without.*

Well, to better illustrate the impact of applying the air surface, let's take a look at a comparison of a glass ashtray with an air surface and one without. Take a look at Figure 8.38.

Here we have two ashtrays. The one on the left has an air surface whereas the one on the right doesn't. Notice how natural the ashtray on the left appears. One of the most striking differences is the apparent thickness of the glass. Notice how the ashtray on the right appears thick while the ashtray on the left seems as thin as paper. I'm sure you also noticed the way the ashes seem to be wrapped around the ashtray on the right. This happened because the light was refracted at twice its normal value, which distorted the appearance. It now becomes painfully obvious that we need to add an air surface when creating glass.

Color Plate 1 *Gizmo's birth place.*

Color Plate 2 *Gizmo acquires his transport vehicle.*

Color Plate 3 *Gizmo's discovery.*

Color Plate 4 *Gizmo searching for spare parts.*

Color Plate 5 *The reality clinic.*

Color Plate 6 *The virtual theater.*

Color Plate 7 *Robby the rabbit's den.*

Color Plate 8 *My desk.*

Color Plate 9 *Virtual living.*

Color Plate 10 *Sunrise in the office.*

Color Plate 11 *Jack!*

Color Plate 12 *Jurassic 3D.*

Color Plate 13 *Dweller's tunnel.*

Color Plate 14 *Now that's a burger!*

Color Plate 15 *Virtual smokes.*

Another great benefit of using air surfaces is the ability to make glass objects appear solid. Take a look at Figure 8.39.

Here we have the same ashtray in a scene with several other objects. Notice how the cigarette boxes are distorted when viewed through the ashtray. This is a marvelous effect that happens when objects are viewed through thick glass. It's a very natural effect that couldn't have been created without the addition of the air surface. The air surface allows us to accurately simulate solid glass objects. Cool, isn't it?

We've covered glass, now what about water? That's simple, water is created the same way as glass. In fact, you need to create an air surface for all transparent surfaces that refract light. In Appendix E you'll find the index of refraction values for all transparent materials, even some rather obscure ones.

ALWAYS USE AIR SURFACES WITH TRANSPARENT OBJECTS.

You need to create opposite facing air surfaces for all transparent surfaces that refract light. If you don't, they won't refract the light properly and they'll fail to appear as if they are solid material.

Figure 8.39 *Creating solid glass objects with air surfaces.*

Well, that about does it for water and glass surfaces. As you can see, you need to carefully study real-world objects before you surface their 3D counterparts. Don't forget, if you plan to create a glass of water with ice cubes, you'll need to create air surfaces for the glass, water, and ice. Otherwise you'll end up with a rather scary looking object.

Looking Ahead

Well, we've covered quite a bit on surfacing fundamentals, haven't we? I don't know about you, but I need a break. Take a moment to clear your head. Get something to eat, see a movie, take a nap; just do something to clear your head so you can attack the next chapter with all your energy. We're going to explore some very cool surfacing techniques in Chapter 9, "Image Map Surfaces," and I wouldn't want you to miss anything.

I'll see you in the next chapter.

9 *Image Map Surfaces*

Nothing makes an object more photorealistic than high-quality image maps. They are absolutely essential if you plan to add realistic details to your surfaces. Real surfaces are full of tiny details that couldn't possibly be replicated without using image maps.

I'm sure you're familiar with image maps. In fact, we've used them many times in the previous chapters. The two most frequently used image maps are color and bump, but there are actually eight types of image maps, which are essential for creating photorealistic surfaces. I guess you're probably wondering what they are? The image map types are color, diffusion, specularity, luminosity, reflectivity, transparency, bump, and clip, which we'll cover in detail later in the chapter.

You'll find that color and bump maps are used in nearly every image, but you don't see too many images that take advantage of other types. The interesting thing is that the majority of surfaces really should use a great deal more than just color and bump. You can't effectively mimic reality without using specularity and diffusion image maps. But I'm getting ahead of myself. Before we cover the specific image map types, we need to explore the foundation of image maps—you know, start with the basics. In fact, there's nothing more basic than finding source material, so let's start with it. What are we waiting for? Let's take a look at source material.

VISIT THE COMPANION WEB SITE FOR TUTORIAL FILES.

Before you begin this chapter, go to Appendix F to learn about the companion Web site. All of the TUTORIAL FILES referenced in this chapter are located on the companion Web site at www.wiley.com/compbooks/fleming. You should also download the color figures from the companion Web site since they will be easier to review than the grayscale images printed in this chapter.

Finding Source Material

Creating realistic surfaces requires an abundance of quality source material since it's difficult to create photorealistic image maps from memory. There are so many subtle nuances in real surfaces that it would be impossible for us to remember all of them. Take rust for example: I'm sure you remember that it's a reddish brown color, but do you recall the other details like the orange splotches, purple dabs, and occasional white spots? Probably not, unless you happen to have a photographic memory. Even then you'd have so much information stored in your head that you'd have barely enough memory left to remember what you were trying to surface. It's important to have the source material in front of you when you create the surfaces to ensure they are realistic.

I have a very comprehensive library of source material, which I draw upon daily to help me create photorealistic images. In fact, my desk is completely covered in source material. You can never have too much source material. It's almost as important as your computer.

There are many ways to acquire source material, but we're only going to take a look at the most useful ones. We'll start with the most obvious one—books.

Finding Source Material at the Bookstore, Library, and on the Internet

There are a number of places you can get source material, such as the library and even on the Internet, but if you are seeking really high quality source material you are better off visiting your local bookstore, or maybe even the on-line mammoth bookstore: www.amazon.com. Bookstores always carry a wide variety of books that feature an abundance of color images, and they have those wonderful children's educational sections. I know it sounds bizarre but you'll likely find the best source material in this section. Children's educational books are always filled with an abundance of color photos, unlike the adult books, which are more words than pictures. I've always preferred books with more pictures—well, that's another story.

Another benefit of getting source material from a bookstore is that you own the book so you can vandalize the books without having a psychotic librarian stalking you. Sometimes it's necessary to remove the pages from the book to scan them and most libraries don't appreciate this. . . . I know mine didn't.

MAKE THE CHILDREN'S EDUCATIONAL SECTION YOUR FIRST STOP WHEN SEEKING SOURCE MATERIAL.

When looking for source material in a bookstore, you should head directly to the children's educational section. You won't find a better source of high-quality color images than a children's educational book.

Of course, libraries aren't all bad. They can be another good place to find source material. I've spent hours in the library digging up great source material. I find that the magazines are probably the best source material in the library since the books have been handled by thousands of people, which can leave them a little worse for the wear. If you're planning to scan images to use in your surfacing you'll find that libraries aren't the best place to go, since you'll want a high-quality, untainted image for the scan. Another drawback of libraries is the lack of color images in the books. It's important that your source material is full color so you don't have to guess at the colors. (Boy, it sounds like I have some deep hostility toward libraries, doesn't it?) Actually, if you're lucky enough to have a city library nearby, I'm sure you'll find some very nice source material.

Of course, the fastest way to obtain source material is through the Internet. While the images may not be very large, they are easily obtainable, usually full-color, and don't cost you anything. I occasionally browse the Internet for images I want to use as a reference for painting the image maps, since high-resolution images aren't necessary. On the other hand, if I need to scan the image I prefer bookstores, since they have large, high-quality originals.

So we know the bookstore is a great place to find source material but what books should we be looking for? I have found a few books that have outstanding color photographs, which make perfect source material. For example: I heartily recommend that you purchase any of the books in the Eyewitness Book Series. These books were created for children, but they feature literally thousands of high-quality color photographs of nearly everything under the sun. Heck, you might even learn something too. Yesterday I found out that there is a giant water bug that actually eats tiny fish. Cool isn't it? I'm sure that's something you've been dying to know.

TELL ME MORE

You'll find a list of outstanding resources for source material in Appendix A: Modeling and Surfacing Source Material.

Where else can we look? Well, the great thing is that good source material is all around you. You just need to be able to bring it back to your studio. For this, you'll need a camera.

Gathering Source Material with an Instant Camera

Quite often you'll discover that the objects you need can't be found in books or on the Web. In these situations you'll need to go into the world and find the objects yourself. For this task, I seriously recommend that you invest in an instant camera. The world around us is filled with an endless supply of awesome source material, which you can capture in an instant (no pun intended) with a Polaroid camera. In fact, for Chapter 11 of this book, I needed to find several items that weren't likely to be in a bookstore or on the Web. Two of the objects I needed pictures of were an aged fire hydrant and an old, rusted water main cover. Fortunately, these items were only 20 feet from the front door of my studio. In an effort to avoid hostility from the Public Works Department, I decided to photograph them rather than dragging them into my studio, which would have been a messy proposition anyway. Let's take a look at the actual photographs I took and the rendered images that were created from these source images.

You can see two Polaroid photographs on the left side of Figure 9.1, which were the source material for creating the fire hydrant and water main image maps. Take a look at the image behind the photographs. This is the final rendered image. It's obvious that the photographs played a major role in determining the surfaces of the objects in this image. Without these photographs, it would have been difficult to re-create the chaotic details of the real surfaces, particularly the discoloration of the fire hydrant and the way rust gathers around the seam at the base. While the quality of an instant picture isn't the best, it does provide you with enough detail to create dynamic surfaces, and it's immediately available, unlike conventional photographs.

CARRY AN INSTANT CAMERA WITH YOU AT ALL TIMES.

You never know when you'll come across a perfect surface while you're out and about. It would be a shame to lose out on such great source material. Always carry an instant camera with you. You don't have to physically carry it everywhere, just leave one in your car so you can easily access it.

I carry a Polaroid camera with me everywhere I go because I never know when I'll come across an awesome surface. In fact, two years ago I had a contract that required a lot of post–nuclear war industrial surfaces. You know, those old

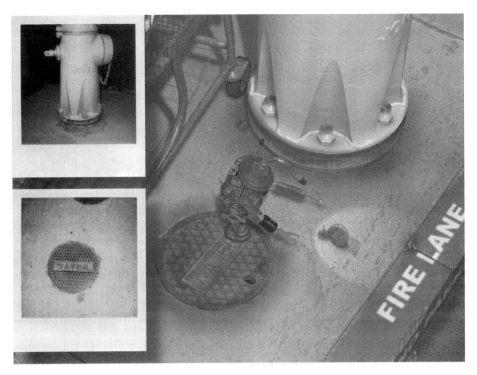

Figure 9.1 *Gathering source material with a Polaroid camera.*

rusty factories with oxidized grunge running down the walls. Well, I just happened to have made a trip to the Magic Mountain theme park the following weekend and discovered that the Batman Park was filled with tons of industrial architecture. Needless to say, I took a great number of photographs—did I ever look like a tourist.

I'm always on the search for great surfaces. I've spent hours walking up and down the alleys behind strip mall shopping centers, gathering killer source material and getting strange looks from mall security. You'll find excellent source material everywhere you look. In fact, let's take a look at another example of great source material that I discovered the other day.

Figure 9.2 shows two Polaroid photographs of a storefront. I just happened to need this very look for the image you see behind the photographs. It would have taken me twice as long to create the image if I didn't have the source material, and it definitely wouldn't have looked anywhere near as good.

Of course, there are times when you won't be able to photograph the source material you need. I'll bet you're wondering when this might happen? Well, I recall a time when I had several Toys R Us employees chasing me around the store because I was taking pictures of the toys. Apparently they thought I was a spy from another toy store who was trying to discover their proprietary toy store

Figure 9.2 *More great source material gathered with a Polaroid camera.*

secrets. Can you believe that's why you can't bring a camera into the store? They even confiscated my photographs . . . well, not all of them. The moral of the story is: "Use smaller cameras when taking pictures in toy stores." Actually, the point is that on occasion you'll have to drag an object into your studio to study it. Of course, this isn't so bad when the object is a G.I. Joe with the kung fu grip.

As you can see, an instant camera is a great tool but it does have one minor drawback. You can't use the photographs as the actual surface for your objects because the quality isn't very good. In many cases you'll want to save time by using portions of a photograph to surface your objects. It sure beats taking the time to manually recreate the surfaces.

If you want to use the photographs as image maps I suggest you use a high-quality 35-mm camera and take the film to a professional developer. Definitely avoid those one-hour photo shops since the quality of prints they produce just isn't worth the time you're saving. You want the photographs to be the highest quality possible so your image maps look their best. It's also a good idea to get enlargements of the really good photos so you have a larger source file for your scans.

Since we're on the topic of using photographs for image maps, I guess we should take a moment to discuss scanners.

Scanning Source Material

A scanner is a necessary tool if you plan to do a lot of photorealistic image maps. There hasn't been a day gone by that I haven't scanned something to use in making my image maps. A scanner allows you to capture images from photographs and books to use as image maps surfaces, or even a source of sampling textures for cloning. I often scan images so I can sample their colors, which I use to re-create the surfaces. It beats trying to mix the colors yourself.

If you plan to purchase a scanner, I recommend that you purchase a high-resolution 24-bit scanner. You want to avoid the lower resolution models since the scans will be too small to be of any use. Try to get a scanner that has a minimum resolution of 300DPI—avoid the 150DPI models. When scanning images, you'll want to capture them at the largest possible size. Once again, you can resample images smaller but you can't enlarge them without sacrificing image quality.

If you already have a scanner, I'm sure you are familiar with the problem of patterns in your scanned images. You see, most color images are printed at a resolution of 300DPI. While the human eye can't see the individual dots, the scanner certainly has no problem seeing them and is more than willing to include them in your scanned image. The best way to remove the patterns created by these dots is to apply a Gaussian blur to the image. Blurring the image will blend the dots so they won't be distinguishable to the human eye. Just make sure you don't use a high level of blurring or you'll end up making the image appear fuzzy, requiring everyone to have corrective lenses to view your images, which doesn't quite have the same appeal as 3D glasses.

ALWAYS REMOVE THE DOT PATTERNS IN SCANNED IMAGES.

It's important to remove the dot patterns from your scanned images, even if they are subtle. If you use images with these patterns to surface your objects you'll find that the patterns will show up in the render as scintillation, which is the undesirable flickering of the image when animated.

It's also a good idea to avoid scanning images from magazines since they are printed on poor quality paper, which makes the dots more prominent. Of course, a magazine cover would work just fine since it's printed on higher-quality coated paper. The best scans come from high-quality coated paper, which you typically find in books. In fact, calendars are always printed on high-quality coated paper and they typically feature crisp color images, which are perfect for scanning.

Scanners are great for capturing images and photographs but what else can you do with them? The great thing about a scanner is that you aren't limited to just scanning images; you can also scan objects.

Capturing Object Surfaces with a Scanner

Scanning objects? That's right, you can put just about anything on a scanner . . . as long as it holds still for you. I wouldn't recommend scanning something like a lizard. They just don't hold still long enough. . . . I know because I tried it once.

There are literally thousands of small objects that can be scanned. I often scan the surfaces on product boxes and books covers. Of course these are the obvious objects since they are printed images, but how about those unusual object surfaces that would be a pain to paint? You know, the ones like carpet, fabric, hamburger meat, lettuce, tomatoes, onions . . . now I'm starting to get hungry again. There are countless objects around your house and studio that can be scanned to create awesome image maps. Take a look at Figure 9.3.

Here we have a nice photorealistic image, with an abundance of really nice organic surfaces. All of the image maps used in this image were scanned from the actual objects. Can you believe I had to sacrifice a perfectly good hamburger for this image?

The image maps play a major role in making the image photorealistic. It would have taken me days to paint these surfaces, but it took me only two hours to scan and edit them.

USE YOUR SCANNER TO CAPTURE OBJECTS AS WELL AS IMAGES.

Don't limit yourself to scanning images and photographs. You can scan literally thousands of objects with your scanner. Just make sure they aren't heavy enough to break the glass.

Sometimes finding the right source image can take a bit of creativity. For example: I needed a carpet surface for many of the images in this book. I could have photographed a portion of my carpet but that would have taken too long, and my landlord advised me that ripping out a segment of the carpet was not a good idea. Instead, I scanned a small portion of the throw rug in my kitchen. It made the perfect source image to create photorealistic carpet. Take a look at Figure 9.4.

Here we have the segment of the rug that I scanned. In the upper left corner you'll find the seamless carpet image map I created from the original scan. I just took a bit of the black rug and changed the color in Photoshop to the desired carpet color. Now I have a very realistic carpet image map. The throw rug made a perfect carpet image map because it has very small fibers, which allows me to

Figure 9.3 *A scene that is completely surfaced with images scanned from actual objects.*

scan a small area and make it appear like it's a much larger segment of a carpet. Five inches of throw rug is the equivalent of three feet of carpet.

Of course, sometimes you need to get a little bizarre when scanning object surfaces. I recall a time where I spread strawberry jam on my scanner so I could get a realistic surface for my 3D jam. It looked great in the final render. I've done the same thing with fruit, toast, tobacco, dirt, and even potato salad. Just make sure you don't close the scanner lid when scanning sloppy stuff, or you'll have quite a mess to contend with.

That about does it for scanning and acquiring source material. So now that we have source material, what's next? We need to paint the image maps, but before we can do this we need to create a painting template for the surface we are creating.

Creating Painting Templates

The creation of an image map begins with a *painting template,* which is simply a visual representation of the surface. It's basically a picture of the model's surface.

Figure 9.4 *A carpet image map created from a scanned throw rug.*

Painting templates are necessary so you can line up the details of the image map with their appropriate location on the model's surface. They are also critical for ensuring that you are creating seamless surfaces. Without a painting template, you'll spend countless, unnecessary hours trying to tweak the image map so it works.

There are a number of ways to create a painting template, but the fastest way is to do a screen capture of the wireframe surface in the modeling program. You simply select the surface you want to paint in the modeling program, hide all the other surfaces, and do a screen capture. Take a look at Figure 9.5.

Here we have a screen capture that shows the lower part of the pumpkin we surfaced in Chapter 8. All the other surfaces were hidden so they wouldn't clutter the screen capture. You want only the surface you are capturing to be visible, or the template will be difficult to use. You can see that a screen capture from the modeling program gives you an orthographic view of the surface. An orthographic view is a flat view, with no perspective. An orthographic view is necessary because you don't want any perspective to be present or the template won't match the surface, causing the image map details to be out of alignment with the model's details. Your image map will also end up being several pixels shy of covering the whole surface, which is a little too sexy for 3D photorealism.

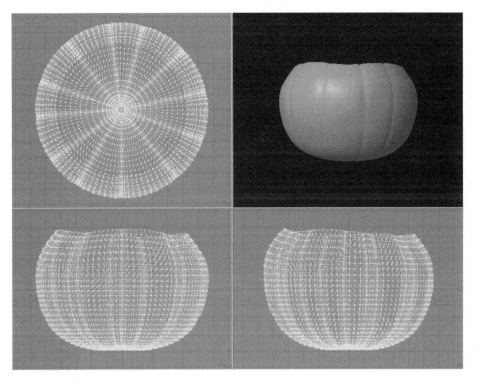

Figure 9.5 *Creating painting templates with screen captures.*

There are a number of ways to capture the screen. If you are running Windows, the fastest way is to press the Print Screen button on the keyboard. This will capture the screen to the clipboard, which you can then paste into your painting program to edit. On the Macintosh, you press Command+Shift+3, which will save the screen dump on your startup hard drive. The images will be named Picture X, where X is the number of the screen capture you just created. These, of course, are fast methods but they can become unreliable if you do too many screen captures. The most reliable method, for all platforms, is to use a screen capture utility. There are many shareware and freeware screen capture utilities available on the Internet. Table 9.1 provides a listing of several screen capture utilities and their URLs.

Screen captures are great but they aren't the only way you can create a painting template. You can also render a template. There are a couple of things to consider when rendering your painting template. The first is whether you want to use a wireframe or shaded view. Quite often you'll find that a wireframe is the most useful method since it will clearly illustrate the unique aspects of the model. Shaded views tend to hide some of the details. Let's take a look at how these two methods compare. Take a look at Figure 9.6.

Table 9.1 Screen Capture Utilities

PRODUCT	PLATFORM	DEVELOPER	URL
PrintScreen95	Win 3.1, 95, NT	Super Simple Software	www.primente.com/~glencj
SnagIt	Win 3.1, 95, NT	TechSmith Corporation	www.techsmith.com
SnapShot 3	Win 3.1, 95, NT	Beacon Hill Software, Inc.	world.std.com/~bhs
Photoimpact	Win 3.1, 95, NT	Ulead Systems Inc.	www.ulead.com
HyperSnap DX	Win 3.1, 95, NT	Hyperionics	www.hyperionics.com
ScreenShot 2.5.5	Macintosh	The Beale Street Group	www.beale.com
Flash-It	Macintosh	Nobu Toge	www.sharewarejunkies.com /flashit.htm
Captivate	Macintosh	Mainstay	www.mstay.com

Here we have two renders of a pager model. You can see that the wireframe view gives you a very clear illustration of the details on the model. Now take a look at the shaded view. Notice how it tends to confuse the lines with shadows. We could have avoided the shadows by lighting the pager from the front but then we wouldn't see any of the details. Both images would be good painting templates, but if you wanted precise placement of detail you should use the wireframe template. Now we need to take a look at the second thing you need to consider when rendering painting templates—perspective.

When rendering the template you'll encounter the problem of perspective being added to the model. This is because cameras are usually set to relatively low

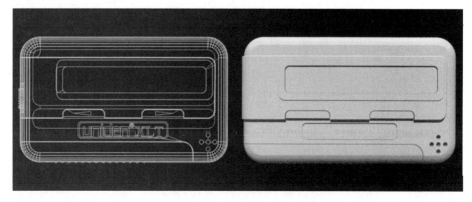

Figure 9.6 A comparison of wireframe and shaded templates.

zoom settings, which adds perspective to the model. In order to prevent this, you'll need to set an extremely high zoom value for the camera. I usually set it to around 100, which moves the camera far enough away that the view becomes orthographic. Let's take a look at how increasing the camera zoom changes the perspective of the model. Take a look at Figure 9.7.

Here we have the same pagers but this time we've rendered the ones on the left with a standard camera zoom of 3.2, and the ones on the right with an exaggerated camera zoom of 100. Take a look at the right side of the shaded pagers and you'll see that the perspective pager on the left has a wider margin between the screen and its edge. It's not a major difference, but if you were to use the perspective view to paint details on the pager's screen, the image map would be slightly out of alignment with the actual screen on the model.

USE A CAMERA ZOOM OF 100 OR GREATER WHEN RENDERING PAINTING TEMPLATES.

A low value for the camera zoom will add perspective to your model, which will make your image maps out of alignment with the actual detail on the model. Using a camera zoom in

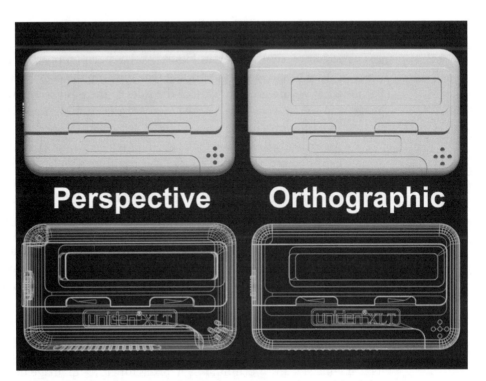

Figure 9.7 *A comparison of perspective versus orthographic view.*

excess of 100 creates an orthographic view, which gives you the best representation of the surface.

It can be difficult to see the difference between perspective and orthographic views when using shaded renders. It's usually better to use a wireframe render so you can be certain you have created a truly orthographic view. Take a look at the wireframe models in Figure 9.7 and you can immediately pick up on the difference between the perspective and shaded views. There is a very dramatic difference in the perspective render, which makes this an undesirable painting template. Be sure that you always use a very high zoom level on your camera when you render painting templates.

You have just created a template for your surface. Now what do you do? It's time to paint the image map, but before we begin painting we need to size the painting template.

Sizing the Painting Template

The first step in sizing the painting template is to crop out the excess information in the image. You want to see just the wireframe portion that represents the surface you are painting. The rest of the image is useless, so just crop it out as shown in Figure 9.8.

The screen capture we saw in Figure 9.5 has been cropped to show only the mesh we want to surface. It's important that you crop the right view of the mesh. For instance: We are going to surface the sides of the pumpkin with a cylindrical image map so we want to use a side view for the painting template. If we used the top view, the image map would not fit the surface properly.

Now we're ready to size the template. This is a very important step in creating image maps because you need to size the painting template before you begin painting.

The size of the template really depends on the use of the model. If you plan to do close-ups, you'll need to create large image maps. If you only plan to use it as a background prop, you could create small image maps but I recommend that you always create large image maps. Why? You may later find that you want to use the model in a close-up and if you have only small image maps, you'll be painting them all over again, and that's no fun. Remember, you can resample an image smaller but you can't increase it without losing image quality. You can always resample the image maps smaller for the distant shots, and then use the larger image maps for the close-ups.

What's a good size? I like to size my image maps to about 1000 pixels wide for standard image maps and around 2500 pixels for close-up image maps. Of course, this all depends on the surface you're editing. These settings would apply to the largest surface on the model. You should always start by editing the largest surface on the object because you need to make sure that all your image maps are in the right proportions. Why is this important? That's a great question. If you're using multiple image maps to surface an object, they need to be proportionately sized or they won't be seamless. This will be easier to understand if we look at an example. Take a look at Figure 9.9.

Here we have our pumpkin again. Take a look at the pumpkin on the left and you'll see a seam around the top where the two surfaces meet. This seam is the result of using image maps that weren't proportionally sized. These image maps were painted with no regard to sizing. Now take a look at the pumpkin on the right. Notice how the image maps are seamless, making the pumpkin appear nat-

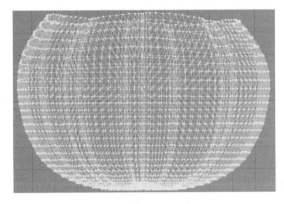

Figure 9.8 *A properly cropped painting template.*

Figure 9.9 *Using proper sizing to make image maps seamless.*

Figure 9.10 *Proportional sizing of image maps.*

Figure 9.11 *Sizing cylindrical image map templates.*

ural. This is because they were created at proportional sizes. Okay, so what's all this talk about proportions? Well, when you create image maps you need to make sure they are equally sized. Once again, this is easier to explain with an image. Take a look at Figure 9.10.

Take a look at the top image. Notice how the painting templates for the top and side have been combined into the same painting template, which is called a Master Painting Template. A *master painting template* is used to ensure that the image maps are sized proportionately. This is particularly important when there is a pattern in the color image map, as we have with the pumpkin. Take a look at the bottom image. You'll notice that there is a subtle repeating pattern in the surface of the pumpkin near the top. It's important that you keep this pattern the same size on the top of the pumpkin or you'll end up with a seam where the two image maps meet, because the pattern sizes won't match. Putting the templates together makes it very simple to size them proportionately. Once you are done painting the surface, you just select the specific surface areas, then copy and paste them into a new file.

This brings up a good point. You always want to keep the template layer untainted since you will need it for reference, and to create the selections for the image maps. If you paint on the template you won't be able to accurately select the individual image maps.

Here's a question I hear a lot. When creating a painting template for a cylindrical object, just how wide do you make the template? This question comes up because the image you screen capture or render is a mere fragment of the actual size of the surface. The answer is quite simple. Your cylindrical image map should be 325 percent of the object's width. Let's see exactly what this means. Take a look at Figure 9.11.

You need to size your cylindrical image maps to 325 percent of the object's width to prevent image map pinching and stretching that occurs when you use the improper size. Now let's wrap up this segment and get on with the fun stuff.

When creating image maps, it's imperative that you start with the largest surface so you can properly size the other surfaces. I'm sure you also noticed that placing the two painting templates together makes it very easy to ensure they are seamless. In fact, there is no better way to ensure image maps are seamless than painting them simultaneously in a master painting template. Now that we're on the subject of seamless image maps, let's take a look at how we can create them.

Creating Seamless Image Maps

Nothing undermines the photorealistic credibility of an object like surface seams. Real-world objects don't have surface seams, especially the organic objects. So how do we create seamless image maps? First we need to look at the two types of image maps: tileable and specific. Tileable image maps are the most common type of seamless image map. They are usually square images of common surfaces like woods, marble, bricks, and such. There are many companies that sell these image maps in libraries. I'm sure you have all purchased one of these libraries at some point.

Creating Nonrepeating, Seamless Image Maps

What if you can't find the seamless image map that you need? You need to make one. It's not as difficult as it sounds. Let's make a seamless tileable image map from the throw rug that I scanned. First you need to make sure that you have downloaded the tutorial files for this chapter from the companion Web site at www.wiley.com/compbooks/fleming. For this tutorial we'll be using Photoshop, but the steps we'll be doing are very basic, which means they can be done in most painting programs. Okay, now we're ready to get started.

Exercise: Creating Seamless Tileable Image Maps

1. Load the carpet.jpg file into Photoshop. Now create a new image that's 800 × 800 pixels. When creating a seamless image map tile, you want to make a template that's twice the width and height of the source image.

2. Now select the entire carpet.jpg file, then copy and paste it into the new file you just created. The carpet image should have a selection around it. It is very important that you don't remove the selection. You should have a square segment of carpet in the middle of your image as shown in Figure 9.12.

3. We need to save the selection that's active. This will be the area of the image that we will be saving as the final seamless tile. Go ahead and save the selection.

4. Now comes the tricky part. First, move the carpet selection to the upper left corner of the screen. Then copy and paste it. Now flip the new selection horizontally and place it to the right of the first piece. You should now have carpet covering the top half of the image.

5. Paste another copy of the carpet segment and flip it vertically. Then place it in the lower left corner.

6. Finally, copy and paste the current selection (it should be the segment in the lower left corner) and flip it horizontally. Then place it in the lower right corner. Well, that was fun. You should now have an image that resembles Figure 9.13.

Why did we flip the image? Well, we wanted to make sure we put the same sides together so there would be a seamless border in the center selection. Now we have to do some cloning to remove patterns in the carpet.

7. Load the selection you saved earlier. We'll be painting in the selection since we don't care about the rest of the image. Take another look at Figure 9.13 and you'll see a circular pattern in the middle of the image. We need to remove this pattern or it will show up as a repeating pattern when we use the image map. You'll also see a light-colored stripe down the middle of the selection with darker bands on either side. These too will create repeating patterns. What we need to do is use the Cloning Tool to sample areas of the carpet outside the selection and paint them over these repeating spots. Make sure you avoid the edges of the selection when you are painting or you'll interfere with the seamless border we created by flipping the images.

8. We've just finished removing the patterns in the selected area. Now there's just one more step to make the image seamless. All you need to do is crop the image to the selected area. Now you should have an image like the one shown in Figure 9.14.

There you have it. A perfect, seamless image map that you can use to surface the carpet in your scene. In some cases you may have to repeat the process to clean up repeating segments, or to correct a border which you might have accidentally altered with the cloning brush.

As you can see, it can be fairly simple to create awesome seamless tiles. Now let's look at the more complicated task of creating nonrepeating, seamless image maps.

Creating Complex Seamless Image Maps

Complex seamless image maps can be a lot more difficult to create. The foundation of any complex seamless image map is the painting template, so let's jump right in and take a look at one. Take a look at Figure 9.15.

Remember how we discussed the importance of proportionately sized image maps? Well, there's another reason for combining the templates into a master painting template—it makes it easier to paint seamless image maps. If you look at the figure you'll see that the images for the side and top of the pumpkin were seamlessly merged using the Clone Tool. Putting the two templates together made it possible to ensure that the image maps would be seamless. Of course, this is a relatively simple example since there are only two surfaces and the texture isn't very specific. What happens when you have a very specific surfacing need?

Well, that's where the fun begins, and I use the term loosely. Once again it all starts with the painting template. Before we make the template we need an object,

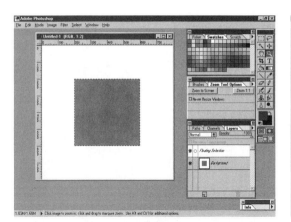

Figure 9.12 *Pasting the source sample into the seamless image map template.*

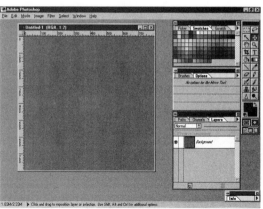

Figure 9.13 *Laying down the carpet selections.*

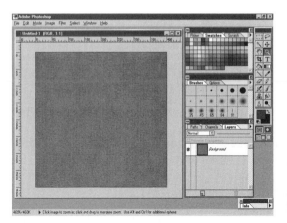

Figure 9.14 *The completed, seamless tileable image map.*

Figure 9.15 *Creating a painting template for complex seamless image maps.*

so let's take a look at a complex object with very specific surfacing needs. Take a look at Figure 9.16.

Here we have the engine segment of a spaceship. Each of the different surfaces has been indicated by a unique color. You can see that we have several image maps to create, which doesn't seem too bad until you consider the amount of detail we'll need to add to the surfaces. Let's take a look at the story behind this object.

This engine is part of an old Roid Hopper spaceship. Roid Hoppers get their name because they are private security patrol ships that tour the asteroid belts of

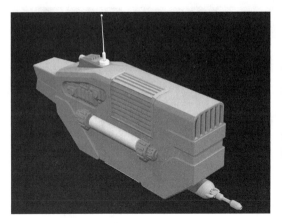

Figure 9.16 A complex object with specific surfacing needs.

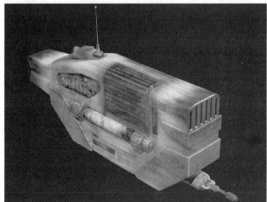

Figure 9.17 The surfaced engine.

Saturn, protecting the mining colonies on its moons. Since they fly through asteroid debris all day long, they tend to be heavily aged. Usually they are covered in dents and dings from asteroid fragments. Of course, this would mean the paint is chipped and probably covered in oxidation. Since they patrol a rather grungy environment they don't waste their time cleaning the ship, which means you can expect to see dirt, oil, and grease stains near all the vents and mechanical parts. Needless to say, the surfacing of this object is rather complicated. Let's take a look at the final surfaced object, shown in Figure 9.17, to get a real nice visual of the challenge before us.

As you can see, creating seamless image maps for this object appears rather impossible, but yet, it was done for this image—so there must be a way. Let's take a look at how we approach the surfacing of complicated objects like the engine. The first step is to create the painting templates, which help us to size the image maps proportionately and ensure they are seamless. This object is more complicated than the pumpkin we discussed earlier so we need to create a more detailed master painting template. We'll use the main engine body as the basis for our discussion, so it doesn't get too confusing.

Once you have created a painting template for each of the five surfaces—front, back, side, top, and bottom—you'll need to combine them into a single master painting template. This is a little tricky at first, but you'll get the hang of it quickly. You start by creating a large image that is big enough to hold all the other templates. Then you start piecing together the puzzle. It's best to start with the Parent Template, which is the one surface with seams that connect to all the other surfaces. You should place this template in the middle of the image, then start placing the other templates in relation to it as shown in Figure 9.18. Make sure that you size all the templates so they are proportional to the center one. Your completed master painting template should look like a box that has been unfolded.

The master painting template shows you all the object's surfaces simultaneously, which makes painting seamless image maps a great deal easier. Now that we have a master painting template for the engine, we need to paint the seamless surfaces. I won't go into the actual painting techniques but I will cover the steps that were used to make the image maps seamless.

The first step was to create the base color, which is the foundation of the seamless surfaces. Figure 9.19 shows the base colors that were created.

Obviously this is a very simple coloration, but you always need to start with a foundation color before you can add the details. Any good painter uses a primer coat. Now the challenge is to create extremely high detail, which is also seamless. Since we have a master painting template, this process becomes a matter of painting within the lines, so to speak. You start by painting all of the seams that are visibly connected in the image. Once you have built the foundation with the connected seams, you need to work on the seams that aren't connected, like the front and back templates, which aren't connected to the top or bottom of the engine. There are actually two ways to do this. You can use the Clone Tool to copy parts from one edge to another, or you can do what I do—copy the whole edge of one surface to another, creating a perfect blend between them. I know you want to see an example because that last sentence kind of confused me, too. Let's take a look at where the top and front surfaces meet in Figure 9.20.

Here we have an image that shows the process of creating seamless blends between surfaces. The master painting template and color layers have been superimposed so we can see where the changes need to be done. You can do the same thing in Photoshop by reducing the opacity of the color layer. Take a look at Cell A; this is the upper left corner of our master painting template. The two edges we need to blend are indicated with the highlighted selections. We're going to copy the top edge of the engine's front to the leading edge of the engine's top by following a few simple steps.

1. The first thing we need to do is copy a portion of the engine front as shown in Cell B, and then feather it so it blends with the engine top surface. I usually use a value of 5 pixels when feathering selections.

2. Now we need to rotate it 90 degrees counterclockwise so it lines up with the engine top surface as shown in Cell C.

3. Next, we move it into place as shown in Cell D, and then we crop the selection a bit so it doesn't cover any of the engine front, as shown in Cell E.

Now take a look at Cell F. Here we have the completed effort. The surfaces have been selected so you can see how their edges will blend. You can see that it actually isn't terribly difficult to create seamless surfaces as long as you are working with a master painting template. Let's take a look at the final color image that was created for the engine surfaces. Take a look at Figure 9.21.

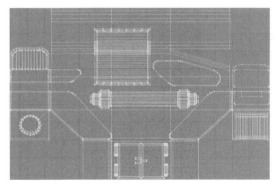

Figure 9.18 *The Master Painting template for the engine.*

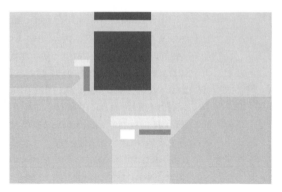

Figure 9.19 *Creating the base colors for seamless image maps.*

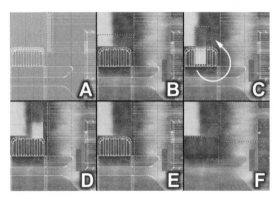

Figure 9.20 *Creating a seamless edge between image maps.*

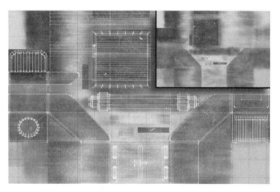

Figure 9.21 *The completed master color image.*

Here we have the completed master color image for the spaceship engine. Once again, the master painting template and color layers have been superimposed so you can see just how accurately the details can be created with this technique. You can see a small overlay in the upper right corner that shows the color image map in its final form. The only thing left to do now is separate the individual image maps and place them on the model. In fact, let's take a look at the actual Roid Hopper in Figure 9.22 to see how it all came together.

Here we have an image of a Roid Hopper patrolling the outer edge of the asteroid belt. You can see how the complex seamless image maps have gone a long way toward making the model photorealistic. In fact, this entire model was surfaced with a total of 109 image maps. If you enjoy sanity, I suggest you avoid developing models with this much image map detail. Honestly, this is a very unusual case. Typically it's a matter of creating only a couple image maps to surface complex objects.

Figure 9.22 *The Roid Hopper—covered in complex, seamless image map surfaces.*

Seamless image maps play a major role in the photorealistic credibility of a 3D image. While they may seem daunting at first, they are actually relatively simple to create once you understand the principle of using Master Painting Templates. Now let's lighten things up by exploring the diversity of image maps.

Getting Mileage Out of Your Image Maps

One of the greatest things about image maps is their unlimited application. You can use one image map as the foundation for creating an incredible variety of unique surfaces. All you need to do is use your imagination. Speaking of imagination, let's take a look at how a simple driftwood image map was modified to surface a photorealistic palm tree. Take a look at Figure 9.23.

While it may be a bit cluttered, this image does show how versatile image maps can be when creating photorealistic images. In the background you'll see three variations of the original driftwood image map, which is in the upper left corner. This image was modified to produce the image maps for the palm leaves. First, it

Figure 9.23 Using one image map to create multiple surfaces.

was turned green to create the surface for the fan leaves on top of the tree, and the new palm leaves around the base of the fan leaf stems. Then two levels of green fade were added to simulate the gradual dying of the lower palm leaves. Of course, the original driftwood image was used to surface the completely dead palm leaves. As you can see, this single image map, which has nothing to do with palm trees, was perfect for simulating the palm leaves. You need to be creative when exploring your image maps.

Since we're on the topic of using an image map from one object to surface a completely different one, let's take a look at one of my favorite examples.

Figure 9.24 illustrates how a crab shell texture was used to make a photorealistic fruit skin. Doesn't that crab fruit look tasty? As you can see, the possibilities are limitless. The most important tip for image maps is to use your imagination. Don't limit yourself to assuming that a driftwood texture is good only for driftwood when it actually makes a great surface for dead palm leaves.

Now that our imaginations are running wild, let's put them to good use by exploring the seven types of image map surfaces. Yes, we're finally going to do it! Here we go.

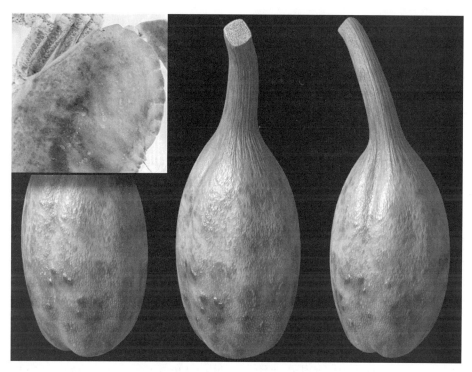

Figure 9.24 *A creative application of source material.*

Exploring the Types
of Image Map Surfaces

You're probably familiar with color and bump image maps since they've been used in nearly every 3D image created. And you've probably used transparency image maps at some point, but have you taken advantage of specularity and diffusion image maps? How about those power image maps like luminosity and clip? Well, you're going to start using them now.

You can't effectively mimic reality without using a variety of image map types to surface your objects. The surfaces in reality are very complex, and nothing about them is consistent. You won't find a single object that has the same level of specularity across its entire surface. The same also applies for diffusion levels. Real surfaces are very chaotic. Therefore, we need to create this same chaos in our 3D surfaces if we hope to effectively mimic them. How do we do this? We start by taking advantage of the other types of image maps at our disposal.

In a moment, we discuss each of the image map types, but first we need to take a look at how image maps work. The good news is that all image maps, except color, use the same principle of determining their values based on the shades of gray in the image. Simply put, the black areas in the image would represent zero effect, while white areas represent 100 percent effect. For example: The white area on a luminosity image map represents maximum brightness, whereas the black area would be completely nonluminous. Now that we understand the principle behind how they work, let's take a look at each of the image map types and get an idea of what they do.

Understanding the Types of Image Maps

There are eight types of image maps that can be used to create photorealistic surfaces. They are color, diffusion, specularity, luminosity, reflectivity, transparency, bump, and clip. It's possible that your program might not use all of them, and in some cases might even refer to them by a different name. Don't worry, it's not the end of the world if you are missing a couple of them. Just experiment with the ones you do have until you acquire a program that uses them all.

Before we take a look at what each of the image map types does, let's examine a model that uses several types of image maps to create a photorealistic surface. Take a look at Figure 9.25.

Here we have a close-up of the Roid Hopper's right wing. You can see that it has very detailed surfacing with a number of chaotic traits. Let's take a look at the subtle details that were created using a variety of the image map types. Notice the grease and grunge behind the weapons. This really helps to make the object appear natural since we can expect debris from the weapon blasts to attach itself to the wing. Now take a look at the leading edge of each metal plate and you'll see little streaks of dirt. This is a subtle detail but very important since the ship has been flying through asteroid belts, which means the dust particles that hit the wing will stick to the leading edge of the plates.

Now look at the front of the wing. You'll notice that the red paint has been chipped away in a few places, exposing the metal beneath. Those must have been some big dust particles. Did you notice the occasionally whitish spots on the wing? This is where oxidation has formed. And, of course, there are little specs of white all over the wing where oxidation has formed in places where the paint has been dented and chipped away. This wing is a mess, but it's very photorealistic, something that would have been impossible to achieve using only color and bump image maps.

Now let's take a look at the types of image maps that were used to create these effects.

Color Image Maps

Obviously, I don't need to tell you what these are. A color image map is the most visible of the image maps. It's also the most frequently used, and for good reason

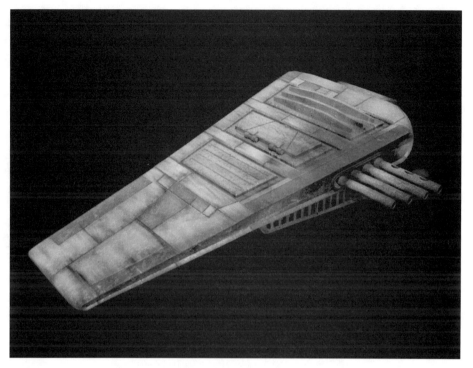

Figure 9.25 *Exploring the types of image maps.*

since our models would look fairly drab without them. A *color image map* gives your surface its color. It's probably the most important image map type since it is responsible for creating the overwhelming majority of visual chaos we see on the surface. It's also the foundation of all the other image maps. You create the color image map first, then you create the other image maps based on the details in the color image map. In most cases you can simply convert the color image map to gray and modify it to be used for the other image maps.

Color image maps are also the only type of image map that doesn't use shades of gray to determine its value. It's just a color, and nothing more. Now let's take a look at the color image map that was used for the Roid Hopper wing. Take a look at Figure 9.26.

You can see that a great deal of detail was added to the color image map, which was essential for making the surface realistic. Take a look at the grease marks where the guns were located. In fact, look at any of the grease marks covering the wing. What are the attributes of dried grease and grime? Well, it's usually dull and porous, which means it will be dark and show very little specularity. You're probably thinking we could add more detail to the grease on the color image map to achieve this effect. Sure, you could, but it still wouldn't look right when rendered since the color cannot image map control the diffusion and specularity of

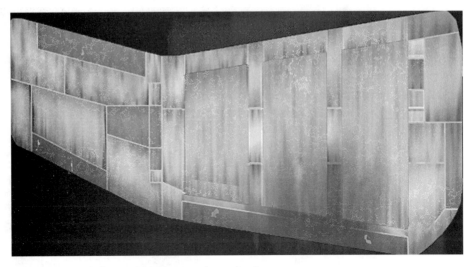

Figure 9.26 *The Roid Hopper wing color image map.*

the surface. In order to make the grease dull we need to apply a diffusion image map. Let's take a look at diffusion image maps now.

Diffusion Image Maps

Very rarely does a 3D surface include diffusion image maps, which is unfortunate since they play a major role in creating photorealistic 3D images. *Diffusion image maps* regulate the amount of light that is scattered by the surface. Simply put, diffusion is the amount of an object's color that the surface will show. For example: Metal objects are very reflective so they have low diffusion levels because they show the surrounding objects on their surface. On the other hand, plastics have a higher diffusion level because they are only slightly reflective. The diffusion image map uses shades of gray to set diffusion levels. Following are the low and high values for diffusion image maps and the effect they produce.

- Black = Dark (none of its own color is visible)
- White = Light (all of its own color is visible)

Now, let's take a look at the diffusion image map that was used on the Roid Hopper wing. You can see in Figure 9.27 that the diffusion image map is very similar to the color image map. This is necessary because we want to modify the diffusion level of the details on the color image map. Notice how the grease marks are very dark; this will lower the diffusion level of the grease so it doesn't react with the light in the scene. We don't want the grease to be illuminated much by the light since it's very porous, which means it absorbs light. You can

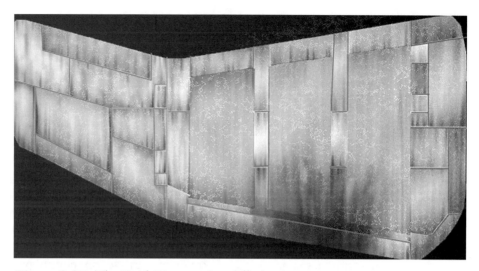

Figure 9.27 *The Roid Hopper wing diffusion image map.*

also see that there is an abundance of white dots on the image map. These represent the oxidized areas of the wing. This is where the oxidation is collecting in dents and dings. Oxidation is whitish so we want to raise the diffusion level fairly high so it maintains its color. Now take a look at the gray lines between the metal plates. These were added to darken these areas on the surface. We can assume grime and crud will make its way to the lowest point on the surface, so we need to diffuse these areas on the wing.

You can see that if we didn't use a diffusion image map the greasy and dirty areas would show too much color, making them appear unnatural. Diffusion image maps are necessary so you can control the diffusion of specific details on the surface.

Specularity Image Maps

Nearly all 3D images feature surfaces that use blanket specularity values, which makes them appear unnatural. There is no object in reality that has a consistent specularity level across its surfaces. There are always subtle elements that change the specularity of the surface. Quite often these surfaces are covered in dust, dirt, and rust, which all have low specularity levels.

As we mentioned earlier, *specularity* is the highlights that occur on smooth and/or shiny surfaces—it's basically a reflection of the light source. The human eye uses specularity to determine the hardness of the surface. Hard objects like plastic, glass, and ceramic typically have a higher level of specularity, whereas softer objects like rubber, wood, and fabric have low levels of specularity. Another factor in determining specularity is the reflectivity of the surface.

Reflective surfaces, like metals, have very low specularity values. I've seen far too many 3D metal objects that had high levels of specularity.

In some cases, like cars, you'll find painted metals with protective coatings, which show a large degree of specularity. It's important to realize that it's the paint and coating that are specular and not the metal beneath. Another example would be an airplane wing. Now these look like bare metal but they too have a protective coat, which is specular. Try this experiment in your studio: Take a chrome object and point a flashlight directly at it. Now, do you see any specularity? Don't be fooled by the bright spot on the objects; it's the reflection of the light emitting object, not the light itself. You're seeing the bright light bulb in the flashlight. In fact, repeat this experiment with a number of bare metal objects to see how low their specularity actually is.

It's important to know that the specularity image map controls only the intensity of the highlight and not the size. The size is controlled by a separate hardness/glossiness control. You must remember to set this control properly to ensure the effect is natural. For instance: Rubber would have a very low hardness/glossiness (16) setting while coated plastic would have a much higher setting (64). Some programs will allow you to set values for the hardness/glossiness while others simply have a low, medium, high toggle. Both are effective, though the numeric control is much more precise.

Following are the low and high values for specularity image maps and the effect they produce.

- Black = Soft and porous
- White = Hard and shiny

Let's take a look at the specularity image map that was used on the Roid Hopper wing.

Figure 9.28 is a rather ugly image isn't it? Although it's not the prettiest sight, it does serve its purpose well. Notice how the grease stains areas are nearly black. Dried grease has literally no specularity because it's a dull and porous surface so we want to make these areas darker on the specularity image map. If we didn't use a specularity image map on the wing, the grease stains would end up being shiny, which would be very unrealistic. Of course, if the grease were fresh, we would have to give it a high specularity level since it would be wet.

Now take a look at the white dots. These are those oxidized areas. Since there are tiny dried crystals in the oxidized areas, we need to make them fairly specular. These surfaces will look great when the Roid Hopper is animated. The specular highlights will flicker as the spaceship passes a light source.

Now let's examine the areas where the paint was chipped away on the color image map. Notice the gray spots on the leading edge of the wing—these repre-

Figure 9.28 *The Roid Hopper wing specularity image map.*

sent the bare metal surface. Since metal has a low specularity value, dark gray was added to these areas on the specularity image map.

Speaking of metals, let's take a look at how we make specific areas of the wing reflective by using a reflection image map.

Reflection Image Maps

Reflectivity is a popular element in 3D images, though it would seem that the objects always have the same value of reflectivity across the entire surface. This just isn't likely in reality. There is always going to be some dust, dirt, or general grime on the surface of the object that changes its reflectivity. Obviously, none of these elements are reflective. It's important to note that these elements won't always be visible to the human eye. More often than not they are very subtle and undetectable, but the impact they have on the reflectivity is noticeable. You should always apply a little value shifting in your reflectivity levels. Following are the low and high values for reflection image maps and the effect they produce.

- Black = No reflection
- White = Mirrors

Let's take a look at the reflection image map, shown in Figure 9.29, that was used on the Roid Hopper wing.

You can see that the surface of the wing will have a variety of different reflection values because of the varying shades of gray. This helps to make the surface appear photorealistic since the surface is rather worn and dirty. Now

Figure 9.29 *The Roid Hopper wing reflection image map.*

take a look at the areas where the paint was chipped away in the color image map. You can see that a light gray color was used in these areas to make the exposed metal reflective. In fact, there are a couple more areas where the surface has a rather high level of reflectivity. Take a look at those little gray spots. Since these are tiny crystals, they will be somewhat reflective. I know it's a little detail to worry about, but it didn't take any additional effort to create since the details were already in the color image map that was used to create the reflection image map.

The last thing we need to look at is the grease stains. Notice how they are black, which will prevent the grease from reflecting the environment. The grease is dried so it's nonreflective. On the other hand, if it were fresh, we would need to make these areas a lighter shade of gray so the grease would be reflective.

Bump Image Maps

I'm sure these aren't new to you. Just about every 3D image uses bump image maps in one way or another. Bump image maps are one of the most important image maps since they add depth and texture to the surface. You can almost get away without using specularity and diffusion image maps but the bump has to be used. You'll never encounter a surface in reality that doesn't have some sort of texture. There are a couple surfaces that don't have a detectable texture, like mirrors and glass, but they definitely do have one. It's just too small to feel.

So what are bump image maps? Yes, I know you know what they are but right now there is some guy on a desert island who has never heard of them. I certainly wouldn't want him to be confused. A *bump image map* is used to create simulated texture depth on 3D surfaces. I say simulated because it doesn't actually alter the mesh but instead creates simulated depth by adding highlights to the surface, much the same way the embossing filter does in Photoshop. The difference is that a bump map will interact with the light source. Following are the low and high values for bump image maps and the effect they produce.

- Black = Low
- White = High

Let's look at the bump image maps that were created for the Roid Hopper wing shown in Figure 9.30.

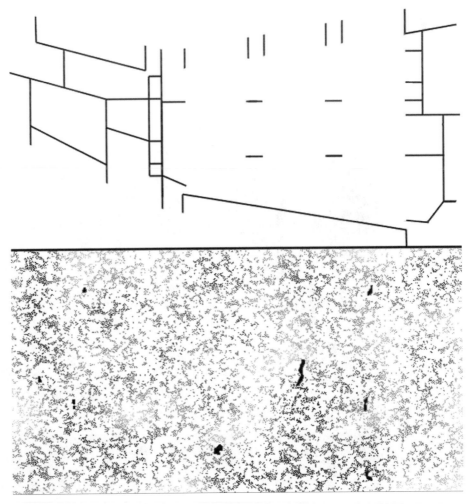

Figure 9.30 *The Roid Hopper wing bump image map.*

Here we have the two bump image maps that were used to add texture to the wing's surface. The top image shows the bump image map that created the metal plates. The bottom image shows the bump image map that was used to create the chipped paint. The metal plate image is fairly obvious so we'll jump right to the paint bump image map.

You can see that there are several black spots. These represent the area where the paint was chipped away, exposing the metal beneath. We had to make these spots black so they would be the lowest point on the surface. Now take a look at the splattering of gray spots. These are the dents where the oxidation has collected. The gray values were varied so the dents wouldn't all be the same depth. It's important that you apply chaos to your image maps so the effect they create is natural.

As you can see, the bump image maps have added a tremendous amount of depth to the wing's surface. Without them, the wing would have appeared flat and artificial.

Well, that about does it for the image maps used to create the Roid Hopper wing. Now we only have three more types of image maps to consider: transparency, luminosity, and clip. Let's take a look at an object that uses all three of these image map types, shown in Figure 9.31.

Figure 9.31 *Using transparency, luminosity, and clip image maps.*

I'll bet you were wondering when we would get around to seeing a photorealistic creature? Well, here you go—and it's a beauty too! Here we have a hatchet fish that lives about a mile beneath the ocean's surface. It has light organs in its lower belly and tail, which it uses to blend itself in with the brighter surface water, making them extremely difficult to see from below. Great camouflage isn't it? They can even control the level of brightness to ensure they match the surface light. It wouldn't be a good idea for them to glow like a lightbulb, since it would be like turning the light on in the fridge. They also have a darker body on top so they blend in with the darkness of the water below. You've got to love Mother Nature's ingenuity.

I'm sure you noticed the little transparent fin on his side and the irregular edges on all the other fins. These are common features on every fish, which we need to include if we want the object to be photorealistic. Let's take a look at the types of image maps that were used to create these effects.

Transparency Image Maps

You'll see a lot of transparent objects in 3D scenes but rarely do you see objects with varying levels of transparency. I'm sure you've seen countless rendered drinking glasses. So how many of them had water spots? Seen any windows with streaks or dirt? What about water marks on a glass table? Get the idea? These are all very common attributes of transparent objects but you won't find them in many 3D scenes, in spite of the fact that they are relatively easy to create using transparency image maps.

A transparency image map determines the amount of light that passes through a surface. Simply put, it controls how much you can see through an object. Following are the low and high values for transparency image maps and the effect they produce.

- Black = Opaque
- White = Transparent

Let's take a look at the transparency image map, shown in Figure 9.32, that was used to make the fishes' fins semitransparent.

Here we have the transparency image map for the hatchet fishes' fin. You can see that it uses several shades of gray, which make some parts more transparent than others. This is important for making the surface realistic. You couldn't just apply a blanket transparency value since the fin is organic and has plenty of chaotic detail, including a spot at the end that isn't transparent at all. This area represents a scar that it probably acquired while escaping a predator. You can also see that the membranes of the fin are less transparent since they are made of denser material.

You can see that transparency image maps are very valuable when creating organic transparency. You could have created water spots on a glass using the same technique that was done with the fin. You would just create several spots that were less transparent by making them a shade of gray. Of course, you would need a color image map to show the minerals in the water spot and a specularity image map to remove the specularity from the spots since the minerals aren't specular.

Now let's take a look at how that cool glow on the fishes' belly was created.

Luminosity Image Maps

This is probably the least used type of image map since there aren't too many things that are luminous in our environments other than lights and digital displays. Of course, both of these effects need luminosity. You'll find that most 3D artists will just apply a blanket luminosity to surfaces which, once again, never happens in reality. Let's consider a lightbulb for a moment. It's obviously luminous but certainly not at a uniform level of luminosity. A lightbulb is lit by a filament, which means that it will be more luminous toward this point and less luminous at the edges of the bulb. You could use a luminosity image map to vary the levels of luminosity on the bulb. How about something less common such as a stove burner? These are luminous but certainly not even. They have stains and hot spots from being used, so the luminosity would vary over the surface of the burner.

A luminosity image map will determine how much a surface appears to emit light. It basically makes the surface bright, but it doesn't make it glow. That's an entirely different effect. Following are the low and high values for luminosity image maps and the effect they produce.

- Black = Dull
- White = Bright

Let's take a look at the luminosity image map, shown in Figure 9.33, that was used to make the fishes' belly light up.

Yes, I know, it's a boring image. I guess I could have made the fish light up like the Vegas strip but that would be like putting a neon sign on a diner. You can see that a light gray spot was added where the belly is located. This will make the belly of the fish fairly luminous. It won't appear terribly bright since the belly is a dark color, but it will be much brighter than the rest of the fish. It's a simple image map but it does the job well.

Now we have come to the last type of image map—clip. Let's take a look at the clip image map and see how it was used to create the irregular edges on the fishes' fins.

Clip Image Maps

Clip image maps are very similar to transparency image maps except they work on the actual model instead of the surface. A *clip image map* is used to cut away

Figure 9.32 *The hatchet fish transparency image map.*

Figure 9.33 *The hatchet fish luminosity image map.*

Figure 9.34 *The hatchet fish clip image map.*

Figure 9.35 *The impact of a clip image map on the quality of a model.*

parts of the model. Actually, they don't cut the model but rather hide the selected portions. Clip image maps work a little differently than the other image maps. You have only two color possibilities to work with, black and white. Anything that is white will be cut out of the render. Note the two levels of clip maps.

- Black = Unaffected
- White = Cut

Clip image maps do have one major advantage over transparency image maps. They completely remove the portion of the model from the rendered image. A transparency image map makes only the portion invisible. This works well if the surface has little or no specularity, but if you have a highly specular surface you'll actually see specular highlight on the invisible portion. This, of course, is very undesirable. On the other hand, since a clip map removes portions of the model from the render, you won't get a specular highlight.

Where do you use a clip image map? There are a number of places, which include trimming the edges on leaves, cutting away the edges of a treasure map or even adding irregular edges to fish fins. In fact, let's take a look at the clip image map that was used to trim the edges of the hatches fishes' fins.

In Figure 9.34 we have a black silhouette of the hatchet fish. The black area represents the solid portion and the white area is everything that will be cut away. Take a look at the tail fin and you'll see that it has a very irregular edge, which really adds credibility to the model since fish have very irregular edges on their fins. If we left the edge smooth, the fish would look like a 3D model. In fact, let's take a look at how the clip map changes the appearance of the model.

Take a look at the fish model on the right of Figure 9.35. You can see the incredible difference the clip image map has made. This model looks a great deal better, and more realistic than the model on the left. It was a great model to begin with, but the irregular edges add the fine chaotic details that make the object photorealistic. Take a look at the top and bottom fins and you'll see very fine details on the edges. This is the kind of detail that convinces the viewer that they're looking at a real object. Of course, the surfaces help a lot, too.

You can see how valuable all the image map types are when it comes to creating photorealistic surfaces. It can take a bit of time to create the different types of image maps but I think you'll agree that the result is well worth the effort. Reality is a complex environment, so you'll need to take full advantage of the image map types to re-create real-world surfaces.

Well, we're actually done with our exploration of the eight types of image maps. We could jump right to Chapter 10, but I think it's time we had a little fun. Let's do a couple exercises that show us the real power of using the different image maps.

Putting the Image Map Types to Work

We've seen several examples of the types of image maps and the effect they have on surfaces, but we haven't actually done it ourselves. Now it's time to put the image maps to work for us so we can better understand the impact they have on making an object photorealistic. Let's get a little exercise.

In this exercise we will use five of the image map types to transform a simple battery model, as shown in Figure 9.36, into a photorealistic battery with both chrome and plastic surfaces, using only image maps.

There are several JPG files that were included in the tutorial file you downloaded for this chapter from the Web site at www.wiley.com/compbooks/fleming, which we will need to surface our exercise object. It's a good time to check and make sure you have all of the files listed as follows:

- E_Color.jpg
- E_Diff.jpg
- E_Spec.jpg
- E_Bump.jpg
- E_Refl.jpg

Great; now that we have the images, let's get started.

Exercise: Energize Me!

1. Load the battery.dxf file into your rendering program and light the scene so you can clearly see the battery surfaces. You should also position the

Figure 9.36 *The basic battery model.*

camera so you have a view similar to the one in Figure 9.36. Next, add a ground plane with an image map surface. We will be making the model reflective and you can't create photorealistic surfaces without having surfaces in the environment to reflect. A simple ground plane with a wood or marble surface will do nicely.

2. Now we can surface the model. We'll start by setting the two surfaces on the battery, chrome, and label, to maximum smoothing and disabling the double-sided feature since it's unnecessary. We won't be surfacing the chrome portion since it would be done with procedural textures and we aren't quite ready to look at those yet. For this exercise you can just load one of the default chrome surfaces that came with your program or possibly one you have created yourself. Let's put some image map on this battery.

3. Select the LABEL surface, open the color layer, and cylindrically map the E_color.jpg image along the y axis. Be sure to wrap the image only once. This, of course, puts the basic color image on the battery. Go ahead and render the battery. You should have an image similar to Figure 9.37.

   You can see that it doesn't look much like an actual Energizer battery. Let's ignore the fact that it has no specularity and focus on the fact that there should be chrome where there is currently a light gray color. Now, we could have created unique surfaces to give these areas a chrome look but that would have been next to impossible considering the level of detail in, and around, the chrome areas. You could spend a year on the model and never reach the photorealistic level. Nope, for this task there is only one method that makes sense—image maps. What we're going to do is use several image maps to create a chrome surface on the battery. Let's start by adding a reflection image map. Take a look at the reflection image map we'll be using shown in Figure 9.38.

   You can see several areas with different shades of gray, which represent the different reflective areas of the battery label. We want to make the chrome areas about 50 percent reflective and the plastic areas about 12 percent reflective. This means the chrome areas on the reflection image map will be light gray and the plastic will be dark gray. Let's put the reflection image map on the battery.

4. Select the LABEL surface, open the reflection layer, and cylindrically map the E_refl.jpg image along the y axis. Be sure to wrap the image only once. This makes the surfaces reflective but the chrome parts still won't look right because we haven't added the second half of the metal formula—diffusion. In fact, they look downright scary because we're adding reflection to a surface that currently has 100 percent diffusion. Go

Figure 9.37 *The battery with color image map.*

Figure 9.38 *The battery reflection image map.*

Figure 9.39 *The battery with reflection image map added.*

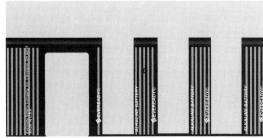

Figure 9.40 *The battery diffusion image map.*

ahead and render the battery to see what I'm talking about. You should have an image that resembles the one in Figure 9.39.

Notice how the chrome area on the label is completely washed out. This is the result of using 100 percent diffusion and high reflectivity. Let's fix this problem by adding a diffusion image map. Take a look at the diffusion image map for the battery in Figure 9.40.

Here we have a similar image to the reflection map except the colors are somewhat reversed. We can see that the chrome areas are very dark, which means they will show very little of their own color. This is important because metals are highly reflective and don't show much of their own color. Lowering the diffusion in the chrome area will clear up the problem we encountered when we added the reflection map. You can see that the plastic areas of the surface have a higher level of diffusion. We definitely want to show plenty of their color since this is the labeled part of the image. Let's put the diffusion image map on the battery label.

5. Select the LABEL surface, open the diffusion layer, and cylindrically map the E_diff.jpg image along the y axis. Be sure to wrap the image only once. Now go ahead and render the battery to see what it looks like. You should have an image that resembles the one in Figure 9.41. Now the battery is starting to look like the real deal. We have only two image map types to go.

If you look at the top of the battery you'll notice the conspicuous absence of a specular highlight. This is because we haven't added any specularity to the surface. We could use a global specularity value but that won't work since metals have very low specularity and shiny plastic has a rather high specularity. We'll need to use another image map so we can provide a different specularity level for the metal and plastic surfaces. Well, I suppose we should take a look at the specularity image map. Take a look at Figure 9.42.

You can see that the chrome area of the battery has a specularity value of zero since it's completely black. This is a typical value for chrome since a specular highlight would only wash out the surface. Now take a look at the plastic region of the image map. Notice that a medium value of gray was used to make the plastic parts slightly specular. This was done because the paper label that covers the battery is somewhat pliable, and if we use a higher level of specularity it will appear too hard. That about does it for the specularity map discussion. Well, what are we waiting for? Let's add the specularity image map to the battery label.

6. Select the LABEL surface, open the specularity layer, and cylindrically map the E_spec.jpg image along the y axis. Be sure to wrap the image only once. Now render the battery to see how the specularity has been added. You should have an image that resembles the one in Figure 9.43.

Now we finally have a photorealistic Energizer battery, or do we? Well, it may be nit-picking but we have one little detail left to add. Take a look at the middle of the battery and you'll notice a notch is taken out of the bands. This is where you'll normally find a couple small letters that have been embossed on the surface of the battery label. To make our battery completely photorealistic we'll need to add the embossing with a bump image map. Of course, this is a very simple image map. It's basically all black with a couple of white letters where we want the bump to be located. I would show it but it's likely you wouldn't even see the letters. Let's get right to adding the bump image map to our battery label.

Figure 9.41 *The battery with diffusion image map applied.*

Figure 9.42 *The battery specularity image map.*

Figure 9.43 *The battery with specularity image map applied.*

Figure 9.44 *The final battery with bump image map applied.*

7. Select the LABEL surface, open the bump layer, and cylindrically map the E_bump.jpg image along the *y* axis. Be sure to wrap the image only once and set the bump value to 100 percent. This will emboss two little letters on the side of the battery as shown in Figure 9.44. If you have image antialiasing it would be a good idea to use it. The antialiasing will smooth the bump so it doesn't seem too rigid.

Now that's more like it. I'd say we've done a pretty impressive job of turning a simple model into a very advanced photorealistic object. You can see how image maps play a major role in making an object photorealistic. In fact, you can use them to create a variety of unique material types on the same surface as we did with the battery.

Now that we have a handle on the basic image maps, let's have a little fun with transparency and luminosity.

Working with Transparency and Luminosity Image Maps

I thought we'd take a stab at surfacing something with transparency and luminosity image maps. We're going to create a photorealistic, burning cigarette by using transparency and luminosity image maps. This cigarette would make the surgeon general proud; it's the only cigarette you can smoke that doesn't cause cancer. There's no safer way to smoke. Enough of the public service announcement. Let's take a look at the cigarette model we'll be using. Take a look at Figure 9.45.

Here you can see a simple cigarette model with ashes protruding from the end. Don't worry about the ashes that penetrate the wrapper. We'll be using a transparency image map to remove the end of the wrapper that covers the ashes. We're going to need a few images in the tutorial file you downloaded from the companion Web site so make sure you have the following images.

Figure 9.45 *The cigarette model.*

- CigColor.jpg
- CigBump.jpg
- CigButt.jpg
- CigLume.jpg
- CigFilter.jpg

Now that we have all the images, let's begin the exercise.

Exercise: Smokin'

The first thing you need to do is load the cigarette.3ds file into your rendering program and light the scene so you can clearly see the cigarette surfaces. You should also position the camera so you have a view similar to the one in Figure 9.45. Before we apply the special effect image maps, we'll need to lay a foundation with the basic image maps. We'll leave the ashes a neutral color since they would normally be surfaced with procedural textures, which we don't cover until Chapter 10, "Procedural Textures." Let's add the basic image maps now.

1. Select the FILTER surface, open the color layer, and planar map the CigButt.jpg image on the y axis. Be sure to size the image so it covers the whole surface. This will create a nasty, tar-filled filter so the cigarette looks like it's been used.

2. Now select the WRAPPER surface, open the color layer, and cylindrically map the CigColor.jpg image along the y axis. Be sure to wrap the image only once. This, of course, gives the cigarette its paper wrapper color.

3. Now for the final touch we need to add a little crinkling to the paper. For this we'll use a bump image map. With the WRAPPER surface selected, open the bump layer, and cylindrically map the CigBump.jpg image along the y axis. Be sure to wrap the image only once and set the bump value to 50 percent. Use antialiasing if you have it. Let's render the cigarette to see where we are so far. You should have an image that is similar to Figure 9.46.

   I'm sure you notice that I added procedural textures to the ashes. . . . I just couldn't resist it. Now take a look at the end of the cigarette wrapper. Notice how the end of the cigarette has a scorched look, which represents the area of the wrapper that has been burned. We'll be using a filter image map to create an irregular edge on the end of the wrapper so it actually looks like paper has been burned away. Now take a look at the ring of orange color near the end of the wrapper, which represents the burning portion of the wrapper. We'll be using a luminosity image map

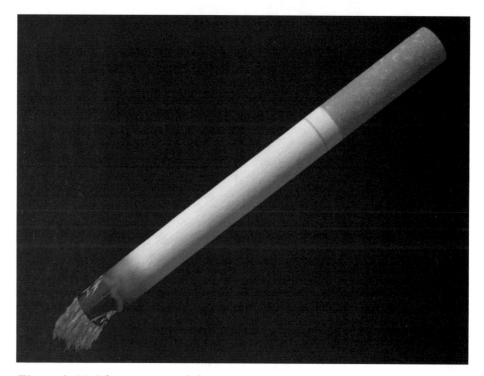

Figure 9.46 *The cigarette with basic image map surfacing.*

to make this area of the wrapper illuminate as though it's actually burning. Let's add these two image maps now.

4. Select the WRAPPER surface, open the transparency layer, and cylindrically map the CigFilter.jpg image along the *y* axis. Be sure to wrap the image only once. This, of course, cuts off the end of the cigarette wrapper in an irregular manner so it appears to have been burned away.

5. Now open the luminosity layer, and cylindrically map the CigLume.jpg image along the *y* axis. Be sure to wrap the image only once. This will make the orange ring at the end of the filter illuminate as though it's burning. Let's render the cigarette to see how it looks. Your cigarette should resemble the one in Figure 9.47.

Now that's a good-looking smoke. Notice how the end of the wrapper has an irregular shape, like the paper has been burned away. Now take a look at the glowing orange coloration around the edge. This makes it look like the cigarette is actually burning. You can almost feel the heat.

Now let's take a look at the images to the right. These images represent the transparency and luminosity image maps that were used to surface the cigarette. The first image is the transparency image map. Notice how it's basically all black

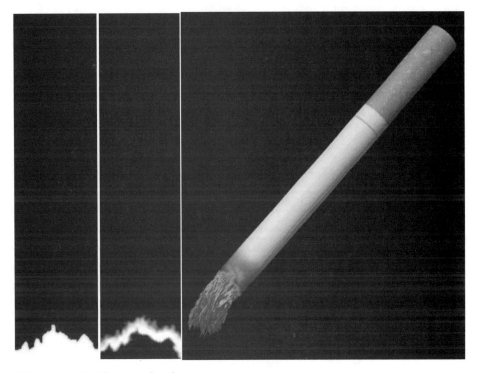

Figure 9.47 *The completed cigarette.*

with a small portion of white at the end. This is the transparent portion of the image map. Now take a look at the image to the right, which is the luminosity image map. Here we have a similar image but this time there is an irregular while line across the bottom, which represents the luminous portion of the image. You can see how these two image maps have transformed the cigarette into a truly photorealistic object.

That about does it for this exercise. You can see that transparency and luminosity image maps can be used to create some rather stunning visual effects. Try to use your imagination when surfacing your objects. You'll be surprised at the number of uses you'll find for transparency and luminosity image maps.

Taking a Breath

That was a whole lot of information on image maps. The good news is that the coming chapter, Chapter 10, "Procedural Textures," isn't nearly as long or intense. Don't get me wrong: The exploration of procedural textures is awesome; it just doesn't make your head explode like image maps do.

Why don't you sit back and relax a moment before you dive into Chapter 10?

10 *Procedural Textures*

Procedural textures are one of the most important elements of 3D photorealism surfacing, since they give you an unparalleled flexibility in creating surface chaos. Unfortunately, they seem to be rarely used when surfacing 3D objects. How often do you see 3D images where the surfaces are completely smooth? How about surfaces that have a consistent coloration, or even a consistent specularity? Well, it seems these are problems with nearly every 3D image. Fortunately, they can be easily corrected with the use of procedural textures.

So what are procedural textures? Well, they are mathematical algorithms that create surface effects in 3D space. Boy, that didn't explain it very clearly did it? Let me try that again. Simply put, *procedural textures* are computer-generated surfaces. They are basically 3D versions of the fractal noise that you have been using in painting programs like Photoshop. Since they are computer generated, they offer you several advantages over image map surfaces:

- They conform to irregular objects without pinching or stretching the surface.
- They are nonrepeating over infinite space.
- They have infinite resolution so surfaces won't be pixilated on close-ups.

Probably the best way to explain the differences between procedural textures and image maps is with an actual image, so let's take a look at Figure 10.1.

Take a look at the object on the left, which was surfaced with a cubic image map. You can see that the image map did a fine job of surfacing the object but unfortunately the surfaces aren't seamless and they are also repeating the same image on every side. This, of course, is undesirable for photorealistic surfacing. Yes, we can seamlessly surface the object with image maps but that would take quite a bit of effort and would require several image maps.

On the other hand, we could quickly surface the object with a procedural texture as shown on the object to the right. Notice how the texture seamlessly wraps

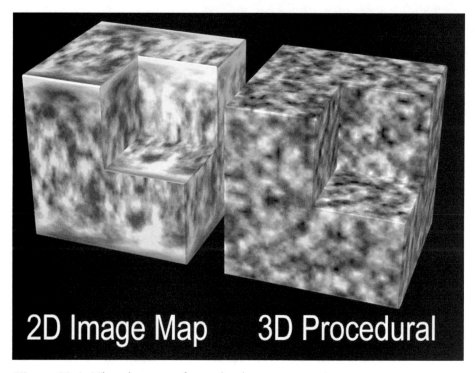

Figure 10.1 *The advantage of procedural textures over image maps.*

around the object. This is one of the main advantages of procedural textures. Now take a close look and you'll notice that the surfaces are unique on every side, which is another advantage of procedural textures. As you can see, there are distinct advantages to using procedural textures to surface your objects.

Of course, this example isn't exactly photorealistic but don't let that fool you into thinking that procedural textures are limited to nonphotorealistic applications. They are actually the foundation of most photorealistic surfaces. There are literally thousands of procedural textures that have been created for 3D application. Some programs have an enormous number of procedural textures, while others merely have a few standard ones. The quantity, type, and application of procedural textures vary widely among 3D programs, which makes it difficult to go into any real detail on specific procedural textures.

Fortunately, there is really only one procedural texture that is indispensable when it comes to creating photorealistic surfaces, and it happens to be common to nearly every 3D program. The procedural texture is called fractal noise. Let's take a look at fractal noise and see how it can be used to add photorealistic surface chaos to all your models.

Creating Photorealistic Detail
with Fractal Noise

Fractal noise is the foundation of all procedural textures. In fact, all procedural textures are built upon the fractal noise concept. *Fractal noise* is merely random noise that is generated based on a few parameters, which include the *x, y,* and *z* size, frequencies, and amplitude. With these parameters you can control the size and volume of the noise. In fact, the surfaces-in-comparison image we viewed in the beginning of the chapter were created with fractal noise.

Fractal noise is the most valuable procedural texture because it is used to apply color, diffusion, specularity, and bump chaos to surfaces, making it the most versatile procedural texture in your surface arsenal. Let's take a look at each of the applications for fractal noise to see how they can add photorealistic credibility to your surfaces. We'll start by taking a look at using fractal noise to create bump textures.

Creating Surface Textures with Fractal Noise

Every surface in reality has a bump texture. While it may be too small to actually feel, there is still a visible texture that has an impact on the specularity, reflectivity, and diffusion of the surface. Therefore, we need to ensure that we apply a bump texture to all of our surfaces. Of course, this could take a great deal of time using image maps, particularly since the bump texture on most surfaces is very small, which would make creating an image map rather time consuming. So what is the solution? Simply use a fractal noise bump texture.

Adding surface texture with a fractal noise bump is very simple. In fact, most surfaces have a very similar subtle surface bump. The majority of surfaces have a very minor bump texture, which actually looks a lot like the gritty surface of sandpaper. Of course, it's nowhere near as gritty but it looks similar just the same. You'll be surprised to know that the surface bump for metal, plastic, paper, wood, marble, and even clay is actually the same. It's simply a pattern of very small bumps that break up the specularity on the surface. Of course, I'm referring to the fine surface bump and not the physical grain. The grain is an entirely different texture, which needs to be applied with image maps since its pattern is very specific, like that of paper or wood.

What is the real impact of a fractal noise bump on the surface? Does it really make that much of a difference? You better believe it does. In fact, let's take a look at an example of how a fractal noise bump texture transforms a rather plain surface into one that is convincingly photorealistic.

Figure 10.2 *The impact of a fractal bump texture.*

Figure 10.2 shows two open-end wrenches that are both surfaced with a chromed alloy surface, but the one on the right also has a fractal bump texture. Notice how the wrench with the fractal bump surface looks more realistic because it actually breaks up the reflection on the surface. You will see only one metal surface in reality that is relatively smooth and that's chrome. In fact, chrome even needs a subtle surface bump texture to appear photorealistic. You can see that the addition of a simple fractal bump texture has transformed the wrench on the right into a photorealistic object.

The actual process for applying the fractal bump texture varies from program to program but the principle is basically the same. If you look closely at the surface of the wrench on the right you'll notice that the texture looks like it's been brushed. Most metals have a brushed surface texture, which is very easy to create with fractal noise. To create the brushed metal look we simply opened the bump layer on the surface and applied a very small fractal noise texture with the following values:

Texture size .0002 (x), .00002 (y), .0002 (z)

Texture amplitude   35%

Frequencies 3

Before we get into what these values represent it's necessary to point out that your program may refer to them by a different name or it may not be able to create the same settings. If this is the case, you will need to do a little experimentation to find the proper setting, but the values just listed will give you a good starting point.

What do these values mean? The first thing we need to look at is the *size of the texture,* which is expressed in inches. You can see that the numbers are extremely small, making them a mere fraction of an inch. In fact, some programs may not allow you to use values this small, which is really just fine since all you need to do is ensure that the texture is tiny. You can see that the *y*-axis value is much smaller than the other two, which is how we created the brushed look. We have basically stretched the texture out along the *y* axis so it appears long and thin, like brush strokes.

Now take a look at the *texture amplitude,* which controls the actual altitude, or strength, of the bump. We want to make the bump relatively strong since we are making a rugged metal surface. You'll find that metal objects are actually significantly more reflective that they appear since the bump texture tends to diffuse the reflection so it isn't as prominent. In fact, you can see this by looking at the wrenches in Figure 10.2. Both of them have the same reflection value, but the wrench on the left appears more reflective because it doesn't have a surface bump. It is necessary to diffuse the reflection of metal surfaces so they look realistic.

Now we need to take a look at the *frequencies* attribute, which creates variations of the texture so it doesn't appear perfect. This attribute is often referred to as a random seed or possibly turbulence depending on the program you are using. You'll find the way your program handles this value may be different, so make sure that you apply some variance to the texture so it doesn't appear perfect.

As you can see, it's rather simple to create a convincing fractal bump texture. The great thing is that this same fractal bump texture can be used on all metals. In fact, let's take a look at another image that shows multiple uses for the fractal bump texture, shown in Figure 10.3.

Here we have four different metals that were surfaced with the same fractal bump texture we just discussed. You can see how it has made these surfaces appear very realistic, and we didn't have to change any of the fractal bump texture settings. Of course, if we did change the settings, we could create an entirely different surface bump texture. If we simply change the *y*-axis value so it's the same as the *x* and *z,* we'll have the perfect fractal noise bump texture to surface rubber and plastic. Let's take a look at an image that shows the fractal bump texture being used to create photorealistic plastic, shown in Figure 10.4.

Here we have a photorealistic cordless phone compliments of the fractal bump texture. Take a look at the receiver cup in the handset and you'll see how the fractal bump texture breaks up the specularity, which adds tremendous photore-

Figure 10.3 *Using the same fractal bump texture to create multiple surfaces.*

Figure 10.4 *Using fractal bump textures to create photorealistic plastic.*

alistic credibility to the plastic surface. The great thing is that this texture is nearly the same as the brushed metal texture; we had to make only one simple change to the *y*-axis value.

The fractal bump texture is a powerful tool for creating photorealistic surfaces, particularly when there is a need for small details. You should make an effort to use it on every surface you create. It's also very useful for aging your surfaces.

Aging Your Surfaces with Fractal Noise

There's no faster way to age your surfaces than using fractal noise because it allows you to add random chaos without spending hours editing image maps. There are two elements of surface aging that can be accomplished with fractal noise. You can use it to add discoloration to your surfaces, as well as diffuse random spots to simulate grease and grime. Let's take a look at an image that incorporates a great deal of fractal noise to age limestone blocks. Take a look at Figure 10.5.

Here we have a scene that is entirely surfaced with procedural textures, except for the bump image map, which was used to create individual blocks. Take a close look at the limestone blocks and you'll see a variety of colors, which were cre-

Figure 10.5 *Aging surfaces with fractal noise.*

ated with a simple fractal noise in the color layer. The great thing about fractal noise is that you can use the same technique no matter where you apply it. Creating the color fractal noise for this image was pretty much the same technique we used to create the fractal bump texture in the examples we saw earlier. The only difference is that you'll want to make the noise texture larger since you'll want to see it clearly on the surface, as in the limestone surface which used a size of 6 inches on all three axes.

Of course, limestone has several colors on its surface so multiple layers of fractal noise were used, each layer being a different color. Some programs actually limit you to a single layer of fractal noise, which can make detailed surfacing difficult. Under these circumstances, you may need to use image maps to apply enough detail to the surface. If you do have the capability for multiple texture layers, you can create an amazing variety of surfaces with fractal noise. In fact, let's look at another image that was fully surfaced with multiple layers of fractal noise.

Figure 10.6 shows the Dweller's tunnel where Gizmo lives. Yes, Gizmo has moved. You see, Papagaio passed away shortly after bringing Gizmo to life, so Gizmo set out to find a new home where he could secretly build a race of cognitive thinking robots without being discovered. If you take a look in the lower left corner you'll see an illuminated tunnel which happens to be the entrance to Gizmo's secret hideaway.

Nearly every surface in this image was created using fractal noise on the color, specularity, and diffusion layers. In fact, the only surfaces that weren't created with fractal noise are the caution signs and the tunnel's metal plate bump. Let's start by looking at the fractal noise on the wall. You'll notice that the wall is gray with a variety of brownish streaks running down it. These streaks were created with fractal noise, much the same way the brushed metal texture was created, except obviously larger values were used so the grime would be visible. In addition to a color fractal noise we also added a diffusion fractal noise to prevent the grimy spots from being too specular. All we did was make the diffusion fractal noise the same size as the color one so they would line up correctly.

You can see that the pipes running through the tunnel are rusted. This rust was created using fractal noise on the color, specularity, diffusion, and bump layers. Basically several layers of color fractal noise were added to create the reddish color and then the fractal noise bump was added to make it look corroded. To really make it look like rust, a specularity fractal noise, the same size as the bump texture, was added to make the tops of the bumps more specular. Finally, a diffusion fractal noise was added to make the lower parts of the bumps darker, which adds depth to the rust surface. As you can see, it took several types of fractal noise to create the rust but it actually took less than two minutes to create. It would take you that long just to set up the color image map for painting. You can see the definite advantage of procedural textures when it comes to quickly aging surfaces.

Figure 10.6 *Using multiple layers of fractal noise to age surfaces.*

I could go on all day discussing the fractal noise effects in this image but I think you get the idea. There is one more effect in this image that deserves attention before we move on. We might as well take a look as to how atmosphere effects are created with fractal noise, since they are rather impressive.

Creating Atmosphere Effects with Fractal Noise

Would you believe that the two fog layers and fire flames were created with a simple fractal noise texture? It's true, and it took only a matter of minutes to accomplish. Let's take a look at how the fog was done first. Actually it's rather simple; all that we did was add a fractal noise texture to the transparency layer, which made parts of the fog object surface transparent. It was really that easy. The fog object was just a simple model with a few bumps and dents to make the fog look like it was sort of rolling through the tunnel.

How did we create the fire flames? The same way we created the fog but this time we added a fractal noise texture to the luminosity layer so the flames would glow brightly. As you can see, it's very easy to create astounding effects with fractal noise. By now I'm sure you're getting the idea that there is literally no end to the number of uses for fractal noise. Well, if there is a limit I haven't found it yet.

Fractal noise is a very versatile procedural texture, which you can use to make countless objects appear photorealistic. Don't limit yourself to simply creating fractal bump textures or even color details; use your imagination and explore the literally thousands of possibilities for fractal noise. In fact, see what you can do with the luminosity layer. I'll bet you can create some awesome glowing fog or even green smelly ooze if you just spend a little time exploring the versatility of the texture. You name it because the sky is the limit. Speaking of sky, how about some nice flowing fractal clouds? Getting any ideas yet?

Of course this is just fractal noise we're talking about. It's likely you have access to even more procedural texture, which you can use to create dazzling photorealistic effects. I would really love to cover more types of procedural textures but I'm afraid we don't have enough pages. A chapter on all the procedural textures would read like *War and Peace.* I'll tell you what I'll do. I'll post more information about procedural textures on the companion Web site. Check www.wiley.com/compbooks/fleming for the details.

It's All About Where You Put It

Well, now that we have a handle on object surfacing we're ready to tackle the challenge of photorealistic staging, which happens to be one of the most enjoyable aspects of 3D photorealism rendering. It's where we get to explore the roots of chaos and get inside the minds of both our characters and objects. Yes, I said objects. They have personality, too, you know.

What are we waiting for? Let's dive in and create a little chaos!

PART IV
Photorealistic Staging Techniques

You've spent hours modeling and surfacing the most perfect photorealistic objects ever, so now what? Well, it's time to put those models to good use. Now that you have a plethora of photorealistic objects you can begin to build realistic environments. Of course, this requires a thorough study of reality.

All too often it seems that 3D artists focus all their energy on the models and surfacing, and completely neglect the staging. It doesn't matter how realistic the models appear, if you stage them improperly you'll end up with a scene that is denied photorealistic credibility. The funny thing is that staging objects is the most entertaining aspect of the 3D photorealism process. It's where you get to become the film director. Actually, it's more like becoming Sherlock Holmes.

You need to discover the clues that make your scene credible. Then you need to include those clues in your scene so the viewer doesn't have to be Sherlock Holmes to understand it. You don't want to make it difficult for the viewer to grasp the concept behind your scene, since the attention span of the average viewer is very short. To maintain their attention you have to leave them enough visual clues so they can decipher the scene. You want to spark their imagination and pull them into the image so they become a part of the story.

In this part, we will be going on a journey of exploration to discover the visual clues that make a scene photorealistic. We'll submerse ourselves in chaos theory, psychology, and even a little herpetology. It's going to be a wild ride, so fasten your seatbelts because we're on our way.

One last thing: There are no rest stops for at least one chapter so you'd better go before we leave. I don't want to hear you complaining about a rest stop after three paragraphs.

VISIT THE COMPANION WEB SITE FOR COLOR IMAGES.

Before you begin Part IV, go to Appendix F and learn about the companion Web site. All of the figures shown in this book are mirrored, in color, on the companion Web site at www.wiley.com/compbooks/fleming. I recommend you visit the site and view the images while you read the book, or download the images for faster reference. There will be details in the figures that you can't see in the printed image.

11 *Planning Your Scene*

Planning your scene is probably the most enjoyable aspect of creating photorealistic 3D images. It's where you get to do a little role playing. Have you ever wanted to be an actor? Well, now is your chance. In fact, you get to be actor, director, writer, and producer. That's a lot of hats to wear. Actually, it all boils down to getting into character with your scene. I know, it sounds a bit weird but it's necessary if you want the scene to be believable.

How do we get into character? That's where the fun begins. It's where you get to be the detective. Actually, it's where you become a 3D Profiler.

Becoming a 3D Profiler

We've all seen those psychological thrillers where the brilliant detective tracked down the genius serial killer. How did he do it? He became the killer. Well, he didn't actually become the killer, but he started to think like the killer. He got inside the killer's mind to see how he worked. The goal is to determine how the killer thinks so you can anticipate his next move. The FBI calls this procedure *profiling*.

There is a parallel between the profiling concept and developing photorealistic staging. To effectively stage a photorealistic scene you have to get inside the minds of characters who inhabit it, so you can understand the way they think. If you don't understand the personality of these characters, you can't possibly stage the scene properly.

How do you become a 3D Profiler? The first step is to gain a working knowledge of the five major personality types. That's right, it all starts with a little psychology. Once you have a handle on the major personality types you can quickly determine the environment for any potential character that would be involved with your scene.

Let's examine the traits of each personality type and explore the impact they have on their environment. There are actually five personality types and they are conveniently named A, B, C, D, and E.

The Type A Personality

Type A is the Midas character—everything they touch turns to gold. They buy swampland and the next day there's a freeway running through it with an off ramp in their backyard. They're those annoying people who always have the right answer and are always in the right place at the right time. Murphy's law doesn't touch these people, but we'd certainly like to get our hands on them.

These people are extreme about everything so you can bet the word moderation doesn't exist in their vocabulary. They are usually entrepreneurs and workaholics so you'll most likely find them sitting in the president's chair, that is, if they actually take the time to sit down. These are fast-paced people who rarely take the opportunity to experience the simple pleasures in life. You definitely won't find any of these people on your local bowling team.

Type As are stubborn, persistent, decisive, very independent, and analytical. They are skilled in many areas, emotionally stable, and easily turn problems into opportunities. They enjoy the challenge and play to win. These are the leaders who inspire people with their dedication and talent.

Simply put, they are the leaders.

The Type A Environment

The type A environment is painfully neat and organized. These are very well organized people who have a filing system for everything. They surround themselves with new things, which they believe helps spawn their creativity and energy. They live in an upscale community, drive expensive cars, and wear expensive clothes. For them the label is more important than the look. They hate antiques and crave high-tech toys. Everything in their environment is a showpiece, a statement of their success.

They can't stand disorganization or clutter, so their space is very neat and well kept. The furniture is art deco, modern, and typically leather. The entire house is lit with indirect lighting that comes from European-style lamps. You can expect a phone in every room and probably one in the bathroom since they are constantly working a deal. They always have an office in the home where you'll find a plethora of high-tech toys. You'll definitely find a computer in their home and you can expect it to be an out of the box brand since they don't have the time or concern to shop around for the best prices.

Good examples of type A characters would be.

Sigourney Weaver in the *Alien* series

Sean Connery as Agent 007

Patrick Stewart as Jean Luc Picard

The Type B Personality

Type B personalities are the happy-go-lucky individuals who you'll find dancing on the table with the lampshade on their head. They are the party people who are filled with energy and crave the good times. They live for today because tomorrow is a long way off.

These people are very impatient, demanding, and sometimes quite childlike. They love parties, traveling, music, and anything to do with a lot of noise and hype. They will talk for hours about anything because they like the sound of their own voice. They are typically salespeople, musicians, artists, or hair stylists. Yes, they love to gossip and they always seem to have way too much energy.

They are creative, artistic, outgoing, talkative, and persuasive people. They are usually cheerful, spontaneous, and enjoy a fast-paced atmosphere. They get bored very easily and usually get along with most people. You usually refer to these personalities as the people that make you laugh.

Simply put, they are the artistic entertainers.

The Type B Environment

Try to picture the eye of a tornado, with everything whirling around in complete chaos and you've nailed the type B environment. Here is an environment that is filled with a plethora of knickknacks, collectibles, and just about anything else you can imagine. You are guaranteed to find a layer of dust on almost everything since they don't have a cleaning person and are too busy flirting with the world to do it themselves.

Their furniture is all cloth and most likely very old. You can bet that nothing in the house matches. It's the type of place you'll find in an interior decorator's nightmares. They are just too busy to worry about how things look. You can expect to find clutter in every room. Their idea of organization is "I know it's in this pile somewhere." The TV is always on and there's probably a radio playing somewhere in the house. You can bet they are always losing the TV remote. You'll find a pile of extraordinary items somewhere close to the door where they empty their pockets as they enter the house.

They are likely to have a computer but it's sure to be a late model, that is, unless they are computer artists. Then the computer is likely to be an off brand since they shopped for the best price. You can bet that they are on-line, frequently chatting it up on the Internet.

Good examples of type B characters would be:

Bob Hope

Goldie Hawn

Dom DeLuise

Martin Short

Robin Williams

The Type C Personality

Type C people take everything seriously. They need structure and direction in their day-to-day routine. They strive for perfection and consistency. They are very low keyed, methodical, not very excitable. They tend to be humanitarians and environmentally conscious. They are usually accountants, lawyers, and politicians.

They are steady, serious, consistent, and patient. They tend to be very detail neurotic, if not completely neurotic and they are motivated by maps, charts, and graphs. Their average decision-making time is around a month, which means their mortal enemy is the used car salesman.

They are very analytical. They spend enormous amounts of time on a simple problem or decision because they can't make a decision until they have thoroughly researched all of the facts and figures. They like nonfiction books, manuals, and educational television programs. In fact, they read the entire software manual before installing the program. They are deep, thoughtful, and sensitive. Simply put, they are perfectionists.

The Type C Environment

Picture a library with a bed in the middle of it and you've got the perfect type C environment. You can expect to find a literal pile of books in every room. Their furniture is older and they probably have a lot of antiques. You can expect to find dust everywhere since they are too busy analyzing everything to clean the house. They aren't messy people but their house is in chaos. There will be piles of paper everywhere you look and the rooms are primarily lit with reading lamps. You won't find many decorative items in the house. You are likely to find collectibles like stamp collections or similar items.

What you will find in their house is absolutely everything they have encountered in their lifetime. These people hang on to everything because they hate waste and actually get emotionally attached to items. You'll find they don't park their car in the garage because it's full of stuff they are saving, which is far more important to them than the car. Everything has a use so they can't possibly part with it.

You won't find many high-tech items in a type C environment. They probably have a black-and-white TV since color is meaningless to them. Everything in their world is black and white. Not the colors, but their approach. The rooms are dimly lit and the drapes are always closed. If they have a computer, it's likely to be several years out of date.

Good examples of type C characters would be:

Commander Data, *Star Trek—The Next Generation*

Sir Isaac Newton

Socrates

Albert Einstein

The Type D Personality

Type D personalities are known as happy-go-lucky individuals who aren't in any hurry. Nothing matters much to these people and we often envy them because nothing seems to get to them. They are content being where they are and with what they have. They float through life enjoying each day as it comes. They are most likely nurses, teachers, administrators, and secretaries. They are more than satisfied with mundane jobs that need to be done. They enjoy doing the jobs that would drive most of us completely nuts with boredom.

They are neither fast-paced nor slow-paced. They tend to be emotionally stable and have a good sense of humor. They are low-keyed, charming, competent, calm, patient, and compassionate. They are good listeners and they like to be involved in everything but rarely accept responsibility for any of it.

They usually need a structured environment and their energy level is consistent and well paced. They are very balanced, persuasive, and charming. They set realistic goals and cope well with problem situations but rarely try to solve them. Basically, they are content.

The Type D Environment

The type D environment is very understated and well balanced, basically a neutral environment that doesn't have too much order or chaos. The items in their environment are neither new nor old. They have some antiques, a few older items, and the occasional new item. They don't have a lot of high-tech toys, but they do have the basics like a color TV, VCR, and stereo, none of which are extraordinary.

You'll find their rooms are relatively neat with scattered spots of chaos that are balanced by areas of organization. We're looking at a fairly neutral environment here.

Good examples of type D characters would be:

Cliff, from the sitcom *Cheers*

George Washington

David Copperfield

Charles Dickens

Sherlock Holmes' faithful sidekick, Dr. Watson

The Type E Personality

The type E personality is very rare. Only one in 1000 people have a true type E personality. These characters can go a number of directions since they are an equal combination of all four types of personalities. They are known as the chameleons since they mirror the personality of the people they are with. This means that their personality changes quite frequently throughout the day. They can be any of the four group personalities at any time.

The Type E Environment

When creating the type E personality, it's basically an "anything goes" situation. You have the freedom to mirror any of the other personality type environments and even mix them. You can have a lot of fun staging a scene for a type E personality. You can combine computers with antiques, clutter, areas of organization, high-tech toys, and complete chaos.

Now that we have a relatively detailed description of each personality type, what's next? You'll find that it's very difficult to neatly squeeze someone into any one personality type. In fact, you'll find that most of us have split personalities. Let's take a look at how this works.

It Takes Two Personalities to Tango

While we may lean toward a specific personality type, we are actually a combination of two. We have a dominant personality with a little bit of another. This, of course, will have an impact on the environment around us, which will end up being a hybrid of the two personality types, with the dominant one prevailing. In fact, let's take a look at a scene and see if we can profile the character who is responsible for creating it.

Figure 11.1 shows Gizmo in Papagaio's workshop. Let's see if we can profile Papagaio. It should be easy to do by simply examining the objects in the image. The first thing we notice is that we are looking at Gizmo, which is an artistic and creative creation. This is a strong trait of type B personalities who are quite often artists. Of course, we immediately notice that Gizmo is made of discarded junk, which means there is no way Papagaio is a type A personality since they would go insane looking at something old and dirty.

Figure 11.1 *3D profiling a rendered scene.*

On the other hand, type C personalities love to collect old stuff and are quite at home with dirt. In fact, they are also concerned about the environment, which means they would be prone to recycling old stuff in an effort to clean up the world. I think it's safe to say that Gizmo is comprised of recycled parts. Speaking of Gizmo, we know that he is a cognitive thinking robot, so we must assume that it required a lot of patience and research to design him, which are additional traits of a type C personality. Hmmm, it looks like we have a winner here.

What does our brief analysis tell us? It would seem that Papagaio is a type C personality with type B traits. He possesses many of the type C characteristics but only a few of the type B. He is best described as a quiet man who is patient, very detail neurotic, analytical, and artistic. We now have a blueprint for creating Papagaio's environment. We can now easily create any room in his house with frightening accuracy.

You can see how 3D profiling is a powerful tool for creating believable environments. There is much more to staging a scene than just dropping a few objects in a room. You need to tell a story with the scene so the viewer becomes intrigued, and the only way you can effectively accomplish this is to get into character with your scene—you've got to become a 3D Profiler.

Honing Your 3D Profiling Skills

A person's personality determines his or her environment, which means that once you determine the personality type you'll be able to stage the scene with great accuracy. It's really a lot of fun.

You now have the personality background information to be an effective 3D Profiler. All you need to do is determine the personality type of the characters involved with the scene and you're well on your way to creating photorealistic staging.

You know, if you're really daring you could turn the focus on yourself and create your 3D profile. Who knows what you'll discover? I'm sure after reading this book, you'll have no trouble determining my personality type. In fact, I recommend that you wander over to your friends' houses and discretely 3D profile them to warm up your 3D profiling skills. I'm sure you'll be fascinated with your findings and you'll probably never look at them the same way again.

That does it for our exploration of planning your scene. It really comes down to understanding the personalities of the character involved with your scene, so be sure to spend some time working on your 3D profiling skills because you'll definitely be needing them.

Time to Wreak Havoc!

Well, it's the moment we've been waiting for. It's time to explore chaos! Now we get to journey deep into the heart of chaos and unearth the secrets to creating photorealistic staging.

Before we dive into chaos, we should take a break. You should definitely approach chaos with a clear head and plenty of energy because Chapter 12, "Adding Chaos—Creating Clutter," is truly a wild ride that will alter the way you look at the world around you. I know it sounds a bit dramatic but you'll soon see.

12 *Adding Chaos—Creating Clutter*

Here we are, back on my favorite topic—*chaos*. As we explained in Chapter 1, reality is chaos. Of course, you probably didn't need me to tell you that. I'm sure you've experienced it many times yourself. No matter how much you may plan or schedule your life, chaos always steps in and alters your plans. If you are ever in doubt, just consult Murphy's Law. I can't count the number of times that Murphy has ruined my day. I really don't like that guy.

So what exactly is chaos? Chaos is that maniacal little criminal who corrupts law and order. It's always lurking in the shadows, waiting to act. Okay, so maybe I got a bit carried away. Simply put, chaos is the unexpected. For example: Newton came up with a marvelous theory, which later became a law of physics. What goes up, must come down. Several hundred years later, chaos stepped in and unexpectedly broke that law with satellites and space probes. They go up, but they rarely, if ever, come down. Well, I certainly hope they don't.

Chaos is always searching for that little loophole in the law so it can present us with something unexpected. A hundred years ago they said we couldn't fly, and then we did. Later they said we couldn't achieve manned space flight, and we did. Then they said we couldn't conquer time travel . . . well, chaos just hasn't gotten around to giving us this little gem yet. You get the idea.

ALWAYS ADD AN UNEXPECTED ELEMENT TO YOUR SCENE.

Chaos is the unexpected. To create a truly photorealistic scene you need to add something the viewer does not expect. It doesn't have to be anything major. It can be as simple as knocking over a chess piece. It just needs to be unexpected.

Did you know there are several species of amphibians that actually change their sex if there is a shortage of the opposite sex? Males become females and vice versa. Now if that isn't unexpected I don't know what is. Speaking of amphibians. There is a salamander, commonly referred to as a mud-puppy, which spends its entire life under water . . . unless the pond dries up. When the water level starts to drop, it actually develops lungs and takes to land, never to return to the water again. In fact, if it does return to the water, it will drown. That's chaos. Reality has been trying to teach us to expect the unexpected. We just haven't learned yet. Just when we think we know the rules, they change. There is only one rule that will always remain constant—reality is chaos.

Are you hungry for a little chemistry? Well, I've got the perfect formula for chaos. Just add two parts Order and blend in one part Chaos. It's that easy. Every scene is a mixture of order and chaos. All scenes start with order. Then chaos enters the picture and applies its magic. Remember the chaos formula we discussed in Chapter 1? Here it is again . . . just in case you forgot.

Reality formula: *Order + Chaos = Reality*

I'll bet you're wondering how to apply the formula to your scene? That's exactly what you'll be learning in this chapter. While the formula seems relatively simple, it actually has many smaller components, which we will explore in detail throughout the chapter. We will go into some very detailed exploration of chaos and how it is used to make your 3D scenes photorealistic. So put on your thinking cap and get ready for a wild ride through the theory of 3D chaos.

The Relationship between Order and Chaos

Order and chaos coexist in the same space. How is this possible? Take a look around your office or studio and what do you see? Piles of things all over your desk. Have you ever had anyone try to find anything in those piles? I'll bet they couldn't, but you went right to it. For you, the pile represented order. You knew where everything was, regardless of how chaotic it looked. For the other person, it was complete chaos because he or she didn't understand the order you've created. Here's another example. Take a look at Figure 12.1. It's a rendering of a desk in my office. On this desk I have a stack of JAZ disks. As you can see in the image, five of them are facing one direction while only one is facing the opposite direction. I have one facing the opposite direction so I know it's blank. For me, this is order. For someone who doesn't know why the JAZ disk is facing another direction, it's chaos. If I were to ask them to retrieve the blank disk, they would have no idea which one to choose . . . especially since I rarely label my disks. As you can see, we tend to create our own order out of chaos.

Not convinced? Here's another good example of order and chaos. Take a look at your filing cabinet some time. You'll see dozens of files that are probably in no particular sequence. They represent order because they contain a specific group

Figure 12.1 *An example of ordered chaos.*

of documents. They also represent chaos because they are probably in no particular sequence. In fact, I'm sure that the documents within the folder are not arranged in any particular sequence. Wherever there is order, there is chaos. We just can't escape it.

Let's look at a visual comparison of how chaos is applied to an ordered scene to make it photorealistic. Take a look at Figure 12.2. Here you see an image with several books on a shelf. You'll notice the scene has a few chaotic items, but the books really stand out because they are arranged by size. Although this looks nice, it isn't very realistic. We have to assume that these books are frequently read. They're all 3D reference books so they probably come off the shelf daily. I know mine do. This seems like a small point to nag, but think about it. When was the last time your books were arranged according to size? Probably the first time to put them on the shelf . . . it was probably the last time too. Books are taken from the shelf frequently but rarely get put back immediately. They gather on your desk until you finally get the energy to organize them, because you can't see your desk anymore. You're probably in too big of a rush to neatly arrange them, so you just put them wherever there's a hole. Sense a little chaos coming?

Now take a look at Figure 12.3. Here we have the same scene with just enough chaos applied to make it appear natural. Notice how the books are no

Figure 12.2 *A scene with too much order.*

longer arranged by size. In fact, a couple of books are sitting on the magazine that used to be neatly arranged with the books. You'll notice the bookend is no longer doing its job. It now appears that the 3D Photorealism book has become the bookend. Hey, there's the remote I've been trying to find for the last week. Now why didn't I think to look here? Ah, yes—it's that Murphy guy again. At last, perfect chaos. Now we're getting somewhere.

Chaos has made the bookshelf scene appear more natural. We like to surround ourselves with chaos. In fact, we get a little weird when things are too ordered. This brings up a good question: Why is chaos so critical for photorealism?

Why Is Chaos Critical for Photorealism?

Humans are wired to be chaotic. Excessive order drives us nuts. Have you noticed that everything we really enjoy doing is chaotic? Think about it. We predominantly enjoy movies, TV, and sports. All of these are pure chaos. We like them because they offer us a healthy dose of the unexpected. We have no idea

Figure 12.3 *A balance of order and chaos.*

what will happen next and we love it. If we thought order was exciting, synchronized swimming would be the most popular sport in the Olympics. We like to be surprised. Don't you just hate it when you're in the middle of a book and someone tells you the ending? How about that blabbermouth who gives away the movie's plot? How exciting is the Super Bowl game the second time you see it? Get the idea? We just love to be surprised. Ironically, we also love consistency.

I bet you drive the same route to work every day, even if you've been told there's a quicker route. How about that one coffee cup you've used since the dawn of time? How long have you been watching the same TV shows? You have many places to sit in your living room but you always seem to sit in the same place. In fact, there could be 10 empty seats in the room but if someone is sitting in your seat you'll ask them to move, or you just might become silently homicidal wishing they would move. Have I struck a nerve yet?

We are actually very well balanced in our lives. We rely on order to keep us going, but seek chaos to break the monotony. You'll find we tend to seek order in the physical sense and chaos in the visual sense. For example: The pile of papers is physically located on the desk, but the individual papers are visually disorganized. Just take a look at the things you consistently do the same and you'll notice they all have one thing in common—they are physically related events: sitting in the same place, driving the same way to work, eating the same foods, and so forth. Now examine the chaos in your life. It's probably purely visual, like movies, TV, and watching sports.

It's important to distinguish the difference between physical order and visual chaos. Physical order means the objects are organized physically. For instance, take another look at Figure 12.3 and you'll see that the books are physically ordered on the shelf. They are all located in an easy to find location. This is physical order. Now take another look and you'll see that the books are chaotically piled on the shelf—this is visual chaos. If you look at Figure 12.1, you'll see the JAZ Disks are physically ordered on the desk, but they are also chaotically arranged. You rarely want to apply physical chaos to your scenes. It will throw them out of balance. You wouldn't want to scatter the books or JAZ disks around the room. It just wouldn't look natural. Of course, if the character responsible for developing your scene is a complete slob like Oscar Madison, then physical chaos would be appropriate.

ORDER MUST ONLY BE IN THE PHYSICAL SENSE.

Order should always be represented in the physical sense. For example: Groceries are physically ordered on the shelves. The chaos is visually represented because they are not perfectly aligned, and there are a variety of different box sizes and labels. You want to avoid making visual order. If the boxes were perfectly aligned and all the same size, shape, and color, they would look unnatural because we are not used to seeing visual order.

Take a look at Figure 12.4. Here we have an excellent example of physical order with visual chaos. Notice how the sofa and loveseat are physically ordered around the coffee table. They are neatly arranged to be parallel with the table's edge. This is a must because these objects are experienced physically. We would feel uncomfortable in a room where these items were out of alignment. Oddly though, we are very comfortable with the throw pillows being chaotically tossed on the sofa. That is because it's a visual effect. The sofa is physically ordered but visually chaotic. It's the perfect combination of order and chaos.

Now take a look at the coffee table. While it's physically aligned with the sofa and loveseat, it's also cluttered with a variety of items. This clutter is important for making the scene appear realistic. A room must appear lived-in to be photorealistic. I doubt there is a house where everything on the coffee table is neatly arranged. It certainly isn't my house. Sure, it's probably done when the house is cleaned, but that won't last long. When was the last time you neatly arranged your mail on the table? If you're anything like me, you walk in the door and toss it on the table. That's realistic.

Figure 12.4 *Physical order with visual chaos.*

Here's an experiment for you. Neatly arrange several items on your coffee table as shown in Figure 12.5. Now sit in front of the table and try to watch TV. You'll notice your eyes are continually drawn to the order on the coffee table. Your first impulse will be to add some chaos to the objects. You'll start to become distracted by the order in front of you. Soon, you won't even know what's on the TV; you'll be obsessed with the order on the coffee table. Try to see just how long it takes before you crack under the pressure of visual order, and are forced to throw the coffee table into chaos. I'm sure it won't take more than a couple minutes at best.

So how does this apply to 3D photorealism? That's a great question. The answer is simple: 3D is a visual experience. We're viewing the images to break up the monotony of our lives. We're looking for some chaos—a form of escape. You can see how an organized scene will be very disappointing when we are seeking the unexpected. Chaos is paramount to 3D photorealism because viewers expect it. The last thing we want to do is pull them even deeper into their daily routine. I know it would disappoint me.

How do we implement chaos? This is where the fun begins. Actually, this is where the chaos begins.

Figure 12.5 *The unnatural look of visual order.*

Applying Chaos and Clutter

Simply put, chaos is natural. In fact, the purpose of chaos in a 3D scene is to make it appear natural. Take a look around and you'll see that few things are completely organized. This is because humans have invaded the environment. We spread chaos wherever we go. Have you ever toured a model home? If you have, you probably noticed that the house didn't feel like a home. That's because it was too organized. Everything was neatly arranged and the house lacked clutter. Basically, it didn't have the lived-in look.

Clutter and chaos make a scene appear lived-in. It's important for 3D photorealism scenes to reflect the lived-in look so they feel natural. A model home isn't natural since it's typically too ordered. In reality, we come in contact with many things in the house throughout the day. Rarely do we bother to neatly arrange these items after we have handled them. How often do you place the TV remote control in the same place when you're done using it? Probably not that often, since you keep losing it. I lose mine constantly. We pick up things as we move through the house and deposit them randomly. This is the natural clutter that is paramount for making your 3D scenes realistic.

YOUR SCENES MUST APPEAR LIVED-IN.

3D scenes must reflect the aftermath of human intervention for them to appear photorealistic. Objects need to be pointlessly scattered throughout the scene so it appears lived-in.

Let's take a moment to examine the impact chaos and clutter have on the photorealism of a scene. Take a look at Figure 12.6. It's a simple scene with a dining room table and place settings in front of each chair. Notice how all the chairs are all rotated 90 or 45 degrees on their axis. What are the odds of this happening in reality? Pretty slim unless you live with a team of engineers. Somehow all the elements in the scene are parallel to an axis. If there is one constant in reality, it's that nothing is perfect. It would take a team of engineers to align your dining room table so everything was perfect, and I don't recommend engineers for dinner guests. It also appears that someone took great care to center the burgers on their plates. I don't know too many people with that kind of patience. It must be those engineers again. What we have here is a whole lot of order and no chaos. This scene is seriously unnatural.

In reality, rooms aren't neatly arranged; they are in disarray—unless you're lucky enough to live with Felix Unger. When I use the term *disarray*, I don't

Figure 12.6 *A typically staged 3D scene.*

mean things are thrown around the room as though it's been ransacked, I mean things are out of alignment. When was the last time you walked into a room where everything was in alignment? Probably the last time you toured that model home.

Take a look at Figure 12.7. This is the same scene with the first principle of 3D photorealism applied—Chaos and Clutter. Notice how the chairs are all slightly rotated and positioned at different distances from the table's edge. In fact, one chair is placed against the wall. This helps offset the alignment of the chairs. It also makes the scene appear natural. We have to assume that the dining table is frequently used, so the likelihood of the chairs' being neatly arranged is very slim.

Now take a look at the place settings. See how they are off center? There are even a couple missing. Many 3D artists feel the need to fill every empty space, like there must be a place setting for every chair at the table. This just doesn't happen that often in reality. More often than not, there is an empty seat at the dinner table. Lately it's been mine.

As you can see, clutter and chaos are critical to making a scene appear photo-realistic. We now know that clutter is an important aspect of 3D photorealism, but how do we determine where and when to apply it? This becomes a question of galactic proportions.

Figure 12.7 *Applying natural chaos to a scene.*

Defining an Object's Galaxy

It's time to get spaced out. All you 3D astronomers should grasp this concept immediately. I know this sounds like a tangent but bear with me for a moment. Consider this: A Universe is a large body that has many smaller bodies within its influence. These smaller bodies are referred to as a Galaxies. These Galaxies have objects within their own limited range of influence. These objects are called Satellites. These Satellites revolve around the center of the Galaxy. There are also objects that freely travel the Universe, but are not a part of a Galaxy. These are referred to as Free Bodies. As you can see, there are four major objects in a Universe. There are actually a lot more but there's no point in covering them. Now that we have covered Astronomy 101, let's see how this applies to a 3D scene.

A 3D scene is very much the same as a Universe. In fact, a scene is referred to as an *Object Universe*. It's a large body that has several small bodies (objects) within its influence. Let's take another look at the dining table scene in Figure 12.7 to see how this works. Since the scene is a Universe, it needs a center object that everything revolves around. This is typically the point of focus in the scene. In this scene, the dining table is the heart of the Object Universe. Everything in the scene is positioned in relation to the dining table.

There are also several small Galaxies that are clearly defined within the dining table Object Universe. Take a look at the place mats. Notice how they have a variety of objects within their influence, like the plate, utensils, napkin and glass . . . in other words, there are several objects that sit upon the place mat. These objects fall into the place mat's range of influence because if it were moved, the objects would move with it. This group of objects is referred to as an *Object Galaxy*. I'll bet you're wondering what we call the objects that fall within an Object Galaxy. Well, those are called *Satellite Objects*. Confused yet? Okay, here it is in a nutshell:

Object Universe:	The entire scene
Object Galaxy:	A group of objects that are under the influence of a single common object
Satellite Object:	Objects within an Object Galaxy
Free Object:	Objects within the Object Universe, but not in an Object Galaxy

These are the four staging elements you'll find in every photorealistic 3D scene. You need to have a balance of all four elements for the scene to appear realistic. Of these elements, the Object Galaxy is the most critical. It lays the foundation for creating clutter and chaos. Let's take a look at all the Object Galaxies in the dining table scene in Figure 12.8.

Figure 12.8 *Defining the Object Galaxies.*

You'll notice that certain objects in the scene are colored. These colored objects highlight the Object Galaxies in the scene. Let's take a moment to examine each of the Object Galaxies.

Place Mats: The place mats are Object Galaxies because there are several items that fall within their range of influence. Simply put, the items are sitting on the place mat. These items are called Satellite Objects because they are under the influence of the place mat. If the place mat is moved, the items will move with it.

Dinner Plates: The plates with burgers on them are Object Galaxies because the burgers fall within the plate's influence. These burgers are Satellite Objects. It's probably a good time to mention that an Object Galaxy can contain other, smaller Object Galaxies. The plate and burger are an Object Galaxy that is a part of the place mat Object Galaxy.

Burger Plate: The plate of burgers, in the middle of the table, is also an Object Galaxy because it has two burgers within its influence. These burgers are referred to as Satellite Objects.

Chair: This one is not so obvious. The chair with the napkin lying on it is an Object Galaxy. If the chair is moved, the napkin will move with it. The napkin is the sole Satellite Object in the chair's Object Galaxy. Some Object Galaxies have only one Satellite Object.

Table: The final Object Galaxy in the scene is the table. It wasn't highlighted because it would have confused the image. It's the largest Object Galaxy since it has many objects within its influence. It also has several smaller Object Galaxies within its influence.

Now that we have identified all the Object Galaxies in the scene, let's find the Free Objects. *Free Objects* are items that fall within the Object Universe but not in an Object Galaxy. There are a couple Free Objects in Figure 12.8. The chairs and wall clock are Free Objects, since they don't belong to an Object Galaxy. They can be moved and nothing will move with them.

Every scene has at least one Object Galaxy. Sometimes they can be difficult to detect but they are always present. It is important to identify the Object Galaxies in a scene so you can determine where to apply the chaos. It's time to put your knowledge of Object Galaxies to the test. Take a moment to examine Figure 12.9 and see if you can identify the Object Galaxies.

Figure 12.9 *Finding the Object Galaxies in a scene.*
(Courtesy of Ian Armstrong, ©1996 Ian Armstrong.)

If you identified three Object Galaxies in the scene you are correct. The table is the most obvious Object Galaxy. It has several items that fall within its range of influence, one of which is the clock, which also happens to be an Object Galaxy. The wooden base is the center object that has influence over the two Satellite Objects, which are the clock and circuit board. The corkboard is the final, and less obvious, Object Galaxy. It has several Satellite Objects that include two papers and many pins. As you can see, it can be a bit tricky to identify the Object Galaxies in a scene.

Now you know how to identify the Object Galaxies, but what relevance does this have in regard to 3D photorealism? That's an excellent question. Object Galaxies are used to determine the amount of chaos that is applied to a scene. Let's take a look at how we determine the amount of chaos to apply.

Determining the Level of Chaos

This is a very important step in the development of photorealistic scenes. If you apply the wrong level of chaos, the scene will appear unnatural. Before you begin to add chaos, you need to determine the proper volume to apply. When you apply chaos to objects in your scene, you have two levels of chaos from which to chose: minor or major. Selecting the right level of chaos depends on the type of object and the nature of the scene. Figure 12.10 illustrates the difference between minor and major chaos. You can see that the stack of JAZ disks on the left displays minor chaos, while the JAZ disks on the right reflect major chaos. I'll bet you prefer the stack on the left. That is because major chaos does not work with Physically Ordered Groups. Unless, of course, you live in Bizarro World. This brings us to the burning question: How do you know which level of chaos to use?

This question is easily answered by consulting the Chaos Volume Guidelines. These simple guidelines help you determine the level of chaos to apply to every object in the scene. Of course, there are exceptions to these guidelines, but these exceptions need to be justified. We'll explore Object Justification later in this chapter. Right now, let's take a look at the Chaos Volume Guidelines.

Physically Ordered Groups require minor chaos: Physically Ordered Groups would be a stack of papers on table, video tapes in a rack, disks on a desk, books on a shelf, or any other group of objects that are arranged for reference. The purpose of Physically Ordered Groups is to organize the objects, so you can't apply major chaos without defeating their purpose. You should make an effort to apply minor chaos to your Physically Ordered Groups. Take another look at Figure 12.10. We now know that the stack JAZ disks is a Physically Ordered Group, which means the stack on the left, with minor chaos, is correct. The stack on the right doesn't work since it is too chaotic and defeats the purpose of the Physically Ordered Group.

Ordered Object Galaxies require minor chaos: These groups of objects are similar to Physically Ordered Groups, except they are not designed to organize objects for reference. Instead, they are organized groups of objects that share a common influence. An Organized Object Galaxy would be any group of objects that are a predetermined form of organization, such as bookshelves, display cases, and cabinets. These objects are designed to organize items. Therefore you cannot use major chaos without defeating their purpose. Let's take a look at the difference between major and minor chaos in the Ordered Object Galaxy in Figure 12.11. Here we have a collection of my favorite Bobblehead characters. I'm sure you found the group on the top to be most acceptable. This is because it has minor chaos applied. The group on the bottom has major chaos applied, which defeats the purpose of the display shelf. Since these figurines are on a display shelf, we must assume that they would be facing the viewer, and placed so they can all be seen. Gathering them together in a huddle is far too chaotic and doesn't permit viewing of the figurines' faces, which is the main detail we would want to see . . . even if some of them are ugly.

Undefined Object Galaxies can use minor and major chaos: An Undefined Object Galaxy would be any common influence group of objects that has no particular organizational purpose, like a sofa, coffee table, or chair—it could even be a sidewalk. These items may have Satellite Objects but they aren't predetermined forms of organization. They are expected to display higher levels of chaos so using major chaos is acceptable. For example: You can pile coats chaotically on a chair, which is major chaos, and it's viewed as natural because the chair doesn't have a predetermined organizational purpose. Take a look at Figure 12.12. Here you'll see a great example of minor and major chaos applied to Undefined Object Galaxies. The coffee table, which is an Undefined Object Galaxy, displays a major level of chaos because it's cluttered with a number of objects that are in no particular order. Now look at the end table in the corner. Here we have an example of minor chaos being applied to an Undefined Object Galaxy. There are only a couple items on the table and they are relatively organized. The minor chaos is evident in the fact that none of the objects are aligned. You can see how either level of chaos is acceptable when used with an Undefined Object Galaxy.

Free Objects can use minor and major chaos: This is the last of the Chaos Volume Guidelines. These objects are not attached to an Object Galaxy, nor do they belong to a Physically Ordered Group. They are free to travel the scene without corrupting the purpose of the object. These objects can have either

Figure 12.10 *An example of minor and major chaos.*

Figure 12.11 *Ordered Object Galaxy chaos comparison.*

Figure 12.12 *Undefined Object Galaxy chaos.*

Figure 12.13 *Free Object chaos.*

minor or major chaos. Take a look at Figure 12.13. This image displays both minor and major chaos being applied to Free Object. As we discussed earlier, the chairs are Free Objects. Notice how one chair is against the wall. This represents major chaos. It has broken the order of chairs that surround the table, yet it is completely natural. Now look at the other chairs. Notice how they are slightly rotated away from the table. This represents minor chaos. They haven't broken the order of the chairs, but they have broken the monotony.

There you have it. The four guidelines for determining the volume of chaos to use with particular objects. Now that we have a firm handle on the amount of chaos to use, we need to know how to go about adding chaos to a scene. This is made easy by following the Three Rules of Chaos Development, which we discuss next. Just when you thought there couldn't be any more rules! Don't worry, we're just about done with guidelines and rules.

The Three Rules of Chaos Development

Chaos is applied to 3D scenes in layers. You start by laying a solid foundation of order, then you add layers of chaos until the desired effect is achieved. The best method for applying chaos to a scene is to follow the *Three Rules of Chaos Development,* which serve as sequential guidelines for determining when and where to add chaos. Let's take a look at each of these rules and see how they were applied to the scene in Figure 12.12.

Use Physically Ordered Objects to Lay the Foundation of Chaos

Physical Order lays the foundation of chaos for the scene. When staging a photorealistic scene, you start by building a layer of order, then you add layers of chaos to make the scene appear natural. You create a layer of order by placing Physically Ordered Objects in the scene. Look again at Figure 12.12. This scene was started by adding Physically Ordered Objects, such as the sofa, loveseat, chair, ottoman, end table, coffee table, and TV. Once they were placed in the scene, minor chaos was applied to make them appear natural.

If you start with major chaos in the first layer, by the time you get to the final layer, your scene will be completely chaotic and rather uncomfortable to view. It will end up looking like a tornado hit the room. This, of course, might actually make sense if you're rendering a child's room, but it isn't usually desired. On the other hand, if you were to make these objects perfectly aligned, the scene would appear staged and artificial. The best choice is to apply minor chaos to Physically Ordered Objects. Take another look at Figure 12.12. Here you can see how minor chaos was applied to make the Physically Ordered Objects appear natural. Notice how subtle chaos was applied to the sofa so it wouldn't be exactly parallel to the wall. You can see the same subtle chaos was applied to the coffee table and footstool so they wouldn't be perfectly aligned. You get the idea. These are very subtle forms of chaos, but they are paramount to the success of the image. They are the foundation of chaos. All other chaos is built upon these subtle nuances.

Now let's look at major chaos. In most cases, you should avoid adding major chaos to Physically Ordered Objects, but there are exceptions to the rule. Maybe you have a murder scene where a struggle took place, like the one shown in Figure 12.14. In this case, you'll want to apply major chaos to simulate the struggle. This, of course, makes the scene uncomfortable to view, but under these circumstances, you want viewers to be uncomfortable so they feel the mood of the scene. Another good example of where major chaos should be applied to Physically Ordered Objects would be a battle scene. In this case, the viewer expects the Physically Ordered Objects to be chaotic, and you don't want to disappoint the viewer. You should always ensure that your level of chaos supports the theme of your scene.

Once you have laid a solid foundation of Physical Order, you need to start adding the second layer, which is Visual Chaos.

Apply Visual Chaos to Physically Ordered Objects to Balance the Scene

Visual chaos is the icing on the proverbial Physical Order cake. Once you have laid the foundation of Physically Ordered Objects, you need to start adding the

Figure 12.14 Major chaos applied to Physically Ordered Objects.

details with Visually Chaotic Objects. These objects are used to offset the structure of the Physically Ordered Objects, so the scene won't appear sterile. Remember our discussion on the balance of chaos and order? Here's where we get to apply the formula for chaos. We added two parts order in the previous layer, now it's time to add one part chaos to complete the formula. This will balance the order and chaos in the scene.

Visually Chaotic Objects are all the objects in a scene that aren't Physically Ordered Objects. Simply put, they are the books on a shelf, the papers on a desk, the videos in a rack, or the toys on a floor. They are the Satellite Objects and Free Objects in the scene.

Take another look at Figure 12.12. All of the items on the coffee table, end table, sofa, loveseat, and ottoman are Visually Chaotic Objects. They were used to subdue the order of the scene and make it appear lived-in. Notice how the Visually Chaotic Objects are evenly distributed on the coffee table. This is important for making the scene balanced. If all the items were on one end of the table, it would appear unbalanced and unnatural. We can see that several people have been sitting around the table by evidence of the CD player on the ottoman, the paper on the sofa and the rabbit doll on the loveseat. This means that the chaos will be evenly distributed on the coffee table.

As you start adding Visually Chaotic Objects, you'll begin to develop Object Galaxies. These groups of objects require their own subtle form of chaos so they don't appear too ordered.

Apply Visual Chaos within the Object Galaxies to Make the Scene Natural

The last layer of chaos is applied to the Satellite Objects in the Object Galaxies. Although the Object Galaxies may not be the main focus of the scene, they are fundamental for creating photorealism. You could have done a flawless job on the first two layers of chaos, but if you skip this layer, the scene will still appear artificial. You need to ensure that all your Object Galaxies have visual chaos.

Before you add chaos to the Object Galaxies, you need to make sure that you have properly identified the type of Object Galaxy you are editing. Remember, Ordered Object Galaxies require minor chaos, whereas Undefined Object Galaxies can have minor or major chaos. Let's take a look at Figure 12.12 again to see how the final layer of chaos was added. First, we need to identify the types of Object Galaxies. Immediately we can see that there are no Ordered Object Galaxies, so we'll jump right to the Undefined Object Galaxies. The sofa, loveseat, coffee table, end table, and ottoman are the major Undefined Object Galaxies. The smaller, and less obvious Undefined Object Galaxies include the book with the beeper, the envelopes on the coffee table, and the dollar bill with remote control. Since these are all Undefined Object Galaxies, they can have either minor or major chaos. A good rule of thumb is to apply major chaos to the larger Object Galaxies and minor chaos to the smaller Object Galaxies. This will balance the chaos in the scene. A small Object Galaxy would have a difficult time supporting major chaos.

You'll notice the coffee table reflects major chaos due to the variety of objects cluttering the surface. This works well because it's a large Object Galaxy, which can support major chaos. On the other hand, the end table is a small Object Galaxy so it has minor chaos. Major chaos would make it appear unnatural. Now take a look at the sofa, loveseat, and ottoman. You can see that these items have minor chaos. These are all seating objects so we expect them to have minor chaos. If they had major chaos there would be no place to sit, which would defeat the purpose of the object.

Now let's look at the small Object Galaxies. Since they are small, they can only support minor chaos. They don't actually have enough Satellites Objects to create major chaos. The minor chaos was created by slightly rotating the objects to break up the alignment. This made them appear more natural.

There you have it, the Three Rules of Chaos Development. That wasn't so bad after all. It may take a bit of time to get the hang of them, but if you follow these rules closely, you'll find your scenes begin to take on a more photorealistic appearance.

Now that we know when and where to apply the chaos, let's look at how we balance it to make the scene appear natural.

Balancing Chaos in Your Scenes

Although it's important to add clutter to your scenes, it's also equally important to add balance. If a scene is too out of balance it will be uncomfortable to view. We have the tendency to seek balance in our lives. Therefore, a solid photorealistic 3D scene combines the chaos of reality with the balance we seek. Whatever you do, don't confuse balance with alignment. Balance means the chaos is evenly distributed throughout the scene, where alignment means the objects are arranged as if they were on a grid.

Rarely do you want the chaos to be focused in a single area in the scene. There are some cases when you will want more chaos in a particular area to draw the viewer's attention to that spot. Maybe you have a murder scene, similar to the one in Figure 12.14, except yours has bullet holes in the wall and a body slumped over on the floor. This is another example of major chaos. You just need to ensure that there is enough minor chaos in the rest of the scene to balance the focal point of chaos. This would be accomplished by knocking over a few items in the scene to simulate a struggle, or items that fell while the felon was fleeing. You probably wouldn't trash your room as much as Figure 12.14 since you want the dead body to be the focal point of the scene. Additionally, the bullet holes tell us that there probably wasn't much of a struggle so there would be limited major chaos.

YOU NEED TO BALANCE THE CHAOS IN YOUR SCENES.

Photorealistic scenes have balanced chaos. Because we seek balance in our lives, we tend to create balanced chaos in our environments. You want to avoid having the chaos focused in one area of the scene. This will throw the scene out of balance and make it uncomfortable to view. Be sure to go over your image when you are finished and ensure that the chaos is evenly distributed.

Let's take a look at Figure 12.15, which is a scene with balanced chaos. Notice how the computer has a floppy disk on it. This is a subtle form of chaos that helps to break the monotony of the computer's beige color. This is a very natural balance of chaos. My computer is literally buried in disks and Post-it Notes. Now take a look at the paperback book on top of the ordered books. This was added to dilute the uniformity of the ordered books. Even though there is minor chaos in the ordering of the books, there needs to be a little more chaos to break up the line that is formed between the books and computer monitor. This is an excellent example of adding balance to the scene. If you look close, you'll notice that a bookmark was placed in one of the books to further dilute the uniformity.

Now take a look at the JAZ disks, which we discussed early in this chapter. These are Physically Ordered Objects so they require minimal chaos to make them appear natural. I'm sure you noticed the pumpkin immediately. It's another element that was added to balance the chaos, but it also serves to offset the neutral colors in the scene. If you have too many similar colors in a scene, it will appear sterile . . . sort of like being in a hospital where everything is white. You need to add occasional color chaos as well as physical chaos to balance your scenes.

Finally, we have the envelope, with cracker, on the corner of the desk. If we had left the corner empty, the scene would have appeared out of balance. Very rarely do we see a lot of empty space on a computer desk. I don't think I've actually seen the surface of my desk in years. The cracker is a great element of unexpected chaos. You wouldn't normally expect to see a cracker on a computer desk. Of course, you would on my computer because I eat them while I work in the wee hours of the morning. If the camera were panned downward, you would likely see piles of cracker crumbs on the floor.

Figure 12.15 *An example of well-balanced chaos.*

Subtle additions of chaos can be very useful in balancing the scene. Adding balance is the finishing touch to your scene. Once you have added all three layers of chaos, you need to go back through the scene and ensure that the chaos is evenly distributed. In the scene we just discussed, the pumpkin, paperback book, envelope, and cracker were added to balance the chaos. If these items weren't added, the scene would have appeared out of balance because all of the objects in the scene were focused on the left side. This made the scene very uncomfortable to view. Therefore, subtle chaos was added to balance the scene.

It's time to look at one of the fun aspects of photorealistic 3D staging—justifying chaos.

Justifying Your Chaos

This is one of my favorite aspects of 3D photorealism. It's also one of the most important. You need to justify the objects and chaos in your scene or you just may lose the viewer. We seek justification in the things around us. If we can't find justification, the environment doesn't feel natural and we lose interest. Therefore, we need to justify the chaos to keep the viewers' interest.

Let me put it another way. When telling a story, you need to justify the elements in the story. You don't need to discuss them, but they need to make sense based on the story. For example: You wouldn't normally have a boat in the middle of the desert. If you did, you'd certainly have to justify it. If you put a tornado in the scene, it would justify the presence of the boat. As we discussed in Chapter 11, "Planning Your Scene," a 3D scene is a story. Therefore, the same rules of justification apply to a 3D scene. For the scene/story to be believable, you need to justify your objects and chaos.

Let's consider an example of justifying chaos. If you created a scene that showed a videotape rack with videos that were seriously chaotic, you'd have to justify their chaos. Normally, these items would be organized. Sure, they'd be slightly chaotic but certainly not seriously chaotic. Now, if you placed a fallen lamp against the videotape rack, it would justify the serious chaos. The viewer can see that the lamp fell over and shook up the videos in the rack. Let's look at a visual example of chaos justification in a 3D scene.

YOU NEED TO JUSTIFY THE OBJECTS IN YOUR SCENE.

A scene tells a story. Since viewers didn't write the story, they need you to justify the objects in your scene. They don't know the background behind the scene. They have to extract the story from the scene. The more justification you provide for your objects, the more likely they will be able to understand the story.

Take another look at Figure 12.14. Here we have the murder scene we discussed earlier in this chapter. You'll notice that the chalk mark and blood on the floor serve to justify the major chaos in the scene. We can see that there was a struggle and someone was killed. If this scene didn't include these elements, we would have a hard time justifying the extreme chaos of the Physically Ordered Objects. A scene with chaotically arranged furniture just doesn't make sense on its own. You need to add elements that justify the chaos in the scene.

If you are animating the scene, you can have objects move through the scene that justify the chaos. You could stage a struggle between two people in the scene and then have them fight their way out of the scene. This would justify the chaos because the viewers saw the fight. Unfortunately, if you are doing still images, you need to include the chaos justification within the scene. This can actually be a lot of fun. It's where you get to be creative in planning your scene.

In addition to justifying chaos, there are cases where you'll need to justify objects in your scene. While the objects may make perfect sense to you, they may not be adequately justified for the viewer. The viewers didn't make the scene, so they need visual clarification to understand the concept behind the scene. For example: If you created a scene that showed a fresh puddle of paint on a sidewalk, you'd have to justify the paint's presence. Although spilled paint is a plausible scene, the paint needs more justification for why it's on the sidewalk. It can be easily justified by placing a paint can next to the spilled paint. As with chaos, if you are doing still images, you need to make sure the objects in the scene are visibly justified.

Now take a look at Figure 12.16. Here we have a scene with a bowl of candy on a coffee table. Even though the bowl of candy is somewhat large, it really doesn't need to be justified since bowls of candy are rather common.

But what if we took a different approach to the scene and scattered the candy over the table. What if we took it a step farther and organized the candy according to their type. Well, we'd end up having a scene like the one shown in Figure 12.17. Take a look at the image. You'll notice that the scene doesn't make any sense because you don't see organized piles of candy on a coffee table . . . or, do you? While it may not be justified in this scene, there is definitely a very logical and common reason for the candy being separated in piles. It's called Halloween. What you're seeing is the aftermath of a child separating trick-or-treat candy in piles, so they can easily access their favorite types. I used to do the same thing so I didn't have to dig through all the candy to find the good stuff.

Now take a look at Figure 12.18. Here we have the same scene with a simple trick-or-treat basket added. Notice how it easily justifies the candy on the coffee table. The trick-or-treat basket tells us that the scene was shot during Halloween. All it takes is one object to justify the unusual objects in a scene.

As you can see. Justifying your chaos and objects is a necessary step in the 3D photorealism process. Be sure to study the story behind the scene to ensure that you properly justify the chaos and objects.

Now that we have a handle on chaos and object justification, let's take a look at the pointless aspect of photorealistic 3D images.

Adding Pointless Objects
to Create Depth

Pointless Objects are an essential aspect of photorealistic 3D scenes. They are used to add depth to a scene and make it appear natural. You need to have completely Pointless Objects in the scene to make it lived-in. Pointless Objects are not critical to the point of the scene. For example: Try putting a piece of crumpled paper on the desk. Scatter tools on the workbench. Chaotically arrange throw pillows and magazines on the sofa. Stack some videos next to the TV. Put piles of paper, books, and magazines on the coffee table. Scatter leaves under the bush or tree. Clutter the bookshelves with knickknacks. Pile toys in the corner of the room, and for crying out loud, knock over a chess piece on the board. You see where I'm going with this. Don't make the mistake of sterilizing your scene by looking for that perfect image—there's nothing perfect about reality. Uniformity makes a scene look 3D and artificial.

Pointless Objects are used to make the scene appear lived-in. Every day we pick up objects and move them around the house. Although they may have a point in their origin, they don't once they are moved. The crumpled paper on the desk has no point, but it would if it were placed in a wastebasket. A TV remote control on the dining table would have no point, but it would if placed on the coffee table, which is in front of the TV. You get the idea.

Figure 12.16 *Objects that don't need justification.*

Figure 12.17 *Unjustified objects.*

Figure 12.18 *Justified objects.*

ADD POINTLESS OBJECTS TO MAKE YOUR SCENE APPEAR LIVED-IN.

Pointless Objects are used to make a scene appear lived-in. In reality, we deposit items in our environment on a daily basis. We are losing TV remotes in all parts of the house, throwing cigarette butts on the streets, depositing books and magazines throughout the house, and scattering disks on our desks. To make your scenes appear lived-in, you need to add Pointless Objects.

While adding Pointless Objects is necessary, don't make the mistake of making them too pointless. The Pointless Objects still need to be justified in the scene. For example: Placing a throw pillow on the dining table wouldn't be justified. This isn't an item that you typically carry around the house. On the other hand, a *TV Guide* or magazine on the dining table would make perfect sense. Basically, pointless items need to be portable. Let's take a look at how Pointless Objects were used to make the scene in Figure 12.19 appear natural.

Here we have a familiar scene from the Dwellers movie. This scene has a number of Pointless Objects that have been used to make the scene appear lived-in. You'll notice that there are a number of cigarette butts lying on the pavement.

Figure 12.19 *Using Pointless Objects to make a scene appear natural.*

These are very common on city sidewalks. They are also very portable items. There are also a couple bottle caps in the scene. These too are common sights on city sidewalks, and most definitely portable. We fully expect people to walk by and discard the bottle caps from their sodas. Now take a look at the rusty oilcan on the ledge. This is another pointless object that feels very natural in the scene. Although it's not a common sight, it certainly is portable. Someone probably changed the oil in his car while parked by the sidewalk, and then left the can behind when he departed. Don't you just hate a litterbug? Now, what about that shopping cart? Well, it certainly is pointless but is it portable? Of course, it has wheels. Someone probably loaded her car by the sidewalk and didn't bother to return the cart when she was done. Or, maybe it was deposited here by a homeless person. Either way, it's a portable Pointless Object that is easily justified.

As you can see, Pointless Objects add depth and realism to a scene. Without them, a scene would appear sterile. Before you call it quits on your next scene, add a little Pointless Chaos—what the heck, add a lot!

Putting the Chaos Concepts to Use

Let's use the techniques we discussed in this chapter to make an existing scene appear photorealistic. Come on, wake up, this is where the fun begins. We'll start with a simple foundation and gradually add the chaos until the scene is truly photorealistic. Let's dive right in!

Take a look at Figure 12.20. Here we have the dining table scene we discussed earlier in the chapter. Let's start by examining the current level of chaos in the scene. You'll notice we have a solid foundation of Physically Ordered Objects. These objects include the dining table, wall clock, walls, and floor. The dining table is the center of the Object Universe. It's also an Object Galaxy. Since it's a Physically Ordered object, it can have only minor chaos. The wall clock is also a Physically Ordered Object so it has minor chaos. If you look closely, you'll notice it hangs a little crooked on the wall.

Now take a look at the chairs. These are all Free Objects, so they can have minor or major chaos. You'll notice the chair against the wall displays major chaos, while the other chairs reflect minor chaos. This adds balance to the chaos in the scene. The minor chaos of the chairs around the table balances the major chaos of the chair against the wall. This covers the major objects in the scene. Now let's look at the minor objects.

The minor objects are all combined into small Object Galaxies. You'll notice that each of these Object Galaxies has a different level of chaos applied. As we discussed earlier, the Object Galaxies include the place mats, chair with napkin, and the dining table. You'll notice that the place mats on opposite sides of the

Figure 12.20 *The beginning of a photorealistic scene.*

table are fairly well organized, reflecting minor chaos. The place mats on the end of the table display major chaos because their burgers are opened. This is a key element in making the scene appear lived-in. It appears two of the people have begun to prepare their burgers. Rotating the chairs at these place settings helped to reinforce the fact that someone has recently been sitting in them. You'll notice that the other chairs are undisturbed, which explains why those place settings are untouched. This is a critical point of chaos justification. The chairs justify the chaos on the plates.

Now let's look at some subtle chaos within the Object Galaxies. You can see that there are three people drinking soda, while only one is drinking water. This helps to break the uniformity of the glasses. It's unlikely that everyone would be drinking the same thing. If you look closely, you'll notice that there is ice in both the water glass and the soda glass on the far side of the table. This helps to break the monotony of the fluid in the glasses. Sure, it's a bit neurotic, but you have to agree that the effect works. You can also see that the water glass is on the opposite side of the place mat. It's a small chaotic detail that helps make the scene appear more natural.

How about the really subtle chaos? Did you notice that the place setting on the near side of the table has the critical blunder of the salad fork being on the wrong side of the plate? How about the fact that all of the utensils are placed in slightly different positions and rotations? You probably didn't notice since it appears natural. If they were all aligned the same way, you would notice immediately, since it would be unnatural. Applying chaos to the utensils helps balance the chaos and removes that sterile, packaged look from the scene.

Now let's take a look at the objects in the scene that aren't justified. Even though utensils wouldn't normally need justifying, we are currently faced with a situation where it's necessary. You see, utensils don't make a lot of sense with hamburgers, which we normally consider a finger food. We have to justify the presence of the utensils. We could just remove them, but they are an important part of the chaos in the scene. Removing them would make the scene appear too empty, so let's take a different approach by adding objects that justify the utensils.

Take a look at Figure 12.21. You can see we've added several bowls of potato salad and a bottle of ketchup. The potato salad justifies the fork and spoon since these utensils are commonly used to eat this type of food. The ketchup was added to justify the knife. We can assume they will be using the knife to spread the ketchup on the burgers. Since the ketchup is new, we can also assume that they will be using the knife to free the ketchup, so it flows from the bottle. Of course, they could pound on the end of the bottle, but then we'd have to add ketchup splatters all over the scene to reflect the aftermath of this poor choice of ketchup extraction.

Now, what do we do next? We're well into the second Rule of Chaos Development: Apply Visual Chaos to Physically Ordered Objects to Balance the Scene, so let's balance the table's Object Galaxy by adding Visual Chaos. You'll notice that all of the objects are at one end of the table. Although this makes sense due to the number of people eating, it's unlikely that the dining table started off perfectly clear. It probably had items that were pushed to one end to make room for the place settings. You'll need a shovel to clear a spot on my dining table.

You'll find that people frequently traffic between the living areas of a home and the kitchen. In many cases the dining table is right in the path. This means that countless items will be deposited on the dining table. In fact, they will likely be placed on the closest point of the dining table, which means that in all likelyhood you'll have very unbalanced chaos on the dining table. This is one of those rare exceptions to the rule of balanced chaos. In the case of our dining table scene, the place settings are located at the closest point to the path of traffic so we'll assume the items have been pushed to the opposite side to make room for the place settings. Now let's see what happens when we add some Visual Chaos to the dining table.

Take a look at Figure 12.22. Now the dining table chaos is a little more realistic. We've added several items at the opposite end of the table. This balances the chaos on the table. You'll notice pointless objects were used to make the scene appear lived-in. These objects are all justified since they are easily portable, and commonly make their way through the house. Unfortunately, we created an alignment problem when we added the new objects. All of the items on the table seem to follow the contour of the table's edge. This looks far too staged. We need to add a little chaos to the new items to ensure they create a natural effect. Let's do that now.

Take a look at Figure 12.23. You'll notice the camera was moved forward slightly to break up the alignment on the outer edge of the table. It's amazing how a minor change can make such a dramatic difference in the photorealism of a scene. The image is really starting to come together. There are just a few problems we still need to correct. The first one we address is the lack of chaos in the rest of the scene. All the chaos seems to be focused on the table. This makes the

Figure 12.21 *Justifying objects in a scene.*

Figure 12.22 *Balancing the scene with Visual Chaos.*

Figure 12.23 *Removing object alignment with chaos.*

Figure 12.24 *Adding depth with random chaos.*

table balanced but tends to throw the scene out of balance. We need to add some minor chaos to the area surrounding the table to make it more believable. My dining table is actually surrounded with stuffed animals, but we'll go with something a little more traditional . . . and expected. It's important that you create chaos that the viewer expects. If you hit them with something too strange, the scene will appear artificial. Stuffed animals are justified in my house but they wouldn't be in most homes. What this scene needs is a little chaos on the walls, which currently seem too sterile. Let's add some chaos.

Take a look at Figure 12.24. Now that's more like it. The image is really becoming more realistic. Two wall outlets have been added to the walls. This breaks up the monotony of the wall texture. They are also familiar objects that add credibility to the scene. You'll notice a power plug was added to the wall outlet under the clock. This really helps to add depth to the scene. Most 3D scenes fail to include power plugs for their electronic appliances, which means they must be drawing current from the static in the air. You can see how the simple addition of a power cord goes a long way toward adding photorealistic credibility. We still have one more wall object to discuss. Take a look at the curtains in the upper left corner of the image. This is a common element seen in dining rooms. Most dining rooms have a window, so the curtains are an expected element. They add a subtle level of chaos to the upper portion of the image, which lends balance to the rest of the scene.

We have one last object to consider. I'm sure you noticed the broom on the floor. This is a great object for adding depth to the scene. Since we have a linoleum floor, we can assume that they use a broom to clean it. The broom on the floor suggests that someone has recently been sweeping the floor. Of course, as with my household, whoever was using the broom neglected to return it to the closet. Thanks to that Murphy guy, you can count on me tripping over the broom every time.

Although this scene has come a long way from the original image, it still lacks photorealistic credibility, because the broom doesn't feel very natural in its current position. One very important aspect of 3D photorealism is to maintain an adherence to the laws of physics. We can assume that the broom was leaning against the wall and fell at some point. The only problem with its current position is that it would have to fall through the clock to reach it. The broom needs to be moved to a more logical position.

In addition to the broom's placement, there is a problem with balance in the scene. Now that we've added the wall outlets and broom, there is a glaring empty spot on the right side of the image. We need to place something in this area to balance the scene. We don't want to clutter this space since that would make the scene too chaotic. Instead, we need to add a subtle object that feels natural in the scene. A piece of carpet should do just fine. Ah, yes, and let's not forget the curtains. Did you notice that they were open? This would mean that sunlight would be shining through the window, yet we don't see the warmth of sunlight in the scene. Let's see what we can do about these problems.

Take a look at Figure 12.25. Wow, what a difference a few changes can make. Now we have a photorealistic scene. Take a look at where the broom landed this time. This position makes sense. The broom was leaning against the wall between the curtains and clock. When it fell, it was pushed away from the wall by the curtains, making it land on the chair. Now take a look at the specularity on the broom handle and table. You can see the warmth of the sunlight coming through the window. This helps to add photorealistic credibility to the scene. Notice how the surface of the table and broom handle are completely washed out with light? This is a natural effect of direct sunlight. Many 3D artists actually strive to avoid this effect. While it may not be attractive, it is what happens in reality. If the effect were softened, it would no longer resemble sunlight. Remember, reality is chaos. Things aren't always going to be aesthetically pleasing.

On to the last change. Notice how the edge of a carpet was added to the right side of the image. This is a very passive object that does a great job of balancing the scene, without adding to the chaos. It's an expected element that helps add depth and realism. Most dining rooms are barely larger than the dining table.

Figure 12.25 *The completed Photorealistic scene.*

Therefore, if we left this portion of the screen unchanged, the dining room would have seemed too large.

Whew, that was a bit of work. Actually, it wasn't that bad. You can see how important chaos is in creating photorealistic scenes. Just take another look at Figure 12.20, then take a look at Figure 12.25 and you'll see that chaos has made a major impact on the photorealistic credibility of this scene. It's worth investing a bit of your time to determine the proper use of chaos in a scene, particularly when the results are dramatically better.

It's Up to You Now

Well, there you have it. Countless mind-numbing rules and principles for photorealistic 3D staging. Okay, so it's not all that bad. Really, once you get used to the idea of analyzing the chaos in your scenes, you'll find it doesn't add much to your development time, though it does add a significant boost in the quality of the image. It takes only a few minutes to add the details that will transform your images from ordinary into unbelievable. Before you wrap up your next image, take a few moments to analyze the staging and make sure that it makes proper use of chaos.

That's enough about chaos. It's time to take a look at something less chaotic—photorealistic camera and lighting techniques.

PART V

Photorealistic Camera and Lighting Techniques

Well, you've toiled away until the midnight hours modeling and surfacing your creations, now it's time to put them to work. This is where things get a bit tricky. Here is where we have to apply photorealistic lighting and camera techniques.

There is much more to rendering a realistic scene than simply staging the scene well. You have to use proper camera angles to elicit emotion in the viewer. In fact, the lighting has a great deal of impact on the viewer's emotional state. You want your creation to be more than a simple image. You want it to be an experience. For an image to be considered "art," it needs to be an experience for the viewer. It needs to spur an emotional response.

Of course, there is also the issue of creating photorealism in your images. To achieve photorealism you'll need to study the effects of light on an environment. You see, you can't simply place a white spotlight in the environment and expect it to appear realistic. You have to study the type of light, its natural color, the amount of light objects in the environment, and the time of day. There is a bit of homework to be done when creating photorealistic images.

In the following chapters we'll be discussing how camera angles and light can be used to create photorealistic images. Hang on to your seats because this is going to be another wild ride.

VISIT THE COMPANION WEB SITE FOR TUTORIAL FILES.

Before you begin Part V, go to Appendix F and learn about the companion Web site. All of the TUTORIAL FILES referenced in this part are located on the companion Web site, which is located at www.wiley.com/compbooks/fleming. You should also download the color figures from the companion Web site since they will be easier to review than the printed grayscale images.

13 *Camera Positioning*

Camera positioning can make a big difference in the photorealistic quality of the image. Far too many 3D scenes are shot so every object is clearly visible. How often does this happen in reality? Never. Think about the last time you took a photograph: Did you take the time to arrange all of the items so they would fit into the view frame? I certainly hope you didn't. Imagine completely rearranging your studio so everything would neatly fit within the boundaries of a photograph. Most 3D images look like the designer moved all of the objects so they are clearly visible in the scene, making the image look completely unnatural.

To create photorealistic images you need to leave something to the imagination. There should be objects that are only partially visible in the scene so the viewer is intrigued about what they are. It's what makes the images interesting. If you pile everything within the camera's view you leave nothing to the imagination of the viewer, which means they quickly lose interest. Let's take a look at an example of good camera positioning, as shown in Figure 13.1.

Here we have a typical office scene, which happens to be a very nice photorealistic image. Notice how there are several objects around the perimeter of the scene that are only partially visible. This helps to make the image appear more natural. In reality, it would be impossible to fit all of the objects in the shot without piling them in on top of each other. This camera position also helps to make the room look smaller. If all the objects were in plain view, the room would seem very large. In fact, it would look too large.

Now take a look at the left side of the image. You can see that the camera angle has cut off the end of the credenza. This is actually very important because it is necessary to balance the image. You see, if the camera was moved over to show the entire credenza there would be too much weight on the right side of the image where we see the wall unit. It would end up looking as if the room was empty on the left side since all we would see is carpet. It's necessary to choose a camera position that balances the scene and makes the environment look full. There really isn't much empty space in reality. In fact, why don't you test this theory?

Figure 13.1 *Proper camera positioning.*

Try this little experiment. First, go find your camera. It doesn't matter what type of camera you have since you won't be taking any pictures. Now pick any room in your home or office and view it through the camera. Try to find a shot where you can actually see some empty space. Difficult isn't it? The average room is rather cluttered and cramped, unless you are fortunate enough to live in a castle. Most of us are faced with the problem of too much stuff and too little space. Therefore it's rather unlikely that we'll ever see a picture with any empty space. You can see that a 3D image, which implies empty space, would be rather unnatural. Let's get back to analyzing the image in Figure 13.1.

NEVER POSITION THE CAMERA SO EVERYTHING IN THE SCENE IS VISIBLE.

One of the fastest ways to sterilize your scene is to position the camera so you can clearly see everything. In reality it would be nearly impossible to take a picture where all the elements were clearly in the image. The only way to accomplish this would be to manually arrange the elements, which wouldn't be very natural. Always try to leave objects where only a portion is visible so your image appears natural.

I'm sure you noticed that the image leaves you intrigued about a few items such as the magazine on top of the television. You can see only part of the cover, which makes you wonder what the full cover image looks like. (Actually, you're really not missing anything. It wasn't that exciting anyway.) Now take a look at the wall unit and you'll see there is something on the top shelf that we can't identify. It may be a subtle element in the scene but it adds a lot of credibility to the camera position since we can't see enough of the object to identify it. The last thing you want to do is make it possible to identify every object in the scene. It would neutralize the viewer's curiosity, which is the exact opposite of what we're trying to accomplish.

The camera position plays a major role in the photorealistic credibility of the scene. Although it's true that the camera position doesn't actually make the scene look photorealistic, it does prevent the image from looking staged, which is what we're trying to avoid. A staged scene looks artificial, not realistic. In fact, most 3D scenes look staged because they have poor camera positions. We've actually come to expect sterile camera positions from 3D images so even if your objects and surfaces are realistic the camera position can make the image look 3D if it's not positioned properly. On the other hand, if you are creative with your camera positions you'll end up strengthening the photorealistic credibility of the scene.

Let's have a little fun by taking a look at how we can create different moods with camera angles. They don't have any real impact on the photorealistic credibility of the scene but they will help you get the most out of your images.

Creating Emotion with Camera Angles

A common problem with many 3D images is that they are shot from sterile angles, which kills the mood of the scene. It would certainly be a tragedy to go through all the effort to create a photorealistic scene only to kill it with a sterilized camera angle. A sterile camera angle is typically an *orthographic view,* looking straight at the scene, with no camera rotation in either direction. Let's take a look at a sterile camera angle to see how it undermines the credibility of a photorealistic scene in Figure 13.2.

Ouch, what a waste of really nice photorealistic work. You can see that the models and surfacing are wonderful but the camera position is far too rigid. It's looking straight at the scene. It's as if our heads were locked in position as though we were in an electric chair—a view we really don't want to experience. If you stare at the image for more than a few moments you'll actually start to get uncomfortable because it inhibits your freedom, and the last thing we want to do is give the viewer anxiety. I'm sure they already have enough of that.

NEVER USE ORTHOGRAPHIC VIEWS TO RENDER YOUR IMAGES.

The goal of an image is to elicit an emotional response. Orthographic views neutralize the viewer's emotions, which leads to boredom. While boredom is an emotion, it's not a desired response. You should try to position your camera so it elicits the proper emotional response. This means anywhere but orthographically.

Proper camera positioning is very important to keep the viewer interested in the scene. The camera angle controls the mood of the scene, and the mood is what pulls viewers into the image and holds their interest. For example: High camera angles add drama whereas lower camera angles create tension. It's amazing how a mere change in the camera angle can completely alter the mood of the scene. In fact, let's take a look at the same scene shot from two completely different camera angles to see how the mood actually changes. First we'll take a look at the scene shot from a typical camera angle in Figure 13.3.

While it's a nice scene, you can see that this camera angle doesn't evoke a major emotional response. In fact, it's a rather comfortable camera angle, which tends to expedite the onset of boredom. We don't want the viewers to be too comfortable or they'll fall asleep. There's actually nothing wrong with this shot; it just doesn't change the viewer's emotions. Now, let's take a look at the same scene shot from a very low camera position in Figure 13.4.

That's certainly a big difference. Immediately we have an emotional reaction to the image. In fact, it makes us feel small and insignificant, as though Gizmo could actually step on us, which in reality would be rather difficult since he's only a foot tall. You'll notice nothing in the scene has changed except the camera angle and yet the entire mood of the scene has been altered. There are literally dozens of emotions we can elicit with this same scene by merely changing the camera angle.

Low camera angles create tension and even fear. What happens with a high camera angle? Well, let's take a look at an example—Figure 13.5, for instance.

Notice how small Gizmo looks in this scene. It now looks like we can step on him. That will teach him not to intimidate us! Suddenly the mood is shifted to a feeling of power, which you'll find most people are very comfortable with. We can safely say that higher camera positions create a feeling of power. In fact, the higher the camera position, the more powerful the viewer feels. You could make a T-rex look insignificant if you positioned the camera high enough. On the other hand, if you put the camera directly beneath him, well, your viewer's hearts will be skipping a few beats.

You can see that the camera position has tremendous influence over the mood of the scene. When positioning your camera you really need to consider the mood you are trying to project, because you can totally reverse the mood of the scene by positioning the camera improperly.

Figure 13.2 *A sterile camera angle.*

Figure 13.3 *A neutral camera angle.*

Figure 13.4 *Creating tension with low camera angles.*

Figure 13.5 *The feeling of power created by a high camera angle.*

Creating Emotion with Camera Rotation

There are times when you'll want your scene to elicit tension from the viewer, and there's no better way to do this than rotating the camera. We spend our entire lives looking at the world head on, which happens to be the most comfortable view for use. Now if we were to rotate our head to the side it would be only a matter of seconds before we started to get tense. Of course, as soon as we felt the tension we would straighten our view out. In fact, why take my word for it? Go ahead, rotate your head to the side and try reading. It really bugs you doesn't it? How fast did you turn your head back? I'm sure it was pretty close to immediately.

A 3D image with a serious camera rotation will definitely elicit tension, particularly since we can't just straighten out our heads to correct the view. You'll have viewers literally crawling out of their chairs to escape the tension. Actually, you'll have them turning their head to the side so the view is comfortable. That is, until they strain their neck.

When should camera rotation be used? It all depends on the scene, but most definitely when you want to create tension. An example of a good use for camera rotation would be in a scene where a murder just took place and you are looking through the eyes of the murder victim. In this case the camera would be low to the ground and rotated at almost 90 degrees. Now that would be a tense image. In fact, let's take a look at just how intense it would be. Take a look at Figure 13.6.

How does it feel to be dead? Pretty tense isn't it? Probably eerie too. You need to resurrect yourself now so we can discuss Figure 13.6. You can see how this camera rotation really adds tension to the scene. I'll bet you even wanted to turn

Figure 13.6 *Creating tension with camera rotation.*

your head when you looked at it. I know I did. Camera rotation can be a powerful tool for eliciting emotional responses from your viewers but it doesn't always have to be tension. In fact, it can also be humor, and in some cases pity. It all depends on how you stage the scene. Most of the time it will be tension because we don't enjoy the rotated view, but the staging can alter the effect, or it can even enhance it. If you take another, and quite painful look at Figure 13.6, you'll notice that the room is in total disarray. This serves to heighten the tension because it's an awful lot of chaos to take in at one time. And as we know, the more chaos the more intense the reaction.

Now let's release a little tension by taking a look at another example of camera rotation, but this time with less chaos in the scene. Take a look at Figure 13.7.

Remember the low camera angle image where it looked like Gizmo was going to step on us? Well he just did. Actually, you are now looking through the eyes of Flash, who is waiting for Gizmo to come over and pick him up. Flash is a Polaroid camera who's been charged with the task of finding spare parts and photographing their location so the Dwellers can find them. Unfortunately, Flash is rather awkward and clumsy so he tends to fall over a lot.

Figure 13.7 *Creating mixed emotions camera rotation image.*

This scene has nowhere near the tension of the murder scene. That's because there is rather minimal chaos. The possibilities for emotional reaction to this scene are actually very mixed. It all depends on viewers and their personalities. They could feel tense, happy, or possibly confused, which of course isn't bad. It's actually quite good since it makes viewers think a bit to figure out why they are viewing the world from this angle. You could always put visual keys in the scene, which help them determine the reason for the rotated view. In fact, you could dump a few items directly in front of the camera to make it look like someone fell over. For that matter you could put a banana peel in the scene, which would make it more humorous—the possibilities are limitless.

As you can see, camera rotation is another powerful tool for eliciting emotional responses from your viewers. Although it doesn't work for every scene, it does have its application when you want to snap viewers out of the trance that typical 3D images put them in.

There is just one more technique we can use to create moods with our camera—camera zoom. Let's take a look at how it works.

Creating Visual Depth

One of the least seen elements in 3D images is depth. I know it sounds weird considering that we're talking about 3D images, but it's true. Most 3D images are shot with a relatively moderate camera zoom, which tends to flatten them out, particularly if it's the standard orthographic view that we so frequently see in 3D images. It seems an awful shame to spend so much time creating 3D models only to flatten them out in the rendered image.

There are a couple of ways to create depth in scenes. You can use either camera zoom or object placement to achieve the feeling of depth. Either one is very effective. Let's take a look at both of them to see how they affect the perception of the scene. We'll start by looking at camera zoom.

Camera zoom can have a significant impact on the depth of the scene. In fact, a small zoom setting will literally stretch the scene out, giving it tremendous depth. The actual zoom levels will vary depending on the program you use but typically a good zoom setting for depth is 2.5 to 3.2. Let's take a look at an image that gained plenty of depth by using a small camera zoom setting. Take a look at Figure 13.8.

Here we have a scene of the Seeker in the Dweller's tunnel. Seeker is the Dweller that Gizmo created to search the water drainage tunnels for parts that he can use to create other Dwellers. He looks like a fish because Gizmo has a sense of humor.

Let's take a look at the depth in the scene. As you can see, a small camera zoom was used in this scene to make the tunnel appear longer by widening the part that

Figure 13.8 *Adding depth with camera zoom.*

is closest to the camera. A low camera zoom level widens the perspective, which creates the feeling of depth because it allows you to see more of the object's mass. Instead of merely seeing the front of the object, you can now see part of its side, which creates depth.

Object placement is another very simple way to add depth without distorting the perspective. All you need to do is place an object close to the camera. An object close to the camera will appear very large in the scene compared to the other objects. This creates the illusion of depth. Let's see how this works. Take a look at Figure 13.9.

Notice how the furniture in the scene looks far away. This is because the television looks as big as the sofa, which we know isn't possible, so therefore we assume the furniture is farther away. It's really as simple as that. As you can see, object placement can be a very quick and effective means for adding depth to your scenes.

What if we want to have the wide angle look of a small camera zoom without the exaggerated perspective? You need to move the camera farther away from the image and use a higher camera zoom. This will flatten the perspective and allow you to view a wider portion of the scene as shown in Figure 13.10.

Here we have a view of Robby the Rabbit's den. Who's Robby? Robby is a tiny rabbit that lives under my vegetable garden. He's quite the character. I can't count the number of times I've lost items in the house only to find them buried in the garden! Robby is a scavenger so his house is filled with wonderful items.

Figure 13.9 *Adding depth with object placement.*

This scene is a shot of Robby in his living room, reading the morning paper, which happens to be printed on gift cards from a stuffed animal in my niece's playroom. His house is tastefully furnished with items borrowed from Barbie's Dream House and on the back wall is the watch I lost more than a month ago! No wonder I keep hearing a ticking sound when I'm working in the garden. Of course, by the door is the missing piece from my Flintstones chess set—Robby wanted a watchdog to protect his home. And finally, in the foreground is the Hotwheels car my nephew lost in the garden last week. Well, now you know everything there is to know about Robby.

The perspective of this image is relatively shallow, which makes us feel like we're in the room with Robby. The view is also rather wide, which allows us to take in all of the detail in Robby's den. Naturally, to make this shot work I had to knock out the wall of Robby's den so I could move the camera far enough back to capture the full width of the room. Don't worry, I put the wall back after I was done.

It's definitely important to add depth to our scenes, which can be done with camera zoom or object placement. While it's not necessary for all images, it can help to add more impact to many of your images.

Figure 13.10 *Achieving a wide angle view with camera zoom.*

That about does it for camera placement techniques. Camera positioning, rotation, and zoom have a significant impact on the quality of your scene. Just remember that you've invested a number of hours developing those wonderful photorealistic models, now don't kill them by shooting and orthographic view.

And Then There Was Light . . .

Wow, I just realized we only have one more chapter to go. And what a chapter it is! Nothing has a greater impact on the photorealistic credibility of a scene than lighting. We're too close to quit now, so let's dive right in and get our feet wet with lighting photorealistic scenes in Chapter 14, "Lighting for Every Occasion."

14 *Lighting for Every Occasion*

Before you begin reading this chapter, you should go to the companion Web site and download the example images.

Lighting is one of the most critical aspects of photorealistic 3D images, and it's also one of the more complicated. It can literally make or break an image, so we need to place a great deal of emphasis on getting it right. It won't do us any good to spend hours modeling, surfacing, and staging our scenes only to undermine the photorealistic credibility with poor lighting. Unfortunately, very few 3D images actually have realistic lighting. It seems they always place a pure white light in the scene and expect it to look natural, but in reality you will never encounter a white light source. In fact, light is anything but white. I know I must sound like a complete madman, but before you sign my commitment papers let's take a look at light and how it affects our environment.

We obviously know what light does, so I won't waste your time with pages of scientific mumbo jumbo that explains the theory of light waves. Instead, I'd rather we focused on how light affects the environment around us. The most critical element of light is its temperature. Yes, light has a temperature. In fact, it's the foundation of photorealistic lighting. For example, the color of natural daylight changes throughout the day. At sunrise and sunset the light looks reddish (warmer), while at midday it look bluish (cooler). These changes are referred to as color temperature, which is measured in degrees Kelvin (K). Warm light, as at sunrise and sunset, has a low Kelvin rating, whereas cool light, such as midday sunlight, has a high Kelvin rating.

What does all this have to do with photorealistic lighting? Most people don't realize that every light source has a distinct color based on its temperature or Kelvin rating. We don't actually see this color because our eyes automatically adapt to changes in color temperature, much the same way auto-white balance on a camcorder does, making any type of light look nearly white. This process is known as *chromatic adaptation*. Our eyes automatically correct the color of the light so it appears white when in reality it's anything but white. In fact, let's take a look at the actual colors of different light sources. Take a look at Figure 14.1.

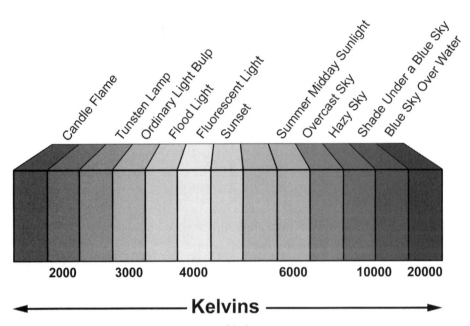

Figure 14.1 *The color temperatures of light.*

Here we can see a chart that shows the actual color temperature of several light sources. You can see that the lower the temperature of the light, the more reddish it becomes. On the other hand, the higher the temperature, the more bluish it becomes. The interesting thing is that although the temperature may be getting higher, the light color is actually getting cooler. Most of us consider blue a cool color and red a hot color, which are very natural conclusions since fire is red and water is blue. Since we have these predisposed notions about colors and temperature, you'll find that light colors will actually change the temperature of the scene, making it appear warm or cool depending on the color.

Certainly if we use the actual light colors for our 3D lights we'd have an image that looked more like a Disco Dance Club, creating an undesirable urge within us to wear bell-bottom jeans, which is a really scary thought. Well, our eyes do correct the color of the light, but it's not a perfect conversion, which means we can still see very subtle evidence of the actual light color. This, of course, means that we need to incorporate these subtle color nuances into our 3D lighting endeavors if we intend to create photorealistic images.

The first thing we need to do to accomplish this is to identify the Kelvin rating of the light source we are emulating so we can determine the proper color. Fortunately, we just happen to have the perfect tool for determining light coloration. Take a look at Figure 14.2.

Here we have a rather detailed chart that shows the light color for a number of specific light sources. On the left you'll find the actual light color referenced

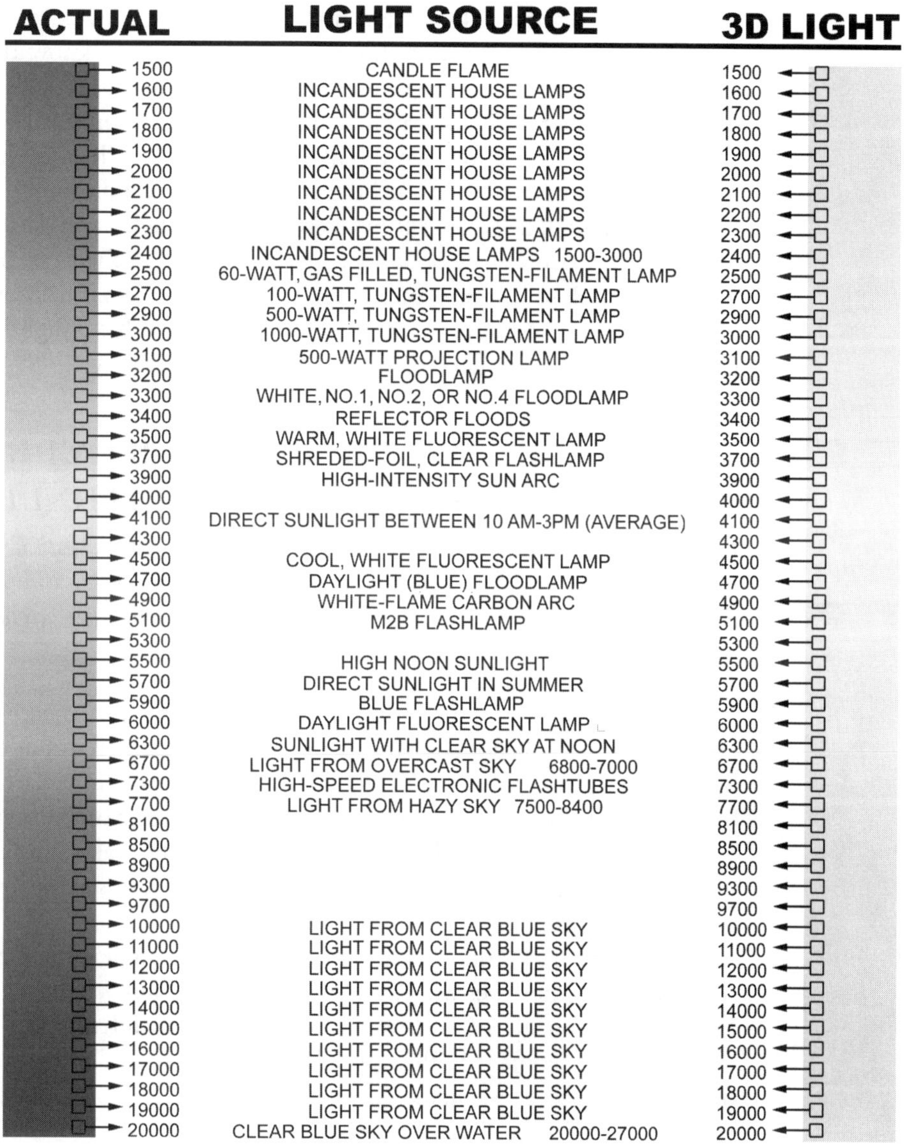

ACTUAL   LIGHT SOURCE   3D LIGHT

ACTUAL	LIGHT SOURCE	3D LIGHT
1500	CANDLE FLAME	1500
1600	INCANDESCENT HOUSE LAMPS	1600
1700	INCANDESCENT HOUSE LAMPS	1700
1800	INCANDESCENT HOUSE LAMPS	1800
1900	INCANDESCENT HOUSE LAMPS	1900
2000	INCANDESCENT HOUSE LAMPS	2000
2100	INCANDESCENT HOUSE LAMPS	2100
2200	INCANDESCENT HOUSE LAMPS	2200
2300	INCANDESCENT HOUSE LAMPS	2300
2400	INCANDESCENT HOUSE LAMPS 1500-3000	2400
2500	60-WATT, GAS FILLED, TUNGSTEN-FILAMENT LAMP	2500
2700	100-WATT, TUNGSTEN-FILAMENT LAMP	2700
2900	500-WATT, TUNGSTEN-FILAMENT LAMP	2900
3000	1000-WATT, TUNGSTEN-FILAMENT LAMP	3000
3100	500-WATT PROJECTION LAMP	3100
3200	FLOODLAMP	3200
3300	WHITE, NO.1, NO.2, OR NO.4 FLOODLAMP	3300
3400	REFLECTOR FLOODS	3400
3500	WARM, WHITE FLUORESCENT LAMP	3500
3700	SHREDED-FOIL, CLEAR FLASHLAMP	3700
3900	HIGH-INTENSITY SUN ARC	3900
4000		4000
4100	DIRECT SUNLIGHT BETWEEN 10 AM-3PM (AVERAGE)	4100
4300		4300
4500	COOL, WHITE FLUORESCENT LAMP	4500
4700	DAYLIGHT (BLUE) FLOODLAMP	4700
4900	WHITE-FLAME CARBON ARC	4900
5100	M2B FLASHLAMP	5100
5300		5300
5500	HIGH NOON SUNLIGHT	5500
5700	DIRECT SUNLIGHT IN SUMMER	5700
5900	BLUE FLASHLAMP	5900
6000	DAYLIGHT FLUORESCENT LAMP	6000
6300	SUNLIGHT WITH CLEAR SKY AT NOON	6300
6700	LIGHT FROM OVERCAST SKY 6800-7000	6700
7300	HIGH-SPEED ELECTRONIC FLASHTUBES	7300
7700	LIGHT FROM HAZY SKY 7500-8400	7700
8100		8100
8500		8500
8900		8900
9300		9300
9700		9700
10000	LIGHT FROM CLEAR BLUE SKY	10000
11000	LIGHT FROM CLEAR BLUE SKY	11000
12000	LIGHT FROM CLEAR BLUE SKY	12000
13000	LIGHT FROM CLEAR BLUE SKY	13000
14000	LIGHT FROM CLEAR BLUE SKY	14000
15000	LIGHT FROM CLEAR BLUE SKY	15000
16000	LIGHT FROM CLEAR BLUE SKY	16000
17000	LIGHT FROM CLEAR BLUE SKY	17000
18000	LIGHT FROM CLEAR BLUE SKY	18000
19000	LIGHT FROM CLEAR BLUE SKY	19000
20000	CLEAR BLUE SKY OVER WATER 20000-27000	20000

Figure 14.2 *The light color chart.*

by its Kelvin rating and on the right you'll find the 3D lighting equivalent. To determine your 3D light color just look up the actual light source on the chart and then drop your color sampler in the little box next to the Kelvin rating. This will give you the RGB (red–green–blue) settings for your 3D light source. You'll find that this chart is an invaluable tool for creating photorealistic lighting in your 3D scenes.

Speaking of lighting 3D scenes, let me ask you this: How many 3D images have you seen where a candle was emitting yellowish light? I know there aren't that many candle scenes, but I'm sure you'll find that almost all 3D artists use a yellowish colored light for the candle flame, a very common mistake. They assume that if the flame is yellow, then the light must also be yellow. It would be great if it were that easy, but it's not since the actual color of candlelight is red. In fact, try this experiment. Close yourself in a dark room and light a candle as the only light source. Now place a piece of white paper to one side of the light, making sure not to get it too close to the flame. I don't want the fire marshal coming after me. Now take a look at the paper and you'll notice that it has a slightly red hue to it. It's not an overpowering coloration but you can definitely see that it's red.

>> ALWAYS USE THE PROPER LIGHT COLORATION WHEN CREATING PHOTOREALISTIC LIGHTING.

Every light source emits a different color so if you want to create realistic lighting you'll need to use the appropriate light color. In fact, you should avoid using white lights since they don't exist in reality. You'd be surprised at how realistic your scene becomes when you use the correct light color.

As you can see, to create photorealistic candlelight you'll need to use a reddish light coloration. Of course, you don't want too much red, but this won't be a problem since you now have the light coloration conversion chart. It's easy to see how the light color plays a major role in the credibility of the scene since different light sources produce different colors. In fact, let's take a look at a scene that was rendered with four different light sources so we can see the actual difference, as shown in Figure 14.3.

You can see that Robby the Rabbit was kind enough to pose for our lighting study. Actually, he loves the camera. Let's look at some lighting. Here we have four different images of Robby, which we lit with different light sources. Let's take a look at the image in the upper left corner, which illustrates the reddish cast that is created by candlelight. Notice how the image feels warm; this is because candlelight emits red light, which we perceive as warm. Now take a look at the image to the right, which was lit with a standard light bulb. Notice how it has a very subtle reddish coloration, which is nearly undetectable. This is the most natural looking image in the group since we are exposed to this type of light more often than any other. You'll notice that it doesn't feel nearly as warm as the candlelight scene because standard light bulbs have a higher color temperature.

Now take a look at the image in the lower left corner. This image was lit with a fluorescent light, which gives off a green color. Notice how the subtle green tint makes it feel cooler than the previous images. You know, it's likely that you are one of the many people who have fluorescent lighting in your kitchen. This makes

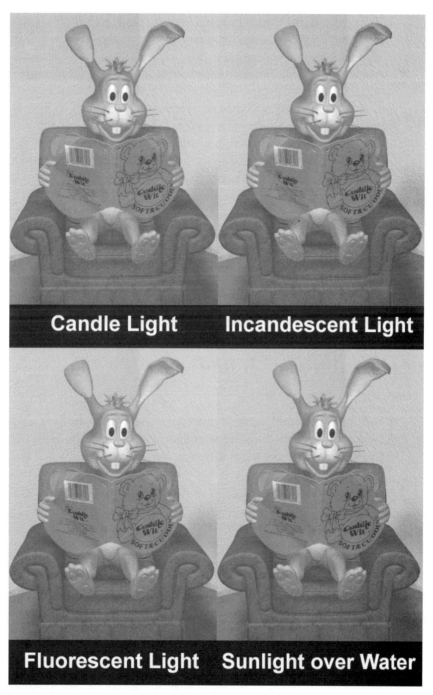

Figure 14.3 *The impact of different light sources.*

for a great comparison of light sources. Take a look at the walls in your kitchen and you'll notice that they actually have a slightly green tint. Now take a look at the walls in your dining room and you'll notice the coloration is different. I bet you never noticed the difference before; most people don't, since your chromatic adaptation is constantly working to correct the light coloration. The last image was lit to simulate sunlight over water, which happens to have the highest color temperature and appears blue in color. You'll notice that the blue tint makes the image feel very cool, as though we were sitting somewhere in the Arctic.

There is a significant difference in light coloration for each light source, which happens to change the temperature in the room. Well, it doesn't actually change the temperature but it does make the room feel warm or cool.

I'm sure you noticed that the coloration added by the different light sources was a bit strong. The light coloration is actually correct but there is something missing in the scene. It lacks the light color bleeding that is caused by radiosity. Color bleeding and radiosity are the most important elements of photorealistic lighting. In fact, they are the most important elements of photorealistic 3D images, period. Let's take a look at how these lighting attributes work.

Creating Realities with Radiosity

Simply put, *radiosity* is the indirect light that is distributed between objects. You see, most real-world objects reflect light, which means the light is bounced back and forth between the objects in the environment. This reflected light is responsible for most of the illumination in the environment. You'll find that the actual light source illuminates only a specific point in the environment, whereas radiosity lights up the majority of the space. Reflected light is commonly referred to as indirect lighting, and is the most common form of lighting you'll see in reality. Natural light is primarily indirect lighting.

To better understand radiosity let's consider an example. I'm sure you have opened the window in the early morning and noticed that light literally flooded the room, even though there were no lights on at the time. How was this possible? The sunlight entered through the window and bounced off all the objects it hit in the room, illuminating the rest of the room with indirect (bounced) light. Which objects actually reflect light? Only the reflective and specular objects reflect any real volume of light. You'll find that dull objects don't add to the indirect lighting. Of course, the object also needs to be a light color to reflect light because darker objects will absorb light. They don't actually absorb the light; they just don't reflect a dark color, which is basically the same thing as not reflecting the light. In fact, let's take a look at an example of radiosity lighting where we can see the dramatic effect of reflected light, as shown in Figure 14.4.

Figure 14.4 *The dramatic effect of radiosity lighting.*
(Rendered using LightScape ©1995 View by View, Inc., San Francisco, CA.)

Here we have a very nice image that was rendered with the LightScape Visualization System from LightScape Technologies, Inc. LightScape is one of several radiosity rendering engines on the market. As you can see, the image accurately depicts the reflection of light. In fact, the only real light source is a window that allows sunlight to flow into the stairwell. This sunlight is reflected off the white walls into the room below, which is filled with indirect light. You can see that the highly reflective floor is bouncing the light upward so it illuminates the underside of the stairs. This is how natural light works, which is why radiosity is so important when creating photorealistic images.

What happens to the light color? The light that bounces off objects actually changes color. In fact, it assumes the color of the object that is reflecting it. This effect is referred to as *color bleeding,* which means the color reflected between surfaces. This becomes an important factor to consider when lighting our scenes. If we don't accurately compensate for color bleeding, our scene will end up looking very artificial as we discovered with the lighting examples we examined earlier. In fact, let's take a look at what happens when we apply color bleeding to the Robby images (see Figure 14.5).

Here we have the same four images of Robby the Rabbit, but this time we applied color bleeding to the scene. The light that reflects off the walls has assumed its cream color, which tends to neutralize a great deal of the color tint that was created by the light source. You can still see a slight coloration but it's not nearly as prominent as before. We now have a very natural lighting scenario for all four light sources. Let's take a look at another image that shows the color bleeding effect.

Figure 14.6 was rendered with the LightScape Visualization System. Notice how there is a green tint to the scene, which was created by the light that is reflecting off the green water. We are seeing a larger amount of color bleeding in this image than in the Robby images because water is very reflective, whereas the painted walls of Robby's room are not. The more reflective the object, the more color will bleed into the light. As you can see, to create natural lighting we need to compensate for color bleeding as well as indirect light. As long as we are looking at this image we might as well take a look at the real influence radiosity lighting has on making a scene photorealistic.

I'm sure your first impression of the image was probably that it looked like a photograph. Of course, upon closer inspection you likely noticed that the models and surface are really rather plain. In fact, they aren't realistic at all, yet the image appeared like a photograph at first. That's the power of radiosity lighting. The light is so natural that we are tricked into believing that the image is a real photograph. Just think, what if we combined photorealistic modes and radiosity? The outcome would be inspirational for sure.

So how do we add radiosity lighting to our images? Well, that's the tricky part. Very few 3D programs have radiosity lighting features. The mathematics for creating radiosity is very complex, meaning few programmers are willing to embark on a journey of madness to create radiosity lighting engines. Of course, as 3D programs continue to evolve we will see more of them incorporating radiosity into their lighting features. If you don't have radiosity capabilities in your pro-

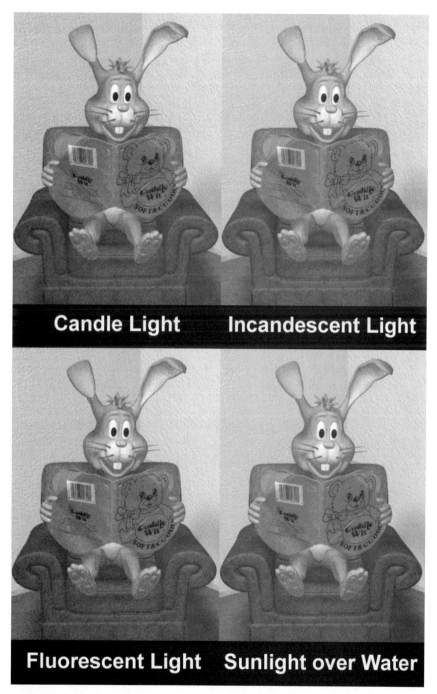

Candle Light

Incandescent Light

Fluorescent Light

Sunlight over Water

Figure 14.5 The effects of color bleeding.

Figure 14.6 *More color bleeding.*
(Rendered using LightScape ©1995 Agata and Andrzej Wojaczek.)

gram you can always purchase one of the third-party products or plug-ins that do radiosity rendering.

On the other hand, there are ways to simulate radiosity without having to purchase additional tools or even suffering the extended render times that come from using actual radiosity. Let's take a look at how that's done.

Simulating Radiosity

Although radiosity is a complex lighting formula it can be simulated fairly easily with success. Of course, the lighting won't be nearly as accurate as radiosity but it will certainly be significantly better than simply using direct lighting. In order to simulate radiosity you'll need to do two things: Add additional lights around the scene and give them color bleeding. It's actually not very difficult to do but it does require a bit of experimentation. Let's see how the radiosity lighting was added to the Robby images. Take a look at Figure 14.7.

Here we have a before-and-after comparison that illustrates the impact of simulated radiosity. Let's take a look at the before image so we can see where the lighting needs improvement. The image on the left is a typical representation of

Figure 14.7 *The difference between direct lighting and simulated radiosity.*

single-light source rendering. Notice the dark shadows in the scene, which really aren't possible since Robby is sitting in a corner with rather light-colored walls around him. The walls would normally reflect light, which would illuminate the back of Robby's head and diffuse the many shadows in the scene. Take a look at the lower right corner of the scene. Notice that a shadow from the chair has completely shadowed the carpet. While there would be some shadowing, it certainly wouldn't be this dark since light would bounce off the wall and illuminate the carpet.

ALWAYS REMEMBER TO CREATE COLOR BLEEDING WITH YOUR RADIOSITY LIGHTS.

When light is bounced off an object it assumes the color of the object. If you don't reflect this color in your radiosity lights, you'll end up with a very artificial looking image.

Let's see how the image looks when we correct these areas by applying simulated radiosity. Take a look at the image to the right and you'll see that Robby is now illuminated from the back and all of the shadows have been diffused to the point where they are only slightly visible. In fact, we can now see the true color of the walls that were previously rather gray and we can also see Robby's natural colors. The simulated radiosity image has made the image much more natural.

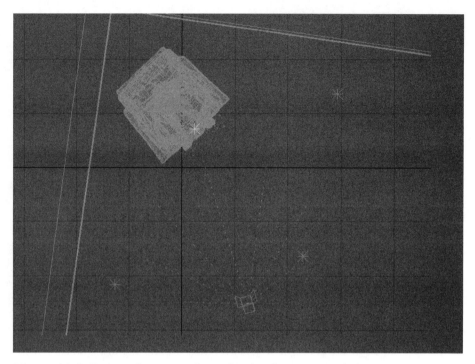

Figure 14.8 *Proper placement of simulated radiosity point lights.*

It's obvious that simulated radiosity is much better than direct lighting but how exactly do we create it? Actually, it's fairly simple. Place several point lights around the scene to simulate the places where the light would bounce. It's very important that you use a point light and not a distant light or spotlight since we want the light to travel in all directions, which is what happens in reality. The placement of the light is determined by the light reflectivity of the objects in the room. In the case of Robby's image, the walls are the main source of indirect lighting so we needed to place lights in relation to the walls. Why don't we take a look at where the lights were placed in the scene? Look at Figure 14.8.

What we have in Figure 14.8 is a top-down view of the scene. You can see that four point lights were added to the scene to create the radiosity effect. Two lights were placed against the walls to create the light that bounces off the wall. Another light was placed above Robby in the corner to create the light that is reflected by the corner of the wall. Finally, a fourth point light was added just below the direct light to simulate the light that is bounced off the opposing walls. Why don't we view the scene from another angle so we can see how high the lights were placed. Take a look at Figure 14.9.

You can see that most of the lights were placed slightly above Robby. This was done because the carpet would actually absorb the light. Placing light any lower

Figure 14.9 *The vertical placement of the radiosity lights.*

would make it look like the carpet was reflecting light. You'll notice that one light is lower than all the others. This light is located directly under the direct light so it was placed lower to avoid hitting Robby with too much light from the front. As you can see, the placement of light is critical when trying to simulate radiosity. The actual brightness of the lights is something you'll have to experiment with since it will vary form scene to scene.

We can't forget the value of color bleeding, which was necessary to make the scene appear natural. All of the point lights in the scene were given a color that was slightly lighter than the wall. This helped to neutralize the tint that was created with the source light, which you can clearly see in the image to the left. You need to avoid adding too much color to the lights since the walls aren't extremely reflective.

ALWAYS TURN OFF SPECULARITY WHEN SIMULATING RADIOSITY.

Specular highlights can be created only by the light source, not by indirect lighting. Therefore, if you don't turn off the specularity for your indirect lights you'll end up with far too many specular highlights on your surfaces, making them appear very unnatural.

There's just one remaining element that you need to be aware of when simulating radiosity—specularity. It's important that you disable the specularity feature of the point lights since you don't want multiple specular highlights on the object's surfaces. Specular highlights are created only by the light source; indirect lighting cannot create specular highlights. If you don't disable the specularity of the point lights you'll end up with a very unnatural number of specular highlights on your surfaces.

Creating simulated radiosity will take a bit of time and experimentation before you get used to lighting scenes in this manner but the result is well worth the time invested.

A surfacing issue arises when we add radiosity lighting to a scene, called color saturation. It can wreak havoc on your surfaces if you don't know how to correct it.

Diffusion and Radiosity

When you start adding lights to a scene to simulate radiosity you run into the problem of surface *color saturation,* which is where the surface actually shows too much of its own color. Far too many 3D artists surface their models with 100 percent diffusion, which is something that will never happen in reality. In fact, most surfaces in reality show only a small fraction of their own color since they rely on the light around them to bring out their color. When you have a surface with 100 percent diffusion, and you add radiosity lights, you end up showing more than 100 percent of the surface's color, which results in surface color saturation as shown in Figure 14.10.

Here we have a simple scene with an office phone where radiosity was used to illuminate the controls on the side of the phone. The phone itself is surfaced with 70 percent diffusion so it doesn't have a problem with color saturation. On the other hand, the table uses 100 percent diffusion so it has several very hot saturation spots where the surface color has been literally amplified by the light. In fact, you can think of lights as color amplifiers. You wouldn't normally see this problem if you used only a single direct light, but when creating photorealistic radiosity lighting you'll need to use several lights, which tend to amplify the surface color of the object.

NEVER USE 100 PERCENT DIFFUSION LEVELS WHEN SIMULATING RADIOSITY.

You should never use 100 percent diffusion levels under any circumstances, but definitely not when simulating radiosity. Light acts as a color amplifier, so if you use 100 percent dif-

Figure 14.10 *Surface color saturation caused by 100 percent diffusion.*

fusion levels your surface will end up with color saturation, which is completely unnatural. Never use 100 percent diffusion levels under any circumstances.

What's the solution to surface color saturation? Lower the diffusion of the surface to a point where the saturation no longer occurs. This may require some experimentation at first but in time you'll be able to predict the diffusion levels you'll need to use. In the case of our phone image, the table should have a diffusion of around 70 percent, which is typical for most wood surfaces. Let's take a look at what the image looks like when we use the proper diffusion setting as shown in Figure 14.11.

This is much better. Notice that there is no sign of surface color saturation. In fact, with the proper diffusion level it will be nearly impossible to add enough light to create surface color saturation. There is a simple test you can do that illustrates the importance of surface diffusion. Take a bright flashlight and shine it on your arm. You'll notice that there is no surface color saturation at all. That is because human skin has a low diffusion level, which means it can't be oversaturated with color.

Another thing to consider when creating your surfaces is image maps. You must lighten the image maps you use since the lower diffusion level will darken them

Figure 14.11 *Correcting surface color saturation with a proper diffusion level.*

significantly. If you use an image map that represents the desired color, you'll end up with something much darker after a proper diffusion level is applied. If you already have a plethora of image maps lying around that need to be corrected you can simply use the Variation tool in Photoshop to lighten them. It's a fast and simple means for creating the proper image map color depth for use with diffusion.

As you can see, diffusion is a major factor to consider when lighting your scenes, particularly if you plan to simulate radiosity. Make sure that you consider the impact of radiosity lighting before you create your next image map. It will save you a lot of time you would spend correcting it later.

Let's take a moment to examine one of the most useful lighting tools for adding depth to your images—lighting gels.

Using Lighting Gels

Lighting gels can be a very helpful for creating complicated lighting effects in your images. A lighting gel gets its name from the film industry where they are used to changing the light color and creating shadow maps. *Lighting gels,* also commonly referred to as *shadow maps,* are used to enhance your lights with color filters and custom shadows. They can be very useful for creating complex shadow effects, such as simulating light passing through a window as shown in Figure 14.12.

In this image you can see a shadow on the wall that resembles the frame of a window. In this case, the shadow map was used to simulate the morning sun pouring through an office window. This effect was created by making a two-color image of the window frame and mapping it to the light. In fact, take a look at Figure 14.13, which shows the actual image map that was used.

The white boxes represent the glass portion of the window and the black lines indicate the frame. Lighting gels work under the same principles as all other image maps, where grayscale values are used to determine the level of the effect. In the case of lighting gels, the white areas represent complete transparency, whereas the black areas represent full opacity.

Another important thing to remember when creating shadow maps with lighting gels is the level of edge blurring you should use. If you plan to simulate early morning light, as done in the sample image, you need to feather the edges of the shadow map. Early morning and late evening light are very diffused, which means shadows will have fuzzy edges. On the other hand, if you wanted to simulate midday light you would keep the edges hard since the sun is very intense during the middle of the day.

Figure 14.12 *Using lighting gels to create shadow effects.*

Figure 14.13 *The window frame shadow map.*

In addition to creating shadows you can also do very interesting color light effects with lighting gels. One of the most popular uses for lighting gels is to create the effect of stained glass windows, which is done by using a multicolored image map for the lighting gel. The image is actually projected on the scene by the light as shown in Figure 14.14.

Here we can see an image of our faithful model Robby sitting in a room with a stained glass window. The image on the right is the actual image map that was used for the lighting gel. Sure, it's a bit corny but it shows how effective lighting gels can be for creating complex lighting effects.

As you can see, lighting gels are powerful tools for creating very impressive lighting effects, which couldn't be created by any other means. Speaking of powerful lighting tools, let's take a look at lens flares.

Figure 14.14 *Using lighting gels to project stained glass images.*

Using Lens Flares

Lens flares are probably one of the most frequently abused lighting effect. It seems they pop up in so many places where they just aren't possible in reality. In order to use them correctly we need to understand how they are created. While they are definitely very cool to look at, they are actually a mistake. *Lens flares* are created in the camera lens when it's aimed directly at a bright light source. They are actually a defect in the capturing system, but since it is often seen on film, we need to re-create it to mimic reality. Besides, they look cool.

The key to creating lens flares is to know when and where to use them. For example, lights that fall into the reddish range in color do not create lens flares. They aren't bright enough to cause the error in the camera lens. I have seen far too many 3D candles and fires that had lens flares. The only proper place to use them is when you have a very bright light source like a star, flashlight, or head-light. Let's take a look at an image that shows the proper use of lens flares, as shown in Figure 14.15.

Here's a familiar character. The very nice lens flare at the end of Gizmo's light, which is a very bright light source, demonstrates the proper use of a lens

Figure 14.15 *Proper use of a lens flare.*

flare. Of course, there are more to lens flares than the rings and stars we are accustomed to seeing. They are also useful for creating the glow of lightbulbs. In these cases you would disable the star and central ring so only the glow is visible. Why don't we take a look at where this type of lens flare is useful? Look at Figure 14.16.

Here we have several lights that use a lens flare glow to make them appear natural. Actually, there are over 300 lights in this scene, all of them with lens flares. The lens flare glow has made these lights very photorealistic. While they are somewhat bright, they don't emit enough light to create a star or ring in the lens flare so we need to remove these elements from the lighting equation.

As you can see, lens flares are very powerful tools for adding photorealistic credibility to your images—but you must use them in the appropriate manner or you'll actually undermine the realism of your image. Don't limit yourself to using the standard start-type lens flares either. Take some time to experiment with them and you'll find there are actually many uses, which can strengthen the photorealistic credibility of your images.

Let's wrap up this chapter by taking a look at lighting source material.

Figure 14.16 *Using lens flares without rings and stars.*

Working with Photographs as Source Material

Photographs can be a great source for gathering lighting information but it's very important that you understand how accurate they are in capturing the true light color of the environment. Film doesn't have the chromatic adaptation that our eyes do, so it has the tendency to capture the actual color of light. Of course, most film has been specially designed to compensate for certain lighting situations. For example, daylight film is balanced for around 5500 Kelvin, which is the typical color temperature of midday, but by sunset the color temperature has dropped to around 3000K which will cause your pictures to take on a reddish coloration. This variance can make the colors in the photograph very misleading.

In fact, most professional photographers will use color filters to correct the light color on the photograph, or even alter it so they have the desired mood for the shot. This means that when you work with source photographs you want to focus on the level of light in the scene and fall back on the light coloration chart for the actual light color. This will ensure that your images reflect the true color of the light source.

On the other hand, if you want to actually find out what the light color is in a given situation, I suggest that you use the wrong film so it captures the true light color. Use daylight film to shoot evening shots and vice versa. Another quick method for capturing the true light color on film is to use an instant camera, which doesn't have the sophisticated color correction of regular film—so you are more likely to get an accurate light color in the photograph.

Photographs can be great source material for lighting but you need to make sure you understand the circumstance under which the photograph was taken to ensure you are getting accurate light color information.

It's All Up to You Now!

Well, what do you know, we're actually at the end of the book. Can you believe that's all there is to know about photorealistic 3D images? Actually it's not but it is all that we could fit into 300+ pages. Don't worry, by the time you master all of these concepts we'll have plenty more waiting for you.

Don't forget to visit the companion Web site at www.wiley.com/compbooks/ fleming and register for our on-line Photorealistic Art Gallery, where we'll be showcasing the impressive 3D images that are being created by you, the readers of this book. I look forward to seeing how the information in this book has affected the way you create your photorealistic 3D images.

It's been great sharing the Principles of 3D Photorealism with you. I hope we have the opportunity to do it again some time soon. Until next time, good luck, good fortune, and remember: *No detail is too small*.

Appendix A
Modeling and Surfacing
Source Material

Ultimate Visual Dictionary
Publisher: Dorling Kindersley
ISBN: 156458640

Over 5000 color photographs of everything from the inside of a golf ball to the surface of the sun, from the skeleton of a platypus to the anatomy of an elephant. This book is an awesome visual reference.

The Eyewitness Book Series
Publisher: Dorling Kindersley

There are 84 books in this series that are saturated with high-quality photos of objects. Each book in the series covers a different subject such as fish, pirates, reptiles, oceans, plants, and so forth. You'll find that they have a color photograph of anything you're seeking.

The Macmillan Visual Dictionary
Publisher: Macmillan Publishing Company
ISBN: 0-02-528160-7

This book features over 3500 full-color illustrations covering a wide variety of objects. Although they are only illustrations, they are still very useful for modeling sources material.

Dorling Kindersley History of the World
Publisher: Dorling Kindersley
ISBN: 0-56458-244-2

This book features over 1500 full-color illustrations and photographs of historical items from the beginning of life to present day.

The Ultimate Book of Cross-Sections
Publisher: Dorling Kindersley
ISBN: 0-7894-1195-4

Thousands of fully illustrated cross sections of cars, trains, tanks, trucks, ships, planes, jets, spacecraft, and other high-tech machinery.

Stephen Biesty's Incredible Everything
Publisher: Dorling Kindersley
ISBN: 0-7894-2049-X

This book features fully detailed cutaway images of historical and architectural items.

Illustrated Encyclopedia of Animals
Publisher: Kingfisher Books
ISBN: 1-85697-801-X

Over a thousand full-color photographs of animals.

Disaster
Publisher: Dorling Kindersley
ISBN: 0-7894-2034-1

If you're looking for chaos, this is the book. It features very detailed illustrations of historical floods, fires, earthquakes, avalanches, and shipwrecks.

Reader's Digest How Nature Works
Publisher: Reader's Digest
ISBN: 0-895-72391-0

Here's a unique source book. It actually features dozens of great science experiments for children but also has more than 500 very nice color photographs.

The Ultimate Dinosaur Book
Publisher: Dorling Kindersley
ISBN: 1-56458-304-X

This is a wonderful book that features detailed profiles on 55 different dinosaurs. It's full of great facts and wonderful source images for those dinosaurs you've been dying to model.

Stephen Biesty's Cut-Away books
Publisher: Dorling Kindersley

There are several books in this series that show fully detailed illustrated cutaway images of ancient to modern-day objects. You'll find eighteenth-century warships, sixteenth-century castles, all the way up to modern-day factories. The cutaway views feature an amazing amount of detail, which aids in the creation of accurately photorealistic models.

Appendix B
Procedural Metal Attributes

Metal	Clr/(RGB)	CH[1]	Lum	Diff	Spec	Gloss	Ref	BMP (Fractal Noise)[2]	Bump %
Aluminum foil	180, 180, 180	Y	0	32	90	MED	65	.0002, .00002, .0002	8
Aluminum foil (dull)	180, 180, 180	Y	0	50	45	LOW	35	.0002, .00002, .0002	15
Aluminum	220, 223, 227	Y	0	35	25	LOW	40	.0002, .00002, .0002	15
Aluminum polished	220, 223, 227	Y	0	35	65	MED	50	.0002, .00002, .0002	12
Brass	191, 173, 111	Y	0	40	40	MED	40	.0002, .00002, .0002	20
Brass polished	191, 173, 111	Y	0	40	65	MED	50	.0002, .00002, .0002	10
Chromed alloy	150, 150, 150	N	0	40	40	LOW	25	.0002, .00002, .0002	35
Chromed alloy 2	220, 230, 240	Y	0	25	30	LOW	50	.0002, .00002, .0002	20
Chromed aluminum	220, 230, 240	Y	0	15	60	MED	65	.0002, .00002, .0002	10
Chromed plastic	220, 230, 240	Y	0	15	60	LOW	50	.0002, .00002, .0002	10
Chromed steel	220, 230, 240	Y	0	15	60	MED	70	.0002, .00002, .0002	5
Chromed (extreme)	220, 230, 240	Y	0	15	60	LOW	85	.0002, .00002, .0002	5
Copper	186, 110, 64	Y	0	45	40	MED	40	.0002, .00002, .0002	10
Gold 18K	234, 199, 135	Y	0	45	40	MED	65	.0002, .00002, .0002	10
Gold 24K	218, 178, 115	Y	0	35	40	MED	65	.0002, .00002, .0002	10
Gold unrefined	255, 180, 66	Y	0	35	40	MED	45	.0002, .00002, .0002	25
Gold yellow	242, 192, 86	Y	0	45	40	MED	65	.0002, .00002, .0002	10
Graphite	87, 33, 77	N	0	42	90	MED	15	.0001, .0001, .0001	10
Iron	118, 119, 120	Y	0	35	50	LOW	25	.0002, .00002, .0002	20
Pewter	250, 250, 250	Y	0	30	40	LOW	15	.0002, .00002, .0002	10
Silver	233, 233, 216	Y	0	15	90	MED	45	.0002, .00002, .0002	15
Sodium	250, 250, 250	Y	0	50	90	LOW	25	.0002, .00002, .0002	10
Soup can	229, 223, 206	Y	0	30	40	LOW	45	.0002, .00002, .0002	30
Stainless steel	128, 128, 126	Y	0	40	50	MED	35	.0002, .00002, .0002	20
Stainless steel polished	220, 220, 220	Y	0	35	50	LOW	25	.0002, .00002, .0002	35
Tin	220, 223, 227	Y	0	50	90	LOW	35	.0001, .0001, .0001	20

[1] Color highlights.
[2] Values are expressed in inches.

Appendix C
Procedural Plastic and Rubber Attributes

Metal	Clr (RGB)	CH[1]	Lum	Diff	Spec	Gloss	Ref	Tran	BMP (Fractal Noise)[2]	Bump %
Detergent bottle	27, 108, 131	N	0	90	60	LOW	5	0	.0002, .0002, .0002	20
Foam rubber	54, 53, 53	N	0	95	30	LOW	3	0	.02, .02, .02	90
Multimedia	20, 20, 20	N	0	80	30	LOW	5	0	.0001, .0001, .0001	20
Multimedia (rough)	25, 25, 25	N	0	60	40	LOW	5	0	.0001, .0001, .0001	20
Multimedia (smooth)	38, 38, 38	N	0	60	30	LOW	10	0	.0001, .0001, .0001	10
Multimedia (dull)	25, 25, 25	Y	0	92	40	LOW	15	0	.0001, .0001, .0001	30
Plastic	20, 20, 20	N	0	80	30	LOW	5	0	.0001, .0001, .0001	10
Plastic (clear)	63, 108, 86	N	0	90	90	LOW	35	60	.0001, .0001, .0001	10
Plastic (high gloss)	20, 20, 20	N	0	70	90	HIGH	15	0	.0001, .0001, .0001	5
Plastic (hard, shiny)	20, 20, 20	N	0	80	80	MED	10	0	.0001, .0001, .0001	10
Plastic (candy shell)	200, 10, 10	N	0	80	30	LOW	5	0	.00002, .00002, .00002	15
Plastic (chocolate)	67, 40, 18	N	0	90	30	LOW	5	0	.0001, .0001, .0001	5
Rubber	30, 30, 30	Y	0	50	20	LOW	0	0	.0001, .0001, .0001	50
Rubber buttons	150, 150, 150	N	0	60	20	LOW	0	0	.0001, .0001, .0001	30
Vinyl	45, 45, 45	N	0	60	40	LOW	15	0	.00001, .0002, .00001	30

[1]Color highlights.
[2]Values are expressed in inches.

Appendix D
Index of Refraction Values for Transparent Materials

MATERIAL	INDEX OF REFRACTION
Vacuum	1.0000
Air	1.0003
Carbon dioxide liquid	1.2000
Ice	1.3090
Water	1.3333
Acetone	1.3600
Ethyl alcohol	1.3600
Sugar solution (30%)	1.3800
Alcohol	1.3900
Fluorite	1.4340
Quartz, fused	1.4600
Calspar2	1.4860
Sugar solution (80%)	1.4900
Glass	1.5000
Glass, zinc crown	1.5170
Glass, crown	1.5200
Sodium chloride	1.5300
Sodium chloride (salt) 1	1.5440
Polystyrene	1.5500
Quartz 2	1.5530
Emerald	1.5700
Glass, light flint	1.5750
Lapis lazuli	1.6100
Topaz	1.6100
Carbon bisulfide	1.6300
Quartz 1	1.6440
Sodium chloride (salt) 2	1.6440
Glass, heavy flint	1.6500

MATERIAL	INDEX OF REFRACTION
Calspar1	1.6600
Glass, dense flint	1.6600
Methylene iodide	1.7400
Ruby	1.7700
Sapphire	1.7700
Glass, heaviest flint	1.8900
Crystal	2.0000
Diamond	2.4170
Chromium oxide	2.7050
Amorphous selenium	2.2920
Iodine crystal	3.3400

Appendix E
Light Colors Rated in Kelvins

Light Source	Kelvins
Candle flame	1500
Incandescent house lamps	2500–3000
60-watt, gas-filled, tungsten-filament lamp	2800
100-watt, tungsten-filament lamp	2865
500-watt, tungsten-filament lamp	2950
1000-watt, tungsten-filament lamp	3000
500-watt projection lamp	3175
3200 degree Kelvin floodlamp	3200
Amber flashlamp	3200
R32 reflector flood	3200
Zirconium concentrated arc	3200
White, no. 1, no. 2, or no. 4 floodlamp, reflector flood	3400
Reflector floods	3400
Warm, white fluorescent lamp	3500
Shredded-foil, clear flashlamp	3800
Cool, white fluorescent lamp	4500
Daylight (blue) floodlamp	4800
White-flame carbon arc	5000
M2B flashlamp	5100
High-noon sunlight	5400
High-intensity sun arc	5550
Direct sunlight in summer	5800
Direct sunlight between 10 AM–3 PM (average)	6000
Blue flashlamp	6000
Daylight fluorescent lamp	6500
Sunlight with clear sky at noon	6500
Light from overcast sky	6800–7000

LIGHT SOURCE	KELVINS
High-speed electronic flashcubes	7000
Light from hazy sky	7500–8400
Light from clear blue sky	10,000–20,000
Clear blue sky over water	20,000–27,000

Appendix F
The Companion
Web Site

The companion Web site contains a variety of support materials for creating photorealistic 3D images. The support materials of the examples discussed in this book are provided in a common format that can be used by any program on any platform. The bonus models on the Web site are available in a 3DS format. The bonus Image Maps are in a JPG format. The *3D Photorealism Toolkit* companion Web site is located at www.wiley.com/compbooks/fleming.

Here's what you'll find on the Web site:

Color Figures and Tutorial files for each chapter are located at:

www.wiley.com/compbooks/fleming/index.htm.

The 3D photorealism gallery is located at:

www.wiley.com/compbooks/fleming/gallery.htm

Free photorealistic models are located at:

www.wiley.com/compbooks/fleming/models.htm

Free photorealistic image map textures are located at:

www.wiley.com/compbooks/fleming/imagemaps.htm

Updates to the book are located at:

www.wiley.com/compbooks/fleming/updates.htm

And links to dozens of photorealism resources are located at:

www.wiley.com/compbooks/fleming/links.htm

Hardware/Software Requirements

To use the tutorial files and free bonus objects on the companion Web site you'll need a Macintosh, IBM PC compatible, or Unix computer with at least 16 MB of RAM.

To view the figures or free bonus image maps files you'll need a picture viewer or painting program such as Photoshop, Photopaint, Fractal Painter or Paintshop Pro. To use the tutorial models or free bonus models you'll need a 3D program such as LightWave, 3D Studio Max, SoftImage, Electric Image, trueSpace or any other 3D program that can load 3DS and DXF files.

To access the companion Web site you'll need a Web browser such as Netscape 2.0 or Microsoft Internet Explorer 2.0, or above, to view the companion Web site. You'll also need a utility that can decompress ZIP or Stuff-it files to extract the chapter figures and tutorial files.

User Assistance and Information

The software accompanying this book is being provided as is without warranty or support of any kind. Should you require basic installation assistance, or if your media is defective, please contact our product support number at (212) 850–6194 weekdays between 9 A.M. and 4 P.M. Eastern Standard Time. Or, we can be reached via e-mail at: wprtusw@wiley.com.

To place additional orders or to request information about other Wiley products, please call (800) 879–4539.

Index

What's on the Companion Web Site?

Check out the companion Web site at www.wiley.com/compbooks/fleming for:

- Color Figures and Tutorial files
- The 3D photorealism gallery
- Free photorealistic models
- Free photorealistic image map textures
- Updates to the book
- And links to dozens of photorealism resources

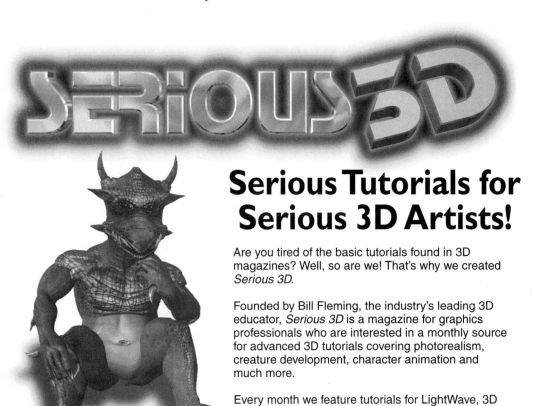